£2-50p

EDGAR MORIN

Plodémet

Report from a French Village

**TRANSLATED BY
A. M. SHERIDAN-SMITH**

ALLEN LANE THE PENGUIN PRESS

Commune en France: La Métamorphose de Plodémet
first published by Librairie Arthème Fayard, Paris, in 1967
Copyright © Librairie Arthème Fayard, 1967

This translation published in the United States of America
in 1970 by Pantheon Books, a division of Random House,
Inc., New York and simultaneously in Canada by Random
House of Canada Ltd, Toronto

Copyright © Random House, 1970

First published in Great Britain in 1971 by
Allen Lane The Penguin Press
Vigo Street, London W1

ISBN 0 7139 0117 9

Printed in Great Britain by
Fletcher & Son Ltd, Norwich

To Johanne,
who was always present,
who loved and helped me to love
the people of Plodémet

No sabemos lo que nos pasa,
y eso es lo que pasa
        —Ortega y Gasset

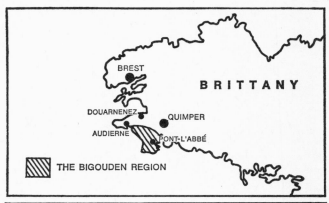

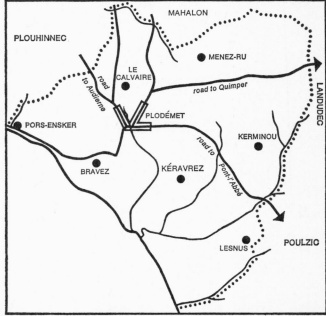

The commune of Plodémet, in the heart of the Bigouden region

Contents

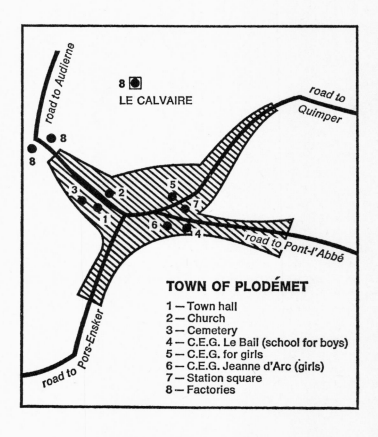

road to Audierne

road to Quimper

8 ● LE CALVAIRE

● 8

● 8

3 ●
2 ●
5 ●
7 ●
1 ●
6 ●
4 ●

road to Pont-l'Abbé

road to Pors-Ensker

TOWN OF PLODÉMET

1 — Town hall
2 — Church
3 — Cemetery
4 — C.E.G. Le Bail (school for boys)
5 — C.E.G. for girls
6 — C.E.G. Jeanne d'Arc (girls)
7 — Station square
8 — Factories

Preface

In 1960 the social sciences commission of the DGRST (Délégation Générale à la Recherche Scientifique et Technique) chose the commune of Plodémet in Sud-Finistère as an experimental field for multidisciplinary research. In 1964, at the suggestion of Georges Friedmann, I was asked to carry out an inquiry into the sociological aspects of the project. From the outset I was fascinated by Plodémet. I successfully applied for additional funds, which enabled me to recruit a team of research workers. I spent the whole of 1965 doing on-the-spot research, and the inquiry has occupied practically all my time since.

Plodémet is neither a village nor a town. It is a *bourg*, or township: it has some industry, a large school (a *collège d'enseignement général*, or CEG), commerce, a working class, and retired people. It is also a commune that takes in a wide variety of highly individual hamlet-villages. It has a coastline, a small fishing port, merchant seamen. The old women wear the tall traditional peasant coiffe; the young women wear slacks. Some of the shops already have neon lights, and there are cottages that are still without electricity. Plodémet is a microcosm.

The character of Plodémet was formed by the changes brought about by the political struggles of the Third Republic (1880–1910). It is now in the midst of a new transformation that began between 1950 and 1955. Everything is changing. The transformation in France as a whole has struck at Plodémet and broken down its isolation from the modern world. Abrupt change, crisis, and rapid progress provide a clearer understanding of social transformation than does a gradual and diffused evolution.

Plodémet, then, is not an "average" commune, or a mini-Middletown conjured up out of a mass of statistical norms. On the contrary, it is a special case, an exception. And because of its uniqueness and diversity, any attempt to see Plodémet as a microcosm is bound to raise a great many problems requiring a highly radical treatment.

This is what fascinated me about this project. I wanted to carry out a study of Plodémet which at the same time would be a study of France, not by avoiding what constituted its originality but by actively seeking it out, and by attempting simultaneously to uncover the underlying forces that were bringing about its transformation.

Of course, it was only because my own project formed part of a wider multidisciplinary research project that I dared to undertake what would otherwise have been an overwhelming task. With the work that had already been done in 1965–1966 and the help of research workers already in the field, I was able to get my bearings quite easily.

But the sociology of the present, as I understand it, cannot respect the boundaries between different disciplines; it must cross them in order to adapt itself to the phenomenon under study.

A method of inquiry was worked out in direct relation to the research field. The principles of this method (a fuller examination of them appears in the Appendix) include:

1. The application of varied techniques of observation.

2. The continual use of the dialogue-interview.

3. Participation, and even intervention, in group activities (social praxis).

4. The progressive autodevelopment of the system of interpretation, through meetings between the research workers, the exchange of research journals written by each worker, and a series of "campaigns," interrupted by periods of rectification, reformulation, and strategic preparation.

This method strives to respect the originality of the field, unlike the usual steamroller methods that try to nullify it; it maintains a permanent dialogue between the thought of the researchers and the reality under study, unlike preprogrammed and prethought inquiries. It is close to the ethnographic approach in the sense that it tries to circumscribe a social group as an original unity, but not in the sense of being primarily preoccupied with the archaic background of this group. It is related to the modern ethnographic spirit, which has adapted to its own use the formula that Hugo von Hofmannsthal applied to poetry: "It makes distant what is near and near what is distant, in such a way that we can feel both." Situated at the extremity of Western Europe, Plodémet is almost exotic, yet at the same time it is part of the society most in need of ethnographic study, our own. Its remoteness enables us to distance ourselves from what is too close; its proximity, to draw closer to what is most distant in our world, our society, and ourselves. Any properly conducted ethnographic research brings us closer to and at the same time separates us from the man whom the gospels call, somewhat prematurely, our neighbor, and who remains, in the ancient biblical term, the *stranger*.

Unlike ethnography, however, the sociology of the present involves a consideration of historical time and therefore of the outside world. Like history, it attempts to understand the event, the break, and the crisis; it concentrates its attention on change, on transformation, on the central problem of Plodémet at the time of the inquiry.

The historian stands downstream from the phenomenon under study; he benefits not so much from a mental distance, which can be acquired, even in the present, by means of an ethnographical distancing, as from the distance that has enabled the past to develop its own future and that now enables the historian to integrate it in a process of change. The sociologist of the present is deprived of any such future. He has to replace the future by a prospective anticipation (which is formed by reference to the progressive sectors of the society under study and to the most advanced states in the world as a whole) and by a thorough study of the process of transformation itself. This study is made possible by the inquiry and by intervention in the living phenomenon.

In general terms, the sociology of the present tries to achieve a true awareness of a phenomenon. It tries by all adequate means possible to make it emerge, to discover its internal and external articulations, and finally, to produce an intelligible account which, instead of dissolving its concrete particularity, may reveal it.

It was this task that demanded the greatest effort. The inquiry,

which lasted one year, was followed by a further period lasting
eighteen months, in which thousands of notes, pages, and yards
of recording tape were broken down and an attempt made to
re-create, out of thousands of fragments, clues, and "snapshots,"
a being which, unlike the paleontologist's dinosaur or the archae-
ologist's Troy, will never have any corporeal existence: a changing
society. We had to compose and decompose, reconsider and reject, examine facts and ideas from a number of different points of
view, meditate, reflect, in short think, in the preindustrial, pre-
cybernetic sense. I realized that the time must come when one
would be able to play on the computer as on an organ, not to
replace meditation, but to emancipate it.

I think I am aware of the gaps and inadequacies in my work.
The richness, complexity, and diversity of Plodémet overwhelm
on every side the enormous quantity of information accumulated.
And this information overwhelms my ability to cope with it.

Moreover, my work suffers from a particular distortion which
I think was hardly avoidable. The special importance accorded
to change forced me to give only secondary consideration to more
permanent aspects, and to regard geography, demography, family structures, tradition, and folklore as mere points of reference.
Indeed, in this respect my study makes no pretensions to being a
synthesis of our knowledge of Plodémet—a task which is now
being undertaken by André Burguière.

But to what extent have I been able to overcome the fundamental difficulties of the enterprise? Every field is "impossible"
in the sense that it does not provide the conditions of isolation
suitable for experiment but remains sufficiently unique to resist
generalization. Plodémet is a particularly difficult field because
of its singularity, and because of its diversity, which at the same
time contradicts and reinforces its singularity.

To what extent have I succeeded in isolating its unique characteristics and re-creating its individuality—that is, the particular
metabolisms through which the general processes operate? What
is the special character of a commune? What do its members have
in common, and to what extent are they just like anybody else?
What is the relation between this individuality and society as a
whole? Since Plodémet is profoundly linked with French society,
and since the process of change taking place there proceeds from

that taking place in France as a whole (with crosscurrents, as will be seen), is it possible to build up a description of Plodémet without creating a second description of the changes operating in France and in the Western world generally? Need this second description be as complex and articulated as the first, or can it be confined to a few unilateral schemata concerning the expansion of an industrial or consumer culture? How can the two descriptions be placed in dialectical relation, when a knowledge of France cannot be inferred from a knowledge of Plodémet, though the latter can contribute to the former, and when a knowledge of Plodémet cannot be deduced from a knowledge of France, though the latter is a necessary part of the former? How can we prevent the dialectic from degenerating into mere intellectual juggling, and being lost either in the particular, concrete phenomenon or in the abstract, general description?

The "impossibility" of my enterprise is apparent on every level. But how can a research program be carried out that does not become an "impossibility" as soon as it confronts the individuality of a group and the particularity of change, that is, the teratology of human reality in the relations between the social individual and society as a whole, and between structure and change? The only merit of the method used here is that it constantly presents the author with these very problems. It cannot be applied mechanically, as a technique. Research becomes a dangerous game, a risk, a matter of chance, an art, incapable of guaranteeing the excellence of its results in advance.

It was not out of any love of difficulty that I embarked on and persevered in this undertaking. It was out of a fatal love for two proud and rival goddesses, the universal and the concrete, the struggle between whom is fatal to both. The universal-concrete (which has haunted me ever since the genius of a Prussian philosopher first introduced me to it) is the hidden, inaccessible, impossible (nonexistent?) God that guides all my search for knowledge. In this myth I wish to unite my two mutually destructive inclinations. The first draws me to generic ideas, the study of the great movements in time and in the world, tries to propel me toward the future and the cosmos freed from any need to circumscribe a feature or to plunge into a particular experience. The other makes me aware of the fascination of particular faces, of close-ups of eyes and mouths, and the attraction of the spontaneous, the immediate, the direct.

For me, Plodémet was an unexpected, unforgettable marriage with the concrete, but a marriage that did not make me betray my bigamous passion. I found there the traces of a tremendous struggle between two worlds. I found there the great movements of our time, the great problems of man, but always incarnated in irreplaceable faces, eyes, lives.

I was led to throw into my experience of Plodémet a mass of ideas and opinions on the contemporary development of France and the world. Some came from my study *L'Esprit du temps* (*The Zeitgeist*), in which I tried to examine the dominant culture of this century through the development of technological-industrial-capitalist-bourgeois-individualistic-consumer societies; others came from articles—essays inspired by the social and political transformation of France. All these rather general, sometimes ephemeral ideas could be used as hypotheses to form an initial approach to the subject of the inquiry. But very soon, in my dialogue with Plodémet, with my colleagues, with my friends, with Burguière, other ideas emerged and continued to emerge that corrected, contradicted, obliterated my initial ideas, and I discovered huge areas of reality hitherto unknown to me. I had the salutary experience of having to adapt myself to Plodémet's singularity. The key ideas that I now hold are not those I took with me, but those I acquired in Plodémet, in the Bigouden country, in the canton of Plogastel, Sud-Finistère.

Acknowledgments

The first draft of this book gained a good deal from the critical reading of Serge Thion. In the final stages of the writing I found the criticisms, corrections, suggestions, and ideas of Bernard Paillard particularly helpful. His experience at Menez-Ru was indispensable to the chapter "The Modern Age." Jean-Louis Peninou wrote the first draft of the chapter "The Wretched of the Earth."

The research team I formed in the field included:

Jean-Louis Peninou (Paris), with whom I have worked in constant dialogue. He was my principal research assistant and was responsible for a number of projects, including the monographic study of the villages. He made a special study of peasant trade-unionist activity (land redistribution, cooperation) and rural transformation.

Bernard Paillard (Rennes) carried out the monographic study on Menez-Ru and a number of interviews with peasants.

Jean-Paul Le Bolloch (Rennes) carried out the monographic study on Bravez and a number of interviews with young married couples and peasants.

Jean-Claude Stourm (Plodémet) attended and recorded all the meetings of the youth club. He is the co-author of the monographic study on Kéravrez.

Jean-Yves Martineau (Rennes), co-author of the monograph on Kéravrez. He took part in the youth club.

Anne Leroux (Rennes) concentrated on youth, young married couples, and women's problems.

Apart from the groups and problems in which they took a special interest, these colleagues took part in many other aspects of the research, and each of us, except for J.-C. Stourm, kept a journal (in principle a daily one), which was a mine of information and suggestions (E.M., 500 pages; J.L.P., 300 pages; B.P., 200 pages; J.Y.M., 80 pages; A.L., 70 pages; J.P.L.B., 60 pages).

The following also took part in the research work:

Romain Denis (Paris), who acted as the catalyst in the youth club (April 1965).

Rosine Fitzgerald (Paris), who carried out interviews with women and tradesmen in the *bourg* (June 1965).

Christian Topalov (Paris), who collaborated with Bernard Paillard on Menez-Ru and took part in the study of the youth club (August 1965).

In addition, I was assisted by André Dubost, who arranged two meetings with leaders of the farmers' union, by J.-C. Kourganoff, whom I brought back to Plodémet three years after his inquiry, and by the stormy but stimulating intervention of Georges Lapassade, who was present at the first meetings of the youth club.

I also wish to thank Johanne, ever helpful, ever curious, ever generous of heart, *sin otra luz ni guía sino que en el corazón.*

My research was considerably helped, particularly during the writing stage, by André Burguière, who was responsible to the Délégation Générale à la Recherche Scientifique et Technique for drawing up the overall multidisciplinary report. He was a constant help throughout our work and I learned a good deal from our many discussions.

During both the inquiry and the preparation of the report, I was able to consult research reports made prior to my own. They enabled me to orient myself fairly quickly, enlightened me on certain fundamental points, and allowed me to measure the progress accomplished between the years 1962 and 1965.

M. Le Lannou (under the direction of): *Rapport d'enquête sur les conditions géographiques de la commune de Plodémet* (1962–1963).

A. Albenque: *État des techniques de production et de con-*

sommation dans l'agriculture et les arts ménagers dans la commune de Plodémet (1963).

J.-C. and M. Kourganoff: *Rapport d'enquête psychosociologique à Plodémet* (1962).

S. Petit: *Enquête d'observation ethnologique; Pors-Ensker* (1962).

J. Maho: *Rapport d'enquête sur la diffusion de l'information à Plodémet* (1962–1963).

N. Tricot: *L'Enseignement à Plodémet* (1963).

M. Izard: *Mariage et parenté à Plodémet* (1963).

F. Bourlière, H. Cendron, and F. Clement: *Le Vieillissement individuel dans une population rurale française, Cahiers du Centre de recherches anthropologiques,* Vols. X and XI, 1966 series, pp. 41–101.

I derived valuable help from an independent study: J. Tranvouez and Montfortain, *Au pays bigouden* (1964).

I also benefitted from the principal findings of the demographic study; I obtained the necessary historical information from conversations with N. Mathieu, C. Capitan, and above all André Burguière. But it was only after the preparation of this book that I was able to consult the following historical reports made under the direction of E. Labrousse and R. Mandrou:

C. Capitan: *La Vie politique de la Révolution aux lendemains de la Libération.*

N. Mathieu: *L'Évolution socio-économique de Plodémet pendant les 150 dernières années (1820–1960).*

Cl. Gasnault-Beis: *La Paroisse de Plodémet à l'époque contemporaine (1820–1920).*

Y. Tyl: *L'Instruction à Plodémet de la Révolution à nos jours.*

J.-M. Caille: *Délinquance et criminalité aux XIXe et XXe siècles.*

F. Laurent: *La Culture commercialisée à Plodémet aux XIXe et XXe siècles.*

I had useful contacts in the field with D. Laurent (ethnography and traditional culture) and M. Jacobi, who carried out an inquiry on the research workers themselves.

I wish to thank the Commission Administrative d'Etudes Scientifiques of the DGRST, which supplied me with the necessary funds while leaving me complete freedom of decision;

Georges Friedmann, who inaugurated this research; Dr. Gessain, who always gave active support to my requests; Jean Stoetzel, who helped me overcome various practical difficulties; M. Saltet of the École Pratique des Hautes Études, who handled with great patience the management of our budget and was an invaluable guide in administrative and financial questions; the secretariat of the Centre d'Études des Communications de Masse (CECMAS); and the secretariat of the Centre d'Études Sociologiques, which helped to supply us with tape-recording equipment.

My research was conducted in collaboration with the CECMAS.

Above all, I wish to thank the inhabitants of Plodémet themselves. Their friendliness made our indiscreet, direct, and omnipresent inquiry possible. I hope this book conveys something of their fine rustic, plebeian culture, their permanent curiosity, their self-taught philosophy, which interrogates the passage of time and the new world it is bringing with it. I wish to thank those whose names I have not disclosed because they have become too close to me, and those whose real names are replaced by pseudonyms, with the exception of Jenny Le Bail, whose surname belongs to history and her Christian name to friendship.

I wish to thank the civil and ecclesiastical authorities, Mayor Maurice, the town clerk, M. Le Neuf, the headmasters of the CEG, the parish priest, Fr. Abel, and his curate, Fr. Azur, who always replied to our questions and corrected our information.

I greet the militants—teachers and trade-unionists—who devote themselves to the good of the community and are always in the forefront, and those engaged in the adventure of the youth club.

Foreword to the English-Language Edition

Nearly four hundred miles separate Plodémet from Paris. Over the last sixty miles, the wind and the rain became stronger and stronger and the squalls beat down on our little Renault 4. Johanne and I arrived on March 14, 1965, at about two or three o'clock in the afternoon, in a sort of long village street with no sign of life anywhere. I stopped outside the Hôtel des Voyageurs, which is also a café, a restaurant, and a cinema. I entered the café. Three men were sitting at a table playing cards. There was no one at the bar. I said, "Bonjour, messieurs," but got no answer as far as I know. I looked along the corridor. Nobody. Rather embarrassed, I turned to the men at the card table. One of them looked up and made an interrogative movement with his chin.

"Is this the hotel?" I asked.

"Yes," said the man, who was rather corpulent. He seemed to be the proprietor, but made no attempt to smile. I said I wanted a room.

"They're not heated," he replied at once, almost as a challenge.

He added that none of the rooms in Plodémet were heated and that central heating had got no further than the Hôtel de Pont-Croix, some miles away.

After settling in at Pont-Croix we came back to Plodémet. We did a bit of reconnaissance, without daring to leave the car very often. I called in at the town hall. It provided the first agreeable impression since our arrival: the town clerk was friendly, and an old peasant welcomed us with a "Not very good weather, is it?" We went back to the car, which by now had attracted the atten-

tion of the few people to be found in the main street. There were
a few shop windows, a crossroads, and some cafés. Plodémet was
too big for a village and almost too small for a town. Johanne
pointed out that the younger women were wearing slacks—and
I had made her wear big rubber boots to make her look more
Breton! I was wearing enormous boots myself, my clothes were
what I had fondly imagined to be rustic, and when I walked I
rolled my hips a bit as if I had spent a good part of my life on
board ship. When we got out of the car—she with the tall, graceful
figure of a model, her black skin, and her sewerman's boots, and
I looking for all the world like some peasant fisherman out of an
operetta—we caused a sensation.

We drove out of the "town," along the coast to the little fishing
village of Pors-Ensker, then on to Audierne, where the sky suddenly cleared. From there, we drove to the Pointe du Raz, the
westernmost tip of Europe. The tourist hotels, restaurants, cafés,
and shops were all shut. Everything was deserted. The sun set
over the Atlantic to the accompaniment of roaring winds and
crashing waves. We felt we were in one of the most beautiful
corners of the world.

Next day, we made our first calls on the simple café-wineshops
known as *buvettes*. Sensing that Peninou, the young research
worker to whom I hoped to leave the day-to-day running of the
project, and himself a Breton, was even more intimidated than
I was, I decided to give him a demonstration of the sociological
human touch. So, summoning up courage, we entered the Rendez-
vous des Pêcheurs at Pors-Ensker. There were about seven or
eight fishermen, probably in their late fifties, and a woman behind
the bar. Imagining that I was dabbling in local color, I ordered,
in as steady a voice as I could muster, two glasses of cider liqueur.
Unfortunately I did not realize, in the first place, that this *alcool*,
or dry liqueur, is called *lambic* in those parts, and secondly, that
its sale is forbidden. The company exchanged sly looks. My confidence crushed, I ordered cognac. The old men looked at us and
talked in Breton among themselves. They were drinking red wine.

"Fine country, isn't it?" asked an old man, who seemed to take
charge of the conversation and who soon introduced himself as
Michel Poullan.

I explained that we had come "for the research project." But old Poullan was surprised that my car did not carry the government plate (DA) on it like those used by the other research workers. I told him I had come in my own car and that I wanted to study the "modern" aspects of life in Plodémet. The word "modern" won general approval. Without further prompting, old Poullan told how, when he was a kid, he had walked nearly three miles to school with nothing on his feet but clogs, and a hunk of bread for each meal. When they got home, he (or one of the others) said, they stole carrots and turnips in the fields and ate them raw. Each of the old men added his own touch to the picture.

"I've been told that people regretted the past," I said.

This met with skeptical, astonished exclamations, laughter, and comments such as "I'd like to know who said that," or "Whoever said that must be crazy," or (old Poullan again) "Perhaps they were some of those rich people who paid you nothing for a day's work." Someone else added, "Yes, some big landowner," and this set off a second wave of condemnation of the past. In the old days you had to fish, grow potatoes, collect seaweed, and hire out your labor as best you could. People hadn't enough money to buy milk and butter and every poor family had to own a cow. Today nobody is poor and you can do without a cow.

Our first visit to a *buvette* surprised and delighted us. The same day we called on other *buvettes*, other cafés, and tried other drinks. Through the open, candid, yet sagacious faces of the peasants, another world began to emerge. But our impressions were already beginning to crystallize when, as we were coming out of the Rendez-vous des Pêcheurs, Poullan led me off to see his old *penty*, with a view to my renting it.

This *penty*—the traditional Breton single-story house, flanked by its two chimneys—was the old family home, now abandoned in favor of a less rude dwelling and rented out to summer visitors. The floor was of beaten earth. There was water from a cistern, a butane-gas stove, and a number of beds. The windows opened onto the sky and the sea. The garden, which had gone to seed, was surrounded by a low wall and looked down from steep cliffs onto rocks and pebbles. I was delighted with the old rustic house, with its platform overlooking the ocean. I dreamed of lobsters, crabs, fresh-caught fish, and an archaic life. That's where we would set up our headquarters on our next visits in April and June–July.

In the next few days the fascination of the landscape, of the faces, and of the problems that flowed in from every side brought us more and more under its power. I was caught, captivated, as if I had fallen hopelessly in love, as if I had been snatched from my own orbit and made to follow a new sun.

Another month saw the first meeting with the "three flowers of the moors" and the meetings with the young people at the Café des Droits de l'Homme, from which the youth club was born. We had settled in at Pors-Ensker and were taking root.

We asked for and were given additional funds, which enabled me to build up a research team. As will be seen later, my research methods gave pride of place to immediate data, conversations, meetings, and notes taken on the spot.[1]

Nevertheless, the result of this inquiry is in no way a piece of *"sociologie-vérité,"* by analogy with *cinéma-vérité*—that is, a montage of data, observations, and confessions. It is true that I had been tempted by this method; I had envisaged just such a project, but in the form of a second volume, a supplement to my study. For it seemed to me necessary first of all to understand what was happening, to understand, that is, the prodigious transformation taking place within a whole social organism, which was passing from a rustic-plebeian civilization that was still very much alive to an urban-bourgeois civilization that was already alive. In order to comprehend this transformation, I would have to try and reconstruct the historical-sociological texture of Plodémet and discover how it had integrated itself within the texture of French life in general.

It was not a simple task: I could not see the transformation of Plodémet as a transition from a "traditional" society to an "industrial" society. Plodémet sprang, not from an immobile, archaic world, but from an extraordinarily complex history. I would have to understand the motive forces of that history, and that would involve going back beyond the French Revolution. Moreover, what Plodémet was entering was not so much "industrial" society (on the contrary, the commune was becoming less industrialized) as a new history, modern, uncertain, and conflicting.

[1] Cf. Appendix, "The Multidimensional Method," pages 255–64.

. . .

A lot has happened at Plodémet since 1966, including, among other things, the "feedback" from the publication of my study. I had imagined that this book would be welcomed at Plodémet, where I would be received with affection and admiration. But I should have reread my Chapter 2 and realized that my book would raise problems. In any case, I would have been surprised by the violence of the mayor's reaction and that of certain teachers who accused me of wishing to denigrate and ridicule Plodémet. This opinion spread to the ordinary folk of the commune, who refused to read such a vile book, convinced that I had abused their confidence.

Of course, I had cut out of my book anything said in confidence and any unpleasant details that cropped up, but there remained innumerable small observations taken straight from life and innumerable opinions noted as they emerged spontaneously from the speaker. Many local people were extremely shocked by what, in cold print, struck me as either good-natured or quite harmless. For example, the photographer Menguy and the teacher Le Bellec protested that I had betrayed their confidence by repeating— actually, in a somewhat attenuated form—their opinions on the youth of Plodémet, and accused me of denigrating these youngsters.

I realized that there could be a dramatic contrast between two truths, one expressed in the everyday, spoken language, the other in the official, written language. For many local people, a book on Plodémet must be part of the official truth, that of civic functions, banquets, tourist guides. It must be like a wedding or family photograph, in which the group must be arranged hierarchically and the correct pose adopted and respected. And of course, I had omitted to refer to the leading lights of the community with the reverence due them. I had taken people in snapshots, as it were, without giving them time to smooth their mustaches or put on a tie. Where I had portrayed them for the general reader as good-natured or praiseworthy, they saw themselves ridiculed. The rumor spread that my book was nothing but a mass of gossip and tittle-tattle. Some people took general remarks as directed against them personally, or against their neighbors. Instead of encouraging greater understanding and friendliness between people, my book aroused rancor between neighbors; I myself had activated the phenomena of "shame" and "jealousy" whose latent presence I had noticed everywhere. Just as the peasants who had gained from land redistribution complained as much as those who had lost, fearing that they would attract "jealousy," so those who were pleased with my book complained as much as if they had been criticized. In the end, the book helped to form an abscess in which was concentrated all the mistrust of the Parisian and stranger, as well as of one's neighbor; and by a sad misunderstanding, everything I had said in praise of a fine rustic-plebeian civilization, especially everything concerning red wine and the *buvette,* was interpreted as an expression of contempt. On the other hand, the affair stimulated friendships that had been born in the course of our research and led to others in Plodémet, in Bigoudennie, and in Brittany.

Meanwhile, the transformation of Plodémet continues. The town has continued to grow, with more houses being built each year. The Café des Droits de l'Homme now has an open-air terrace, and this Mediterraneanization, which attracts the summer visitors, still intimidates the locals. Running water has now been installed, the new roads made possible by land redistribution are being built, and the new secondary school is nearing completion —which will bring back to Plodémet its dispersed young people and restore to the commune its former scholastic pre-eminence.

During May 1968, everything seemed to be calm in Plodémet, as if the fantastic upheaval that was shaking France was an exclusively urban affair. One night after a dance, however, some youngsters—some of whom had been in the youth club whose rise and decline I describe in this book—built a barricade across the main street, stopped the traffic, and singing loudly, mounted guard. The police were called from Pont-Croix; the barricade was dismantled and a few arrests made. It was the only young people's barricade in Bigoudennie—even, it seems, in the whole of Brittany. Once again, Plodémet had shown its astonishing originality in the very movement that set it in profound resonance with the events in France.

E. M.

Paris, August 1968

PLODÉMET

Report from a French Village

1
First Appearances

In Brittany, the westernmost region of France, in the westernmost area between Quimper and the Pointe du Raz, where the West ends, lies the commune of Plodémet.

One feels that this is land's end in the violent wind sweeping the length of the coast of Cornouaille, which prevents trees from growing and dries out the ground even though it is exposed to an ever-present drizzle. The commune is battered by the ocean along four miles and more of pebbles, rocks, and breakwaters, which gradually rise into a small cliff toward Pors-Ensker. Seventeen miles to the west, at the end of an increasingly bleak peninsula, is the Pointe du Raz, turbulent, utterly remote. Yet in the commune itself the violence of the ocean is soon forgotten; just a few hundred yards from the shore, the first trees, isolated and puny, appear behind houses, and the hollows of the shallow valleys manage to shelter tall poplars.

The ancient, wild Armor is acutely felt in the moors and pine woods that flank the commune to the north, but the wildness is almost immediately broken up, absorbed, and dissolved in cultivated fields.

One witnesses another world as people flock in from the countryside for Sunday mass. The old men wear round hats, black velvet tunics buttoned at the side, and varnished wooden shoes; the old women wear tall cylindrical coiffes of white lace, and satin or velvet aprons over ample black skirts. They speak Breton. This is the ancient territory of the *pou*[1] of Bigoudennie.

[1] *Pou* is the Breton equivalent of the French *pays*, meaning land or country. The *pou* corresponds to an ancient ethnic or territorial division which survives in a sense of belonging or in regional costume and accent.

Those under fifty wear their Sunday suits and dresses and speak French.

Enveloped by sea and moors, suffused with Bigouden culture, the commune of Plodémet, population 3,700, forms a rough triangle whose northern base adjoins the Capiste country[2] and whose southern tip points in the direction of Pont-l'Abbé. The southwest side is the shoreline and the east-southeast side cuts toward Landudec and Poulzic.

The *bourg*, or town of Plodémet, population 1,200, is not in the exact geometric center of the commune but a little to the northwest of it, slightly over a mile from the coast, as the crow flies. It stands at the junction of four roads, one to Quimper (the prefecture of Sud-Finistère, twenty-one miles away, population 40,000); another to Audierne (a lobster port in the Capiste country, six miles away, population 4,000); a third to Pont-l'Abbé (the "capital" of Bigoudennie, a market town with a population of 5,800, nineteen miles distant); and a fourth toward the sea and the little port of Pors-Ensker at the northwest end of the commune.

Rural elements are present even in the center of the town: *pentys* (small one-story farmhouses) that are aligned not in relation to the streets but to the paths of the wind; a meadow where a cow or two sometimes graze bordering on the main square; two lanes flanked by modern shops, hidden behind large gates that open to let an old woman wearing the traditional peasant coiffe pass with her piebald cow; opposite the large general school, a time-worn windmill still standing among more solid structures.

One realizes in any number of ways that the town has no urban depth; the visitor, even the hasty explorer, sees Plodémet as a village. Yet the town, though still imbued with rusticity, is already shifting toward an urban civilization, testified to by the appearance of its houses, the rows of shops along its main roads, five wholesale businesses, three schools, three factories, two hotels, a movie theater, and a football field.

Plodémet's long history as a parish center is evident in its Gothic church, but as a center of urban civilization the town is not historical. Apart from an eighteenth-century building (demolished in 1966) and the *pentys* that the town has engulfed in the course of its development, almost all the houses date from the twentieth century and are suburban in appearance.

[2] The Capiste country extends from Plodémet to the Pointe du Raz.

These rectangular parallelepipeds with two-sloped roofs competed during the interwar years with another type of suburban house, the *pavillon*, a modest-sized villa in the Norman, Swiss, Basque, Gothic, or classical style. Since World War II and especially since the mid-1950's, the *pavillon* has been far more popular. The *pavillons* are obliged by town-planning regulations to follow a traditional form (two-sloped slate roof flanked by symmetrical chimneys, white rough-cast walls), but they express individual personalities in the charm of their front steps, rounded windows, varying façades, and small flower gardens and hedges. More recently (1965), a neoclassical or rural-modern building style has made its appearance in the center of town, with imitation stonework, mansard roofs, and tiled porch roofs.

The prevailing shape of roofs and chimneys gives the town a decidedly Breton appearance, interrupted only by the suburban fantasies embodied in the *pavillons*. There are no apartment buildings, only separate family houses. These are working-class or lower-middle-class dwellings, except for a few large villas and a single upper-middle-class house hidden by a high wall and a wrought-iron gate, the residence of the Le Bail family who ruled from the town hall for almost a century.

The town has two centers, formerly separated by the Maison Kérizit, now demolished and replaced by a parking lot. One of these centers is where the main roads meet; it has two bus stops, five cafés, and four shops. The Café des Sports is decorated in the style common to urban cafés of the interwar years. Football scores are posted in the back room, which has a pinball machine and a small shooting gallery. The café also serves as tobacconist's shop, agency for the sale and distribution of newspapers, stationery store, bookshop, ammunition supply center, and insurance agency. The café Au Vaisseau des Droits de l'Homme lacks a glass front but has modernized its interior with neon lighting and decorated its walls with shells and fishing nets. It is frequented by teen-age boys and is equipped with a jukebox, electric billiards, a miniature football game, and a miniature shooting gallery. Marie, the proprietress, a handsome woman between fifty and sixty, wears the traditional Bigouden coiffe and wooden shoes, hums the latest pop songs, and fetches her cow from the meadow. The Ty-Koz *café-crêperie* has a neorustic façade for the benefit of tourists; crêpes are seldom made out of season, when the Ty-Koz reverts to its essential functions as café, bus stop, and parcel depot.

The town's second center, a more institutional one, accommodates the town hall and the church, antagonistically facing each other across the square, as well as the cemetery and the post office. Sunday mass is attended by about a quarter of the population. Men and women, adults and children, are separated during the service. The town hall was built in 1935, as was the post office next door. Tutelary photographs of three mayors of the Radical Socialist dynasty that ran the commune between 1877 and 1951, and of Émile Loubet, President of France from 1899 to 1906, guard the entrance to the town hall.

At the post office the telephone kiosk is rarely used. Whenever old farmers cash a money order, they slip a small coin to the clerk, who cannot refuse it (as we shall see later on).

Near the church is a simple calvary. A bust of Georges Le Bail looks out from the town hall, in front of which is a statue of "two Breton buglers"—the prize given to the small commune for having built a large school by the Minister of Education, Jean Zay, before World War II. Between the town hall and the church, the war memorial of 1914–1918 depicts a Bigouden at the foot of a monolith; a more modest memorial for 1939–1945 also shows a Bigouden, but reduced to bust size.

The cemetery is near the church; it has not yet ventured to surround it and is reached by a path that skirts farmlands. The graves are marked by large stones placed over family plots, constantly tended and supplied with flowers. There are few imposing tombs; in the cemetery, as in the town, there are no ostentatious residences. Crosses are everywhere except on the grave of one Dr. Sartre who died in 1938; there the inscription tells us that the dead survive only in the spirit of the living. The cross over the grave of Albert Le Bail is encircled and painted red. The cemetery rises gently toward a low wall, beyond which lies open country. One can look down from there and survey the town on one side and the coast on the other. The town appears to be huddled around its church tower, and the coastline is dotted with small white houses. Between earth and sky, the horizontal slice of the sea is suspended in space. In changeable weather, the clouds send light and shadows chasing each other across the land, and splashes of sunlight caress the waves and the white houses. In good weather, the diluted blue of the sky and the deep blue of the sea seem to spring from the same cosmic substance.

Plodémet's industry is located to the northwest of the town (whereas the Hanff factory is right in the center of the neighboring town of Poulzic). It consists of two canneries, one for fish on the Audierne road, the other for vegetables, now put to some other use, whose tall chimney faces toward the suburb of Le Calvaire. A small factory and four workshops produce rustic-style Breton furniture.

Wholesale trade activities are situated nearby, to the east of the main crossroads where the sheds and depots of the bus company are also located. There are four wholesale businesses dealing in coal, beer, wine, and groceries. A little further east, the sight of three schools, with a total of 750 pupils, is a surprise in a town of hardly more than 1,000 inhabitants. The CEG (*collège d'enseignement général*) named after Georges Le Bail, built in 1932, is a long gray one-story building with sixteen windows in a line. The CEG for girls, which stands back from the Quimper road, competes with the Catholic Jeanne d'Arc school, near the Le Bail CEG.

In the same part of the town, the station square is half empty and barely used since the railroad was discontinued and the station demolished. A rather lifeless market is set up every month on the large rectangular site. The two hotels are located in this particular part of the town because of its proximity to the station that was. Both are rustic, despite the influx of visitors during the summer; their restaurants refuse parties that are too large in summer and parties that are too small in winter.

The economic stagnation of the area around the station is counterbalanced by the growth in the building of part-suburban, part-Breton villas for retired people.

The movie theater is housed in the Hôtel des Voyageurs and struggles along on two shows a week; its owner handles the box office, refreshments, and the projector. The football field attracts the supporters of the "La Plome" team every two weeks. Three cafés are equipped with mechanical games and jukeboxes. There are five large halls, used mainly for dances and weddings, and occasionally for meetings: the Hôtel de la Gare, the Hôtel des Voyageurs, the Café des Droits de l'Homme, the Ty-Koz *crêperie*, and the bar-*cum*-butcher's shop.

The shops run the gamut of retail commerce and artisanship: groceries, hardware stores, haberdasheries, electricians, plumbers, tailors, two hairdressers' salons, a photographer, a pharmacy, a furniture store, and a paint shop. Shop windows are more numerous, more modern, and more attractive in the town center; here an electrician and a pork butcher are in the avant-garde of neon and plate glass.

The pork butcher makes his own pâté and sells factory-made meat products, dairy produce, and chickens. He has an electric spit, and in the last few years he has taken up preparing cooked dishes for the summer visitors. The electrician floods his panoply of household gadgets with neon lighting—refrigerators, gas stoves, hot-water heaters, electric mixers (called anthropomorphically "Charlotte" and "Marie"), television sets, record players, records (Adamo, Johnny Halliday, Hugues Auffray in 1965).

The pharmacy window invites us to buy mink oil and "Urgo" bandages. A variety store lures with seasonal attractions; the summer banishes sweaters and dressmaking materials in favor of a grouping of Breton dolls gathered in a Lilliputian public square, but in the autumn the knitting wools come back into their own.

As one leaves the center, the stores no longer have display windows, fronts, or even signs; they are merely converted ground floors of houses.

The modern and the old-fashioned mingle in many enterprises in the grocery-bar at Le Calvaire; the grocery part has been turned into a self-service supermarket, but the bar remains a Breton tavern. A café-bakery has a window display consisting of ball-point pens, ping-pong balls, rulers for schoolchildren, rolls of cellophane paper, pears in a fruit bowl, and small bags of candy and peanuts.

The town is expanding fast. Along the four main roads, new houses are eating into the fields, especially on the Pont-l'Abbé road where the hamlet of Méné-Kermao is about to turn into a suburb, with a garage–repair-shop and a gas station as advance guards. To the north, the village suburb of Le Calvaire is in the process of being absorbed, and here the two extremes of the commune are in apparent juxtaposition. Next to the old village, a nucleus of urban life has established itself around the COOP (Société Générale des Coopératives de Consommation) factory;

it was in Le Calvaire that the first supermarket was opened. The factory has undergone a series of crises, however, and the working-class population has largely dispersed. Right now, despite the huge brick chimney on the horizon, Plodémet is not being dominated by industry.

The townspeople rise early, dine early, and desert the streets by nightfall. By midnight, when the street lights are turned off, the windows have long been dark, and the only light throughout the night is the intermittent flash from the Eckmühl lighthouse. Men wear dark shirts or sweater shirts, well-worn jackets, and very rarely, ties. Girls wear sweaters and slacks, older women the traditional coiffe. There is always activity in the bars and shops, and around the trucks, cars, motorbikes, and bicycles that carry on the intercourse between the town, the countryside, and the neighboring towns.

On Sunday morning there is an influx of people to the church, the cemetery, the cafés, and the food stores. But it is especially on holidays, above all on All Saints' Day and during the summer vacation, that Plodémet really comes to life. Three busloads of children studying in *lycées* elsewhere arrive; students and relatives now living in cities come home. Beginning in June, cars bearing British, German, and Paris license plates travel through to the Pointe du Raz. Dances and weddings follow one another. The town is enlivened and rejuvenated until September. During the winter it is lifeless, rainy, and old; it becomes once again a village.

Plodémet is the capital of a large commune of 6,422 acres with a population of 2,500—a density of 260 people per square mile. The land slopes gently from the interior toward the sea, gradually becoming more diversified. The geographic contour separating inland Brittany from coastal Brittany traverses the land, not in a continuous line, but in fine shadings and erasures which indicate extremely varied soils.

The mediocre land of Lamarzine, which looks like a finger of a glove on the map, and that of Menez-Ru, which looks like a large pocket, land retrieved out of moors and woods, end at the Quimper road. To the south of this road, the plateau undulates gently and the land becomes diversified, with some particularly fertile enclaves around Kerlaeron, Kervern, and Kerminou. South of the Pont-l'Abbé road, the land becomes spectacularly varied. Five dipping valleys rising to unequally accentuated ridges form slopes of differing exposures, and these carve out fields either protected from the wind or in its path, either sunny or shaded. Alluvial soil, streams, and trees in the hollows of the valleys add to the diversification. The nearer one gets to the coast, the stronger the wind driving away the rain, and the brighter the sun. Micro-climates are juxtaposed, separated by a few hundred yards, actually different in one plot of land than in the next, here favoring the growth of spring vegetables, there the growth of cereal crops.

The conjunction of all these factors has produced extraordinary ecological fragmentation reflected adversely in the habitat, as well as in the composition of the rural society, which is divided into numerous singular little components: isolated farms, seventy-seven named habitations with two to ten households each, ten hamlets with ten to twenty households each, five to six villages with about one hundred inhabitants each.

At the time of our inquiry, the commune's state of development was exceedingly uneven. Centers of modernization such as Ker-minou or the model farm of Pors-en-Breval—which had become an agricultural enterprise rather than a farming operation—were next door to pockets of technological backwardness such as Menez-Ru, and to anachronistic survivals: a few houses without electricity, an old man or two keeping farm animals indoors, an old woman who was convinced that the sun moves around the earth and that the Russian cosmonauts "will end up meeting the Lord."

The area is not entirely populated by farmers. The villages have their craftsmen (masons, tailors), tradesmen, and merchant seamen. The seamen (fishing and merchant marine) are becoming predominant in the coastal villages of Méné-Gored and Pors-Ensker, favored also by retired people.

Prevalent conditions make it difficult to divide the territory into clearly defined sections, as the dissimilarities are innumerable, commingled, and microscopic. The most one can do is make an outline of a number of areas in an indescribable puzzle.

A fertile, sunny area devoted to truck farming lies parallel to the coast. The farms are very small, selling their produce in the

Quimper market. Bravez is the capital of this zone, which is traditionally "red" in politics.

Another zone—a center of modernization and agricultural trade-unionism—consists of the hamlets of Kerminou, Penquer, and Merros in the eastern area. Here the "white" influence is dominant in politics. It extends eastward to the frontier region which is under the economic and political influence of Poulzic, whose cannery absorbs its labor force and produce, and whose parochial school draws Catholic children away from the small state school at Lesnus.

The pocket-ghetto of Menez-Ru is cramped and isolated, a blind alley in the unproductive land of the northeast. Cows and people wander about the muddy roads of the village, equally indifferent to strangers. Menez-Ru has been very slow to accept modern methods, and its stubborn backwardness makes it the laughingstock of the whole commune.

On the coast to the extreme northwest, Méné-Gored and the little port of Ensker, intersected by a stream, are the centers of maritime life in the commune. The men always wear their blue caps. Old men fish from the shore. Fishermen's families tend to move to the port of Audierne, where the lobster boats are moored.

Thus, at first sight, one notes that the commune of Plodémet is a microcosm of maritime, rural, and urban life, extraordinarily diversified and bristling with peculiarities.

This microcosm is in continuous flux. Town and country are changing rapidly. Villages are dying. Houses for retired people and summer visitors are being built in great numbers. The 1966–1967 land redistribution has filled in sunken roads and leveled hills. New roads are being built. At the time of our inquiry the whole landscape of Plodémet was being transformed.

2

Others

Investigator and Subject

This study, you don't know what it's all for. But it's bound to be useful later on. They explained it all at school. It's for history, sociology, and all that. But I don't understand what your study is all about. It won't make any difference to things here, except perhaps in the long run. Anyway, it must have some purpose or you wouldn't be doing it. It must be logical, it must have a purpose. My mother thinks it's of no use at all and that I'm wasting my time with you.
(Marie, age 22, Menez-Ru)

We were very much afraid of finding an overresearched region and sneering peasants. Anthropometric and medical examinations had been carried out on a large scale. A team from the Musée de l'Homme in Paris, under the direction of Monique Gessain, had made a film that was in part concerned with the population of Plodémet. Representing the social sciences, J.-C. and M. Kourganoff, Albenque, Izard, Maho, Solange Petit, and Donatien Laurent had spent nearly a year at Plodémet, and except for Laurent and Petit, all had circulated questionnaires. More than 1,000 people had come into direct contact with the multidisciplinary inquiry. Most of them, however, had undergone only anthropometric, diagnostic, or gerontological examinations. The work in the social sciences had affected about 400 individuals and 350 households.

Two out of three persons had not been interviewed in the course of the multidisciplinary research, and two out of three households had not been included in the sociological inquiries, which in any case usually consisted of a single session with a questionnaire. At the other extreme, there had been too much interviewing of officials and prominent citizens. Every researcher questioned and requestioned the mayor, the town clerk, the parish priest, school principals and teachers (who were particularly subjected to intensive questioning), the leading farmers, and other notables. But as we shall see, it was not the excessive questioning alone that caused dissatisfaction. The questionnaire was not without a certain allure for those who saw in it a ceremonial element, or those who felt flattered that attention was being paid to the insignificant details of their everyday lives. The baker's wife in Menez-Ru was annoyed because Paillard, unlike three previous researchers who had accorded her the honor of a questionnaire, was content to talk to her. Those skipped by the study felt unjustly neglected. Still and all, the questionnaires were not always welcomed.

"One has been here already. He asked strange questions. You don't know what to answer, but you have to say something. As a matter of fact, I am not interested in all this . . ." (Menez-Ru).

On arrival, then, we benefitted from our subjects' familiarity with such inquiries. At the same time we did not find an over-studied field (the myth of the researcher who thinks he has exhausted that field which he has worked in); what we did find was that the questionnaire had been discredited. We would refrain from using it at any rate. What is more, we were to discover gradually that the social science researcher himself had been already secretly ethnographized and sociologized by the people of Plodémet.

The research worker is never regarded simply as teacher or scholar. He is always a "DA" (*délégué de l'administration*); the initials, inscribed on the license plates of our three Citroën CV2's, marked us irrefutably as "government agents." However, we were at least not taken for some sort of tax inspectors or special police. As the patriarch of Pors-Ensker told us, our "chief," Dr. Gessain, had explicitly reassured the inhabitants of Plodémet on this score at the very beginning. This was subsequently backed up by the cooperation of the municipal authorities, the filming, the medical examinations, and the confidence placed in the research workers by the population when we settled down to live among them.

We must have seemed all the more strange because people had to combine their image of a university professor with that of a DA, which was something of an uncertain nature in itself. The formidable multidisciplinary task force aroused an unquenchable curiosity which was renewed at each contact.

"If you don't mind my asking, what exactly is this study about?" inquired a wine merchant who had seen research workers come and go for the past four years.

"People want to know who you are. You know everybody, but they don't know anything about you" (Eliane, age 18, Menez-Ru).

It is useless to reply "multidisciplinary scientific research, sociology." People want to know *what it is for.*

"What is the purpose of this?" asks the farmer, the teacher, the storekeeper. (I have asked the same question myself.) The "disinterested" nature of the inquiry is difficult for them to understand. In the first vague stage of curiosity, Monique Gessain's film explains matters, and our tape recorder seems to confirm the cinematographic nature of our enterprise. In the second stage, curiosity becames more demanding. If we say that we are studying "the modern," someone will exclaim, "Ah! It's for modernization!" An old man in Kerlaeron asked us if it had to do with poles for overhead power-lines, thereby associating the study with the government.

The more rustic the interviewee, the more he is likely to believe that the study will lead to some kind of government intervention. Having recorded a conversation among discontented old farmers in Bravez, my colleague Le Bolloch was asked by one of them, "Who are you going to get to listen to that?"

"My boss," he replied.

"And what will he do about it?"

Nevertheless, the pragmatic-governmental aspect is perhaps offset by an image of the research worker as collector of folklore and of the picturesque. This view was made popular by the film maker and ethnographer Donatien Laurent, who lived in Plodémet in 1964–1965. He was well liked by the old people and well known for his interest in old stories, old customs, and old objects. The research worker who is identified as a colleague of Donatien's becomes an amusing, harmless collector of local curiosities. A farmer in Kerfurunic invited us into his house and insisted on showing us some old drinking mugs and copper pans. "They're bound to interest you people," he said.

Thus two images are superimposed on that of the "scholar"— the pragmatic-governmental and the ethnographic-aesthetic. The

former is never completely absent and can become disturbing.
"They believe you're here to find out what they think and that
there is some other reason behind it which might eventually go
against them," said Eliane, who is from Menez-Ru where people
are particularly distrustful. Even when they are cooperative, interviewees remain on their guard and can easily turn sullen.

Toward the end of our stay, the town was aroused by a questionnaire inquiring into eating habits; among other things it was
suspected that the questions about drinking concealed a secret
attempt to compile a list of alcoholics. The proprietor of a café,
perhaps fearing the arrival of the interviewers, placed a milk
bowl filled with red wine in his dining room, where the telephone
was. I happened to ask to use the telephone that day and went
into the dining room. He went to his table, picked up the bowl,
and without taking his eyes off me, began to drink from it. In his
haste, he spilled the wine on his shirt. He interpreted my embarrassed smile as the smirk of the detective who has found
damning evidence, and that evening he accused me in the presence of a colleague of having come to spy on him.

Michel Loïc, tailor and town counselor, Goémon, commercial
traveler, Gaelic, a Bravez farmer, and the proprietor of the Café
des Sports all referred to the tape recorder as "the snoop" (*le
mouchard*) at the beginning of interviews. Only when the conversation was well under way did they manage to forget its
presence, or substitute a broadcast fantasy for a spy fantasy.

The patent mistrust of the DA was combined with the reserve
toward strangers which is well concealed by the affability of the
people of Plodémet. Their reserve results partly from a sort of
timidity, a fear of being misjudged, which takes the form of
worrying about "talking nonsense" to the educated Parisian, or
of being careful to conceal shortcomings from the stranger. This
law of silence covers not only the family but the whole village.
For example, a girl from K. who became very friendly with Anne
Leroux described to her all the people in her village, but omitted
a mentally ill individual. In Menez-Ru, not a word was said to
Paillard, who was living in the village, about a brawl one night
when the police had to be sent for because a drunkard had threatened to kill one of his neighbors.

The people of Plodémet dislike giving personal information to
strangers about individuals, especially names of personal enemies

or political adversaries. Only in moments of great anger would
those who considered themselves shortchanged in the land redistribution mention the names of favored rivals. Names, especially nicknames, are protected by a sort of communal taboo ("that's
our business"), an almost clannish code of honor by which to
name is to denounce.

Where politics is concerned, the sense of privacy is not just
communal but also personal. The refusal to discuss politics is
not merely a matter of "that's our business," it is also a belief that
"each man must decide for himself." These two feelings are
blended in Menez-Ru, where the Breton word *ru* (*rouge*) denotes
the village's traditional support for the Communist Party. Yet
when Paillard questioned the villagers on the usage of the term,
they feigned ignorance or deliberately tried to mislead their questioner—"because the soil is red," or "because the wine is red."

To be exact, the political activists see the government's antennae sprouting from the interviewer when he touches on local
politics, and vaguely fear some form of meddling in municipal
affairs. For example, I asked the town clerk whether there had
been any propaganda activities during the first round of the
presidential elections, knowing that the teachers had waged a
campaign.

"No, none at all . . ." he replied.

Our friend and fellow research worker Stourm, a teacher in
Plodémet, wrote to Peninou to tell him that a group of teachers
had put up a large number of posters, but added that he would
not tell us the names of those involved. "You will understand that
I am not in a position to do so," he wrote. Nevertheless, a certain
political connivance could be established between research
workers and subjects, who were mainly Catholics or Communists,
and the ties of friendship succeeded in overcoming the law of
silence.[1]

[1] Speaking of Peninou and myself only, we did not identify completely
with the traditional "red" point of view and remained alien to that of the
"whites." We were able to sympathize with agricultural syndicalism, even
though it was of "white" origin, because we saw a trend toward self-manage-
ment in the cooperative movement, and we could sympathize with the youth
club, although it was infrapolitical, for reasons that will become apparent
later in this book. By getting on close terms with both of these heterodox
movements, we avoided the danger of being regarded by either as followers
of the other, although at the same time it lost us the confidence of more
doctrinaire groups.

Owing to the natural friendliness of the population, the prestige of university affiliations, the cooperation of authorities, and the amicable familiarity established by previous research workers, our study benefitted from especially favorable conditions. Still, these conditions did not completely compensate for the original blemish of our being both strangers and DA's.

Reserve and distrust are not the only obstacles to communication. Certain methods of inquiry may arouse resistance of another kind, which might be called *the refusal to be categorized ethnographically.*

L.B. does not like people studying what he eats: "We're not savages. We're just like everyone else." Anthropometric measurements, which have no apparent medical utility, cause griping comments. It is conceded that one can be interested in folklore and the past, like Donatien Laurent, but to be regarded as some curious species or as "natives" is not acceptable. Plodémet is willing to be subjected to sociological but not to ethnographic and even less to entomological study.

Finally, the subjects of our study gradually learned to criticize the expertise of the research workers. When the film on Plodémet was shown, it produced something of a boomerang effect. An old woman was shown preparing and serving a *bouillie* (a boiled beef dish). *Bouillie* is a symbol of past deprivation and not served nowadays. There was a lively reaction among the spectators: "They're not going to show that to other people, are they? We don't eat like that here any more!" People felt not only that they were being ethnographically classified, but erroneously so. The old woman served the *bouillie* on a table covered with oilcloth, using her best dinnerware, which was incongruous with the frugality of the food. They were greatly amused by the trick the old woman had played, in all innocence, on the research workers. They discovered that scholars could be fooled and were fooled. They learned to mislead deliberately, and on the last of the questionnaires some gave farcical answers to questions which they did not regard as serious.

The leading citizens of the commune became more and more skeptical about the rationality of a procedure in which one research worker after another had asked the same questions for five years, without any explanations or tangible results. The element of mystery ceased to operate in favor of the hidden scientific god, and the question, "What is the purpose of the study?" was posed with increasing insistence. Criticism was sometimes directed at the selection of the interviewees, owing to unfamiliarity with sampling techniques. Efficacy was equated with duration. "Your predecessors talked a lot of nonsense. They were in a hurry to get back to Paris. They only spent two or three weeks here," the parish priest told one of us. Here again the general criticism was aimed at a disdainful stranger anxious to get back to Paris, and revealed the basic need of the people of Plodémet to be treated with respect and friendship by the research worker.

The teachers from the state school constituted the group that felt this need most strongly, and they were the ones to feel hurt —thus their eventual reticence was in proportion to their initial good will. On the very day of our arrival, a teacher we met in a café launched into an attack that can be summarized in three main themes: (1) What is the point of the study? (2) Statistics are misleading. (3) The study cannot be objective because each research worker has a personal bias.

Weariness of being constantly solicited and skepticism about the fallibility of the team cannot fully account for what became a fundamental criticism. The meaning and purpose of the multi-disciplinary project were becoming more obscure rather than clearer to the teachers, and they felt that they were not being taken into our confidence. The teachers, like their pupils, were left in the dark. Deprecating the study became an understandable act of revenge. It did not lead to refusal to cooperate but sometimes found release in a flash of irony at the expense of a young research worker.

The mayor, a former principal of the CEG, to Jean-Yves Martineau as they met in the street: "Still cutting up Plodémet and turning it into sausage?"

A justifiable dart. Did we deserve it?

The French spoken in Plodémet is clear and precise, even in the country. Breton is so far removed from the national language that it cannot pervert it; the French spoken in the commune, though colloquial and even slangy, retains its schoolroom origins and has not turned into a patois. Among the older people in the countryside, Breton is still the everyday language, and while all the men can speak French, there are still old women who know only Breton. Knowledge of Breton would certainly have helped us to establish immediate rapport and given us access to certain marginal sectors of our study, yet our lack of it was not an obstacle to communication, the obstacle being psychological, not linguistic. Saying a few words in Breton and drinking red wine —another way of saying a few words in Breton—are the rituals of friendship and respect which break down the barriers between strangers and reduce the distance between them.

The tape recorder magnifies that distance at the beginning of an interview, as the interviewee is afraid of "talking nonsense." Although it arouses inhibition, shyness, and reticence, it can also encourage, with the help of friendliness and respect, curiosity, a certain seductive appeal inherent in the microphone, and an increased individual identity. As André, eighty-one years old, so admirably put it, it both accentuates and abolishes the tremendous abyss between metropolitan technology and ancient coastal bedrock: "Well, well, it records even Breton!"

In sum the research worker presents a composite image, part scholar, part DA, part film director, part collector of oddities, and part Parisian. One or another part may predominate depending on circumstances, such as the relationship between interviewer and interviewee, or the latter's age or social position. Distrust of the alien DA increases in relation to age though it disappears among the retired. Refusal to be classified ethnographically is strong among the middle class of the town, which wishes to be and already sees itself as urban. Communication with the young and the agricultural syndicalists was not impeded by fantasied distrust, partly because they could see a practical answer to the question, "What is the purpose of the inquiry?" It acted as a catalyst and ally of youth, while the agricultural activists had their own answer to the question: "It might serve us."

Friendliness and Distrust

Perhaps we'll see you again. People usually come back to our little faraway land.
(Menguy, age 40, photographer)

Almost all the people in Plodémet are natives of the commune. The immigrants include many leading citizens, from the Le Bail family to the present mayor, and are mostly from Bigoudennie. There are very few Bretons who are not from Bigoudennie, and

only three non-Bretons—the two doctors and the dentist. Plodémet adopts its immigrants more easily if they come from nearby
or if they marry into the commune. It was difficult to determine
how people felt about the "foreignness" of the dentist and one
of the doctors, both from Normandy, because sentiments were
complex and ambivalent. On the other hand, I observed a definite
attitude of reserve toward the other doctor, a Jew who had converted to Catholicism. A sailor (Communist) referred to him not
as "the doctor" but as "the Jew." A middle-class woman said, "I
don't know where he comes from; he is a Jew," though she knew
that he was a Parisian. Conversion seems to have complicated the
doctor's position rather than clarified it. There must be something
wrong with being a Jew, it is believed, or he wouldn't try to cover
it up. Someone even remarked, "He became a Catholic only out
of self-interest." In other words, the Jew is all the more obviously
a Jew by having become a Christian. Is this a revival of outside
anti-Semitism in a region where Jews have been unknown? Or
distrust aroused by an identity that cannot be clearly defined?

In any case, the visiting stranger is given a friendly welcome,
but adoption into the community involves adaption on the part
of the visitor. He must be "simple" and "natural." He must not be
disdainful and haughty, or consider himself superior. At the same
time, of course, he must not meddle in what does not concern
him. The development of tourism has somewhat distorted this
relationship because after all, for the hotel owner and the merchant, tourists represent a large slice of profits. One or two tradesmen have already learned to juggle prices, weights, and measures.
But as soon as the visitor becomes familiar, he will get the prices
designed for friends (somewhere between local prices and tourist
prices) and gradually will benefit from the traditional hospitality.

The exotic stranger is not a cause for scandal. There is no
racism, and no ostracism is displayed toward the black African
who married a schoolteacher in the neighborhood. People are
more distrustful of the *pied-noir* ("blackfoot," meaning former
French colonist in Algeria) in Plouhinnec, who arouses a fear
of foreign colonialism. In other words, the stranger as such has
no shock value. Johanne, a tall black girl who dressed in an un-
accustomed way—whom I tried in vain to "Bigoudennize" during
the first few days so that she might go unnoticed—was neither
stared at in the cafés nor spied on from behind windows; she
did not even make people's heads turn in the street. At Plodémet,

it is normal for strangers to be different. Moreover, people felt not at all humiliated to have a black woman make inquiries into the habits of white people. Johanne played a very successful "Doctor Schweitzer" role for the women in Pors-Ensker by advising them to halve their daily ration of potatoes and twenty slices of bread, or by supplying them amylase.

To a native of Plodémet, friendliness is a Bigouden virtue particularly typical of Plodémet. Because he regards himself as natural and simple, he expects strangers to possess qualities that facilitate communication; thus being friendly and being liked are complementary. "I think the tourists like our attitude . . . We are usually very communicative" (P., age 28, roofer). Each village thinks it is the friendliest in the commune. "In all of Plodémet, our district is the pleasantest, and people get along best here" (Mme. S., age 43, Kéravrez). "Kéravrez is the most beautiful area and people here are the nicest" (T., age 41).

The people in Plodémet think they are friendly both to strangers and with each other, and don't see themselves as distrustful or aggressive in any way. Yet they make such frequent references to "jealousy" that they themselves construct an image of Plodémet as both a little kingdom of friendliness and an enclave of distrust.

Jealousy is a malevolent interest in one's neighbor. "People are too concerned with their neighbors, they are slanderous" (Mme. G., age 35, shopkeeper).

Jealousy is a thing unto itself. People do not try to explain it in terms of aggressiveness, rancor, or hate; on the contrary, jealousy explains aggressiveness, rancor, and hate. Everyone feels threatened by it. In town, jealousy operates anonymously; in the countryside, it lurks at one's neighbor's. Failure is attributed to jealousy: "He wanted to come to Plodémet, he was too trusting; his trouble was that he came back to his home town. Jealousy, you see!" said Mme. M. about her husband, a jewelry craftsman. Success fears the attack of jealousy: "When someone takes on responsibilities and becomes more competent, the others are jealous because he sees things more clearly and modernizes his farm more quickly. The others destroy him out of jealousy" (Astérix, age 26, farmer). Madeleine S. was elected beauty queen: "People say it was all arranged in advance" (a female relative). Kermélec, one of the initiators of the new agricultural syndicalism, is saddened by the jealous reactions of others. He is reproached with "thinking he is somebody, being president of this and of that."

Quarrels over land redistribution are attributed to the jealousy of neighbors, and the antennae of the first television sets were hidden in attics for fear of jealousy.

Friendliness and jealousy are the antagonistic and complementary forces that determine relations among the citizens of Plodémet, as well as between them and strangers. They are general categories, yet Plodémet thinks that friendliness is a trait peculiarly its own whereas jealousy is a trait of human nature. Friendliness is condensed in Plodémet's character; jealousy is externalized onto human nature. People are jealous, neighbors are jealous, but the citizens of Plodémet are friendly. These two notions enable them to look upon the stranger both as sympathetic alter ego and potential enemy, and to approach him cordially while remaining distrustful.

Distrust springs not only from jealousy but also from a sense of shame. Shame touches on something that lies between the old sense of honor and the new bourgeois respectability. Shame is what makes one blush, lose face, and diminish in the eyes of others. It is very widespread in Plodémet and covers feelings that range from shyness (of the young toward adults, of country people toward town people, of the ignorant toward the educated, of natives toward strangers) to dishonor (for example, for old people it is a dishonor to sell land or to be in debt).

The fear of shame and jealousy requires constant watchfulness bordering on distrust in regard to others, which contrasts with and yet complements the profound friendliness of Plodémet. There operates in effect an encompassing friendliness-watchfulness-mistrust complex, where friendliness is the immediate, obvious trait and watchfulness-mistrust the latent, recessive trait. At first sight, friendliness is dominant and distrust only affects certain spheres, but deeper down the dividing line between them is very narrow.

Is this trait peculiar to Plodémet? Or to Bigoudennie? Can it be pinpointed as a definable temperament, a "basic personality"? No, it is too general a trait and the notion of temperament is too vague, while that of basic personality is too rigid. Before we describe and refine this characteristic, we must try to identify the singularity of Plodémet in time and space.

3

The Personality of Plodémet

Bigoudennie

On some maps Brittany looks like a lion's jaws. Plodémet is situated below the lower lip, which is the Pointe du Raz, on the coast of Cornouaille, in southern Brittany. The commune is part of the Bigouden country and belongs to the canton of Plogastel in the department of Sud-Finistère.

The south of Finistère is farming and fishing country, less fortunate than the north of the department in soil, seaports, and communications. It has no access to the main Paris–Brest highway and railroad networks. Its links with Paris, 370 miles away, are tenuous, and it is far removed not only from national but also from Breton centers of industry. There are few factories, most of them working in food processing. Isolation has long hindered economic development, as it still does, while at the same time it has protected Bigouden singularity.

Bigoudennie is neither a natural region nor a province. It is an ancient ethnic unit lacking geographic homogeneity; although igored by feudal, ecclesiastic, and departmental divisions, it has not disintegrated over the centuries. Even today, the rivers Odet and Goyen serve as its visible ethnic borders. Despite the development of the general market in Quimper, Bigoudennie remains a largely isolated ethnic unit. Nothing can dramatize the extent and duration of its isolation more vividly than the fact that it was a peculiar congenital hip dislocation, widespread among Bigouden women, that initially attracted the attention of anthropologists and demographers, starting the chain reaction that culminated in making Plodémet the subject of a large multi-disciplinary research project in the social sciences.

The Bigouden country—recognizable by the tall white coiffes worn by old women—covers approximately the cantons of Pont-l'Abbé and Plogastel, with a population of about 50,000. It is bordered on the west and south by the ocean, on the east by the rivers Odet and Combrit, and on the north by the river Goyen. The frontier is fluid on the northeast, where the development of the region around Quimper, an administrative center with a mixed population, is diluting and absorbing Bigoudennie.

Bigoudennie contains and sustains within itself the contrasts and fragmentations peculiar to southern Brittany. The most obvious contrast is that between inland Brittany, which is agricultural and Catholic ("white"), and coastal Brittany, which is based on harbors and is urbanized ("red"). Bigoudennie covers both these areas of Brittany; they are clearly differentiated if one examines its northern pole (Guiler, Landudec) and its southern pole (the ports of Guilvinec and Saint-Guénolé), but they are intermingled geologically as well as sociologically in a number of communes, such as Plodémet.

Bigoudennie has no economic or administrative center; the cultural capital, Pont-l'Abbé, occupies a peripheral position. Besides Guilvinec, this is the only town with a population as large as 5,000. More than half the Bigouden population lives in the ports and towns, and urbanization is most advanced in the south.

Bigoudennie is thus maritime, urban, and rural. The rural population is either dispersed, grouped in hamlets or villages, or sometimes even surrounded in pockets within the towns. Poverty, underdevelopment, and the uncertainties of today's market operate in favor of general farming, yet geological and climatic differences have facilitated agricultural diversification. Truck farming is developing in the coastal areas while cattle breeding is expanding inland.

There is, then, no geological, geographical, agricultural, economic, social, political, or religious homogeneity in Bigoudennie; and apart from the clearly defined differences between the northern and southern poles, there is no simple, juxtaposed duality of an inland and a coastal Brittany. The differentiation between north and south is vague, erased by nature, and blurred by varied and unequal development from one commune to another and even within a single commune. Thus the north has its "southern" enclaves, the south its "northern" enclaves, and it would be impossible to delimit a central zone. Yet Bigoudennie, without a center of gravity, without a spinal column, is unified by the resilience of its ancient ties; its ethnic and cultural specificity remains real.

Situated on the northwest frontier of Bigoudennie, the commune of Plodémet contains within itself the complex and varied characteristics of the region as a whole. Whereas the northern coast lacks ports, Plodémet has Pors-Ensker; although unsuited for deep-sea fishing, it is linked to the lobster port of Audierne six miles to the north.

Plodémet is the only one of the eight Bigouden towns north of Plonéour with a population of more than 1,000. It is the administrative, parochial, scholastic, and commercial center of the large commune, as well as the focal point of communications at the junction of roads linking the cultural capital (Pont l'Abbé), the departmental capital (Quimper), and the maritime capital (Audierne).

One of two communities north of Plonéour where canneries have been located, Plodémet no longer has a rural majority. Of heads of families in the commune, 40 percent are peasants, 20 percent craftsmen and tradesmen, 15 to 20 percent workmen and office workers, 8 percent professionals (including 2 to 3 percent teachers), and 12 percent sailors (including 9 percent in the merchant marine).[1]

Diversity is not the only original characteristic of Plodémet. Agriculture shows signs of decay and backwardness resulting from the survival of very small farms. The town's two public schools (CEG's) for boys and girls have achieved exceptional scholastic standards.

The CEG brings us to perhaps the most singular feature of Plodémet, namely, the steady predominance of the red party in municipal life, even though the surrounding countryside, including partially maritime Plouhinnec and above all industrialized Poulzic, is white.

[1] The statistics are imprecise; there are some cases where either the husband or the wife has another job. Here and in subsequent instances we have brought the figures of the 1962 census up to date on the basis of our own estimates and other sources.

Far from diluting Poulzic's adherence to the white tradition, industry has strengthened it. The cannery has been integrated into rural life. The peasants who supply the town with vegetables and pork, the country people who work in the factory whose satellite Poulzic has become, the storekeepers and craftsmen, all have accepted and confirmed with their votes the authority of the Hanff family—the white dynasty of factory owners who have ruled Poulzic for as long as the red family of notaries, the Le Bails, have ruled Plodémet. Poulzic turns its back on the sea despite its modest sea front, and the factory enables town and countryside to support each other, forming an introverted commune. In Plodémet the factory has no monopoly on the economic life of the town; the seamen, the fortnightly arrival of the truck farmers, the CEG's, the town's fortuitous location in relation to the highways, all bring currents of influence from sea and city. Plodémet is an extraverted commune.

Plodémet, therefore, is not only a microcosm of Bigoudennie, itself a microcosm of Brittany. It has distinctive traits of its own, and we must seek out the interconnection among them. In what ways are Plodémet's agricultural backwardness, high scholastic standards, red politics, and extraversion linked together?

Red as in Republic

An old woman in Bravez is knitting a red sweater. Jean-Pierre Le Bolloch is watching her. "Red like the Republic," she says.

In 1877, Plodémet was a rural commune with a population of two hundred. There was hardly any commerce, very few craftsmen, no seamen, and the port of Ensker was not yet laid out. Diversity was lacking.

Yet Plodémet was already red. It was one of the few parishes that accepted a priest loyal to the civil constitution during the Revolution and retained one until the Concordat of 1801. Regarded with contempt by the bishops and watched closely by the prefects during the Restoration, Plodémet attracted the republican notary Roland Le Bail to take up residence in 1830, and then elected his son Lucien notary at the beginning of the Third Republic.

The red peasant base in Plodémet was formed by the Revolution, but we must go back further than 1789 in order to understand its native roots.

In the eighteenth century, the feudal nobility did not directly control Plodémet. The commune was a dependency of the Marquis of Pont-Croix and had no resident lord of the manor. Even as late as the sixteenth century, Bigoudennie and the Capiste country had not been securely converted to Christianity. The Jesuits, who carried out a full-scale sixty-year missionary campaign in the seventeenth century, still encountered in some places a "paganism" so thorough it was ignorant of Christ, and came up against the resistance of "secret societies" inspired by "the devil."

In the period immediately preceding the Revolution, neither the nobles nor the parish priest nor the constabulary was in control of this territory that covered 9.6 square miles. Roads ended halfway to the sea, ignoring Menez-Ru. In the eighteenth century, as today, the neighborhood of Plodémet—including the large villages of Bravez, Menez-Ru, and Ensker—had but two churches, one on the southern and one on the eastern periphery. The "pagan" areas were those that were only tenuous feudal appendages and were poorly integrated into the monarchical order: the extreme cases of Menez-Ru and Ensker lend support to this hypothesis. These two quasi-tribal villages had long remained fiercely isolated, two culs-de-sac, one turning its back to the sea (Ensker did not become a port until the late nineteenth century), the other encircled by woods and moors. Both subsisted in autarky and deprivation, almost wholly outside civilized society, always half dissident from established authority. In the eighteenth century, Menez-Ru was reputed to be a refuge for outlaws and Ensker a den of shipwreck plunderers with no churches. With no permanent affiliation with a parish, despite sizable populations, both dared to accept outdoor services given by Protestant ministers in the late nineteenth century. Both villages have been staunch and total supporters of the red party from the beginning.

At the other extreme, the rich enclaves in the eastern and southeastern areas of Plodémet where noblemen's fields were planted for cereal grains have had access to the Quimper and Pont-l'Abbé roads since the eighteenth century. They sold off part of their crops and made use of the churches at Lesnus and Saint-Ronan (built, or rebuilt, around 1750). They were of the

fabric of the old social system, and in the nineteenth and twentieth centuries they established the white bastions in the commune.

External political, economic, and religious influences have
been uneven and diffuse. Roads and railroads did not reach here
until the nineteenth century. As late as the end of the eighteenth
century, isolation and poverty ruled the enclaves where feudal
lord, admiralty, and royalty signified taxes or repression, and
where the Church, which also signified taxes, was unable to fulfill its role of integrator and consoler.

Thus Plodémet became red, not because the *ancien régime* had
become decadent, but because it never developed here. It was
lack of contact that favored the grand affair with the Republic
while, paradoxically, in the nineteenth century improved contact
favored the growth of republicanism. Isolation facilitated integration into the republican Grande Nation whereas white areas,
which were more highly developed, contrariwise became isolated.
Backwardness promoted political avant-gardism, obsolescence
favored progress.

Evidently, backwardness coincided with poverty, with proletarian virulence, and with profound egalitarianism, affecting
Plodémet's sympathy with the Revolution. Because the Revolution brought a popular message of emancipation, it broke down
the old isolation and bred a political avant-gardism, although
unable to raze archaic structures. As early as in 1675, the revolt
over duty stamps which had spread from the Monts d'Arrée to
Bigoudennie aroused, for the first time, the latent aspiration of
the backward peasant masses in their proclaiming an egalitarian
republic.

Plodémet joined France when, and because, France became
a republic. This did not happen overnight, for the message of the
Revolution continued to ripen throughout the nineteenth century. It was, as always, the reaction of the monarchy and the
clergy that lit up the face of the Republic. During the decades
of white domination, a fervor came into being and intensified to
a point where the aspirations of the peasantry—fired by the
gospel of Liberty-Equality-Fraternity and reinforced by the lib-
eral-republican ideas disseminated among the middle class—
turned into palpable demands.

From 1800 to 1848, Plodémet was subject to the authority of

the Le Guellec family. Charles Le Guellec was an educated man, a miller who had grown rich by acquiring mills and land, having benefitted from both the Revolution and the counterrevolution. He was mayor throughout the Bonaparte years and the Bourbon Restoration. Plodémet was dominated by the clergy and the notables who sat on the municipal and parish councils. A class of large-scale farmers (fifty to a hundred acres) was developing through the purchase of formerly feudal lands by the town bourgeoisie, establishing domination over the proletariat of day laborers, tenant farmers, and smallholders, who were compelled to market their labor in order to survive.

The economic inequality between this rising class and the rural proletariat widened during the 1870's. At the same time, the number of partially self-supporting smallholders increased, as did the number of peasants who saved themselves from total proletarianization by buying or leasing a few plots of land while continuing to work for prosperous farmers, constituting perhaps as much as 40 percent of the peasantry in the middle of the nineteenth century. Was the upward movement of day laborers, who were becoming partially independent smallholders, matched by a corresponding downward movement of smallholders who were becoming partially dependent? In every way, the process that continued until the Baillist era was marked by a double ambivalence. On the one hand, peasants on the lowest rungs were becoming property owners, although the inequality between "big" landowners and "small" ones was increasing. On the other hand, the situation of the partly dependent, partly independent peasantry bore within itself the possibilities of either vassalage or emancipation. Vassalage triumphed in 1848, emancipation in 1876.

The shock wave of 1848 did not reach the countryside. Isolated from the urban movement, suffering through the terrible famine of 1847–1848, the impoverished peasantry of Plodémet sought individual rather than collective relief.

But the underground dissemination of the republican spirit was renewed under the Empire. Sustained in and by adversity throughout the century, now taking a radical turn, it spread among the peasantry, more acutely than ever aware of its dependence within a partial independence, of the threat of general vassalage, and of the steady growth of inequality. Far from repudiating the color red (by which the white forces wished to identify it with communism, whose "specter rose over Europe" in 1848), republicanism adopted it as its flag.

Thus, in the course of seventy years the white political and economic revival evolved parallel to the maturation of a red rural proletariat. After the collapse of the Second Empire, Lucien Le Bail became mayor in 1870, but was removed from office by President MacMahon in 1875. The following year, with the birth of the Third Republic, Plodémet triumphantly re-elected him.

Plodémet had missed out on republicanism in 1848 but attained it once and for all in 1876. Lucien Le Bail was a middleclass republican. He was a notary like his father, and it was his seal that authenticated the smallholder's right to his plot of land: the man of law became the embodiment of the people's legal rights.

The republican party had at its command an extraordinary group of militant activists: tailors. It is a unique feature of Plodémet history, never adequately explained, that sixty families of tailors, all reds, lived in the commune at the end of the nineteenth century.

The tailors were an integral part of peasant life, even though they were transients. They stayed with the peasants just long enough to make the clothes they needed. Experts in tall tales, they drew customers from far and wide. They were living newspapers, storytellers during long winter evenings, transmitters of information, postmen. Traveling from village to village as they did, they served as intermediaries in marriages and disseminated ideas. They were members of an ancient and powerful guild, constituting a sort of freemasonry, and propagated its *Aufklärung* —in actuality, the spirit of the eighteenth century—throughout the region. The red villages of Kéravrez, Menez-Ru, and Bravez all had their civilizing tailors. The era of these village guides, these secular pastors, lasted until the period between the two world wars.[2] Throughout the Baillist period, the tailors provided

[2] A few of these red patriarchs are still alive, and their recollections ought to collected and preserved. There is, for example, an eighty-year-old tailor in Menez-Ru, a former municipal councilor. He introduced first secular, then communist ideas in his village, and tried to accommodate it to the modern world. He calmed the villagers terrified by their first sight of an automobile by explaining, "Its four legs are wheels, and inside there's a very powerful horse."

in effect a nursery for what turned out to be first-rate militant cadres, who were to replace the former notables. In 1965, the Plodémet town clerk, a large number of CEG teachers, and some university teachers born in the commune, such as the rector of the Academy of Rennes, are tailors' sons.

Ever since its rise to power the local red party has had at its command a unique leadership (the bourgeois Le Bail family to whom it has displayed loyalty for three generations), an ideological leaven and political cadre (the tailors), shock troops from Menez-Ru and Pors-Ensker ready to brandish clubs outside the polling booths, and a rural base of peasant population which has adhered to Baillism with all the force of its will for emancipation.

The beginning of the Baillist era is inseparable from economic progress and social diversification. A transformation took place between 1880 and 1910 when agriculture, virtually unchanged since the eighteenth century, was modernized. Chemical fertilizers, leguminous plants, and new equipment made possible an intensification and extension of cultivation. Land clearance almost doubled arable areas between 1859 and 1909. Market gardening was introduced and spread along the coast. The establishment of canneries encouraged the cultivation of peas and the raising of hogs.

The diversification of agriculture made smallholdings profitable at last. From 1880 on, the tendency toward large holdings was reversed, and the subdivision of land continued until 1950. In 1860, out of 380 farmers, 18 held between 74 and 98 acres each, 30 had properties between 49 and 74 acres, while the rest were only partially independent. In 1960 only 2 landowners held more than 74 acres each, 14 had properties between 49 and 74 acres, while 400 farms, almost all of them independent, included 80 of less than 2.5 acres, 156 of between 2.5 and 12.5 acres, and 97 of between 12.5 and 25 acres.

The partially independent smallholders and the agricultural proletariat disappeared along with the large white landowner. As the Le Bails acquired land they either replaced the white landlords with red laborers, as at Menez-Ru, or systematically installed red farmers and tenants, thus turning the exploited into clients. The family consolidated its red politics as it built up its property, which grew from 49 to 274 acres between 1842 and 1900 and stabilized around 345 by 1954.

Within twenty years, Lucien Le Bail completely routed the white party. Having first lost their political power, the notables, churchwardens, landowners, and mill owners subsequently lost their economic power; in general the white restoration was disintegrating. Of course, isolated white pockets survive, especially in the southern region around Poulzic, but Baillism has fulfilled the promise of 1789: land for the peasants! The subjugated rural proletariat has become a class of smallholders. Baillism has been the instrument of agrarian reform.

The promises of the Revolution could not have been fulfilled except through economic progress, and local growth resulted from the general progress of the French economy in the second half of the nineteenth century. The first factory was opened in 1890 (the Gouret furniture factory), followed by two canneries (1920). Ensker became a port, consequently a center of maritime activity. The village of Plodémet became a town, consequently a center of urban development; its population grew from 180 in 1866 to 631 in 1901 to 800 in 1911. By 1910, the transformation was complete. Plodémet's diversity was a product and condition of its red axis.

This transformation consolidated and broadened the red party. It had broken the power of the white notables, reduced the large estates, and politically crushed the Catholic countryside; it had extended its influence over the small peasantry, smallholders and tenants alike, and over the new social class of seamen, craftsmen, tradesmen, factory workers, and office workers. The red party became a coalition movement, united not merely by memories of emancipation but increasingly by the desire for upward mobility. As the big landowners declined, the lower classes rose. Members of what had been the agricultural proletariat became independent farmers and even acquired land, or went to work in the towns; partially independent farmers became fully independent; some of the peasantry turned tradesmen, craftsmen, or seamen; the demographic surplus, compelled in the past to migrate without a chance to acquire skills, now received the education necessary for state careers in the police, the customs service, or the armed forces.

Primary education, secular and compulsory, laid the real foundations of the Third Republic; in Plodémet it served to acculturate children of rural families to urban occupations, and at the same time formed a secular and republican outlook.

The transformation turned Plodémet outward. Tailors, seamen, and tradesmen had mobility and increased contact with the outside world. Baillism broke down the isolation of the coastal areas with roads and railway, completing the process in 1913 by extending the Pont-l'Abbé—Audierne railroad to Plodémet. Though genetically still self-contained, red Plodémet maintained economic relations with Quimper and Audierne, and social and political relations with all of Republican France.

As Plodémet joined the nation for the second time, it also entered the modern world for the first time. The transformation was linked to the introduction of new tools and machines, chemical fertilizers, specialization in market gardening and vegetables, and new educational and medical services. However, technical modernity, like ideological modernity, brought not a decline but rather a revival of Bigouden culture and a development not of modern but rather of traditional arts. In Plodémet, as in all of Bigoudennie, the improved standard of living did not change taste but enriched it. The great period of tailors was also a great period for embroidered ceremonial waistcoats. The elaborate Breton beds of the region, as well as dressers, cupboards, and other furniture, were embellished with carved and studded ornamentation. Around 1900, after the long years of paralysis, came a revival of the traditional tall white coiffes of Bigoudennie. During that era Plodémet attained its diversity and its red character and at the same time rediscovered its true Bigouden identity.

The personality of Plodémet, as constituted in 1900, was thus clearly the result of a progression wherein geographical conditions were utilized by the dynamic forces of history which brought out red potentialities and suppressed white elements. The white establishment could have conquered Plodémet in the seventeenth and eighteenth centuries with missionary activity or economic progress, in the nineteenth with reacquisition of land, and in the twentieth with domination by a Catholic family of industrialists, as was the case in Poulzic.

It was not maritime influence that turned Plodémet red, as might be supposed from its geographical position. On the contrary it was red Plodémet that turned to the sea, extending to it its roads, opening the port of Ensker, and making use of the non-Bigouden port of Audierne. The red movement sprang up from deep roots in the land and came to fruition with and by the Revolution. Baillism accomplished the promised alliance between the bourgeois revolution and the people of Plodémet. The Le Bail family—of non-Bigouden origin, bourgeois, Jacobin—embodied the continuity between the First Republic and the Third. Plodémet took for its guide and instructor the republican bourgeoisie. The Le Bails were such guides, guardians, and one might say chieftains, in the sense that they were more than tribal chiefs but less than princes, and their authority, founded on patronage and pressure, was feudally based but more than electorally endorsed.

Economic and agricultural development might have taken place without Baillism, but popular egalitarianism based on the smallholder, the transformation brought by social diversification, the partial deruralization, the opening up of the coastal region, and urban acculturation can hardly be dissociated from Baillism, even if it might be difficult to determine to what extent it acted as a catalyst, driving force, and organizer. In any case, the interests of the Le Bail family coincided with the great transformation.

Plodémet entered the 1950's with the economic and social structures of the 1880–1900 era still intact—as did France herself —even though the first half of the twentieth century was disrupted by two cataclysmic upheavals. The war of 1914–1918 took every ablebodied man in the commune, killed 250, and left an indelible mark on the survivors, for whom the war remained the unbelievable adventure, the unforgettable experience of their lives. Even today, whenever old men get together for a drink or for a celebration of some kind, they sing the songs of World War I. World War II caused the deportation of 250 prisoners of war to Germany, brought German uniforms, restrictions, and the Resistance. The two cataclysms disrupted and destroyed individual lives, but did nothing to remodel the social structure. The character of the commune was altered less by the two wars than by progress before 1910 and after 1950.

Nevertheless, World War I accelerated and amplified most of the developments set in motion between 1880 and 1900. Four years of hardship and "Hey, you, Breton!" from sergeants made the Bigouden conscious of his membership in the great Breton family, which became a new fraternity. The uniform, the helmet, and the German enemy completed the process of integration into the Republic, into the French nation.

At the same time, the infantrymen of Plodémet discovered France—"half a pint of wine every day, cans of sardines, and some pâté," the large, well-equipped farms in the north, the towns and their amusements. The soldiers came back with new habits, with needs for different foods, conscious of their backwardness and determined to bring their part of the world up to the level of the rest of France for which they had fought.

The women, having received allotments during the war that were higher than the wages their husbands had earned for long hours of labor, were making the same discoveries at home that the men had made in the north and east of France. The disasters of the war sharpened their sense of better living standards and progress.

The 1920's saw the formation of an egalitarian society of small-holders in Plodémet, almost all of whom owned their own houses and land. The rural proletariat greatly decreased in number; industry, which used either seasonal labor (in the canneries) or craftsmen (in the furniture factory), did not create an urban proletariat. Apart from the opening of the Azur cannery and the furniture factory (1920–1921), the economy barely advanced. The real advance lay in changing attitudes toward freedom and relaxation. The quasi-patriarchal family relaxed its fierce grip on its members, who gradually acquired the right to choose their own marriage partners. The fraternization inspired by war and the improved living conditions brought by peace dispelled traditional violence; the fights that used to take place at election time between reds and whites, between citizens of Plodémet and Poulzic, were a thing of the past. The café discussion replaced the club.

The flowering of Bigouden arts (1880–1914) was followed by the era of the tavern (to which I will return) and of the dance halls. The large dance halls were built around 1920 and became more and more popular, despite the clergy's threat to excommunicate "any person organizing dances other than for weddings" and exclude from the sacraments "young people who take part in unauthorized dances."

Compared with life in the nineteenth century, people were undoubtedly better off, but Plodémet aspired to attain the national standard of living. This aspiration sought expression, not in technical or economic advances that were impracticable within a framework of smallholdings and small businesses, but in the advancement of the younger generations through education and migration from the region.

Ever since 1905—secular laws having violently revived the

red-white conflict—the school has been at the center of political battles. During the interwar years, while continuing to be the nucleus of political struggle and the keystone of integration with Republican France, the school was becoming more and more the key to social advancement.

In the nineteenth century, the population surplus had to leave the region in order to find jobs as laborers and menials. The general improvement in conditions in the twentieth century did not absorb the demographic surplus; on the contrary, it increased it by reducing infant mortality and by raising expectations. First the primary school, then, even more markedly, the CEG transformed migration into mobility and mobility into migration. The first Baillism of internal mobility was succeeded by the second Baillism of external mobility.

Georges Le Bail, the mayor from 1898 to 1937, was not merely the local chieftain; he was repeatedly re-elected councilor and deputy, and was an influential member of the Radical Socialist Party. It was he who succeeded in achieving for Plodémet the extraordinary privilege of its CEG. In 1934 a banquet attended by 1,500 guests celebrated the completion of the school.

The CEG made Plodémet into a secular capital and accentuated its difference from the neighboring communes where religious education was dominant. It became the means of mobility and migration for sons of laborers, peasants, clerks, craftsmen, tradesmen, and seamen. During the 1930's, the Georges Le Bail CEG graduated an average of 25 students a year. Plodémet took the lead in red Bigoudennie and Sud-Finistère, which were already exceptionally well served scholastically. In 1962, the percentage of its children in secondary education was very high in relation to the national average: 85 percent for the commune, over 80 percent for the rural areas. The percentage of students receiving higher education was more than double the national figure, and triple that for sons of farmers (12.5:5 and 10:3.6).

From 1900 to 1914, Baillism had fought for a school representing its policies; during the interwar years, it fought successfully for the policies represented by the school. The CEG remained, until 1955, the pivot of Plodémet's future. The red social classes accepted and insisted that all local policies be subordinate to the policies of and in behalf of the school. The CEG set off a great wave of mobility through education, that is, mobility outside Plodémet.

The white forces fought not only against the secular character of the school but also against the school's policies. They opposed mobility and migration, and propagated a policy of keeping the peasants on the land. They made a distinction between communal facilities—roads, water, and electricity—and facilities of the commune. They contrasted Plodémet, which was transferring its vitality to an urban-style society, and Poulzic, which was finding work for its population at home and concerning itself with the economic development of the commune.

On several occasions between 1910 and 1930, Georges Le Bail thought of devising a policy of agricultural modernization, but in fact scholastic pioneering was a cause of agricultural backwardness. By the same token, the difficulty of modernizing an agriculture based on smallholdings and the negligible size of industry in Plodémet were the factors that committed the commune to the policy of mobility through education.

THE CRISIS

The backwardness of agriculture worsened during the period 1930–1945, but became less and less apparent. The strength of its multicrop farming protected Plodémet from the depression of 1931 and placed it in an advantageous position during the deprivations of 1940–1947. The Occupation actually put a premium on backwardness; the black market concealed economic problems; the crisis in small-scale farming was deferred.

Although occupied, Plodémet suffered less from World War II than from its predecessor; the second war took 250 prisoners whereas the first had killed that many. Geography made Plodémet a negligible link in the Atlantic Wall and an ill-suited terrain for the *maquis*. Plodémet was not occupied in strength, nor was it a focal point for resistance, nor did it experience the worst kind of repression. As was generally the case in the occupied areas, the commune was unaffected by the influence of the Vichy government and a resurgence of white power could not be launched. Moreover, there was no nucleus of Breton separatists to encourage collaboration—in Plodémet both reds and whites were hostile to the occupying forces. The Resistance was organized in networks and movements in which Albert Le Bail and many Baillist militants took part. The Communist Party, already strong in Audierne and the organizing force behind the National Front in 1941, and later the *maquis* inland, became firmly entrenched in Plodémet. A mismanaged parachute landing illustrated both the activities and the limitations of the local Resistance. When the Germans left, Plodémet burst into celebration; the enemy returned unexpectedly and fired on the procession, killing three.

Although Albert Le Bail was in the Resistance, Plodémet changed its political skin under the Occupation. During the interwar years, local radicalism was able to absorb socialist and communist trends introduced by the tailors, seamen, and teachers, but during the Occupation renewed communist pressures broke through. Under the leadership of the Poullan family, Pors-Ensker went over to the Communists, as did Menez-Ru, propagandized by the "patriarch" Menguy, though with less homogeneity. The Communists then held between 30 and 40 percent of the red electors, and the Socialists also began to gain followers.

The reds were divided into three mutually hostile parties. After the Liberation, Albert Le Bail was re-elected mayor out of loyalty to his family. At his death in 1951 the Radicals split into two groups; one, led by the industrialist Azur, tried to form an alliance with the whites, the other remained faithful to the old anticlerical alliance. Finally in 1959, a coalition of Radicals, Socialists, and Communists succeeded the old homogeneous radicalism that ruled under the Third Republic. The new mayor, Maurice, was a Socialist, therefore a link between Radicals and Communists. Also headmaster of the CEG, he represented red unity.

The political thaw between 1945 and 1955 contrasted with the economic stagnation which prevailed despite the return of the prisoners of war. Many of these had been assigned to work on German farms, and some had naïvely identified with the German lands of which they had been both masters and servants. Almost all had admired the equipment and learned modern techniques. "They're a hundred years ahead of us! Their cowsheds are better than our houses" (Kerveil, from Menez-Ru). "Better equipped and organized . . . collectively owned machinery . . . they already had land redistribution when I was there" (Yvon, from Kéringard).[3] However, their desire for change was dissipated

[3] To most of the peasants in Plodémet who are over forty, it is not America but Germany that symbolizes modern techniques.

after their return by daily routine, the difficulties of small-scale farming, or personal problems.

Beginning with the 1950–1955 period, the economy of Plodémet, especially agriculture, entered a time of crisis, and stagnation was regarded as backwardness. Backward economy and immobility, though originally allied, now combined to deprive the commune of its younger generation. Yet at the same time an extraordinary transformation began to take place, affecting every aspect of communal society. It has not yet erased the basic features of the character of Plodémet, but it has begun to muffle them.

The Statue of the Bigouden Women and the Bust of Georges Le Bail

GWINN RU

The character of Plodémet, formed during the metamorphosis of 1880–1910, reached its maturity in the plebeian-rustic culture of the interwar years. This was foreshadowed by the late flowering of Bigouden arts at the beginning of the twentieth century, even though in a strict sense it was not oriented toward the arts. Moreover, facing competition from the standardized products of urban civilization, the traditional arts of furniture and apparel began to decline after 1918, as did the wearing of embroidered clothes and tall coiffes. The culture of Plodémet had little to do with painting (pictures other than religious ones found their way into people's homes only much later), reading (except newspapers), music (there was no choral society), or architecture. The teachers, although they played a dominant role in the life of the commune, tried neither to safeguard culture in the folk sense of the term nor to popularize it in the bourgeois-artistic sense. On the other hand, they helped to develop one of the two sources of Plodémet's culture: ideological and political passion.

Plodémet is a remarkable center of political culture. The people of this faraway region where two conceptions of the world, of man, and of society confront each other are passionately concerned with ideas and argue about the existence of God, the virtues of science, and the reality of progress. They name a café "The Rights of Man," a fishing boat "The Love of Humanity."

Politics dominates everyday life; it is a major subject of conversation in cafés and homes.

In the nineteenth century, cabarets and dance halls sprang up throughout France, centers of a popular culture characterized by public consumption of red wine. Bigoudennie had its *buvettes* (small bars) where people could express themselves, free of the bourgeois world and ecclesiastic control. The *buvette* is a completely secular institution, both communal and anarchistic (lacking any hierarchy), an oasis, a positive utopia in the life of ordinary people.

The inexpensive, modest wine of the south of France became available in Brittany at the end of the nineteenth century and reached Bigoudennie at a time of critical change and progress. In Plodémet it coincided with the entrenchment of the red party, and wine consumption also became a daily practice among soldiers in World War I. Red Plodémet was not subject to the constraints of morality, bourgeois dignity, or religious authority, influences that might have stopped the flow of *gwinn ru* (*vin rouge*). In 1880, there were 15 licensed bars; in 1930, 80; in 1962, 33. Today, Bravez, with a population of seventy, and Scantourec, with fewer than sixty, each have three *buvettes*.

The *buvette* reached its maturity in the years before World War I, at the same time as public dances and traveling shows, which accompanied, and actually dominated, religious feasts honoring saints. Red wine—*gwinn ru*—accompanies, assists, and develops communication with others, so the *buvettes* became centers for discussion, comment, and exchange of pleasantries. The glass of red wine became the universal rite of communication, not only in the *buvettes* but also in the homes, where the bottle is brought out at once for the visitor. One communicates in order to drink, as one drinks in order to communicate.

The fundamental ambivalence of alcohol makes it adaptable to the most contradictory needs. One drinks to rediscover oneself as well as to forget oneself; one drinks in company and also because of loneliness; one drinks to celebrate and also to drown sorrows. Like art, wine liberates fantasies, stimulates imagination, mixes dream and reality.

Like poetry, *gwinn ru* contains the potentiality of union with the world and escape from it, and, like poetry when it is the ally of unhappiness, it brings dissipation and death. In Plodémet, red wine inspired communication more than it caused alcoholic dissipation. Plodémet was not submerged by alcoholism. There was an extraordinary capacity—among fishermen, for example— to absorb several quarts a day without apparent damage. A man who could drink six quarts in succession told us, modestly, "It's not much." Self-regulation was strong enough to prevent degeneration. Yet it seems that every family has been struck at least once by alcoholism, although it is difficult to be sure; the collective sense of shame conceals cases of cirrhosis, delirium tremens, and hospitalization from the stranger. Some families were ruined by the father's alcoholism; a few became alcoholics together. Alcohol destroyed especially those already ruined by misfortune. The agricultural proletariat suffered most; a man drank because he could not escape his circumstances, and he could not escape them because he drank.

During and after World War II, alcoholism began to diminish. The women, who had been unable to prevent its rise, intervened with the increased authority derived from progress in female emancipation. Some even threatened divorce, although not yet daring actually to use this new weapon. Others continued grappling with the problem and succeeded in tearing their husbands away from their Sundays at the *buvette*. The younger generations drank less and less as they remained in school longer; among them daily drinking was replaced by bouts of drunkenness at dances and during public holidays. Clubs were founded to combat alcoholism, and they had three cures to their credit in the town.

In the end it was the growth of the middle class that reduced both the incidence of alcoholism and the number of *buvettes*. These days, only a few solitary drinkers while away the evening in the bars. Life is centered more and more around home and television; urban civilization has brought other tranquilizers and intoxicants, other escapes, other fantasies.

Nevertheless, the *buvette* remains an active part of life in Plodémet, and it has a counterpart for women, the *petit café,* or coffee session. Every afternoon, in town and village, neighbors and friends meet over coffee and cake. Today's *petit café,* however, is quite different from the social convention of afternoon tea among bourgeois women in that it is the expression of what has become a habitual need to communicate.

Basically, the *buvettes, petits cafés,* and dances are representations in Plodémet of a popular culture that since World War I has supplanted—except in sullen villages like Menez-Ru—the ancient distrust among neighbors along with the violent excesses that formerly accompanied political battles. An amiable sociability has settled over the commune where bands of children from one village once fought bands from another, where the slightest quarrels once turned into fights and election disputes caused fatalities.

The disappearance of violence, rooted in the catharsis of 1914–1918, is undoubtedly linked to the profound political and social stabilization during the period between 1919 and 1940, and to the evolution of the agrarian class of smallholders enjoying at long last its first experience of better living standards.

It is remarkable that so few traces of aggressiveness remain in evidence in Plodémet today, if one applies the following criteria:

1. The drunks one encounters are affable.
2. At dances, quarrels are quickly smoothed out, and are not exacerbated by groups of friends.
3. According to expert opinion, land redistribution gave rise to fewer conflicts and less violence than have occurred in other communes in the region, causing only quarrels and a few fights.
4. Physical violence in political disputes has disappeared.
5. Schoolchildren are "timid," according to teachers from outside the commune.
6. The adolescent revolt against parents and authority is moderate.

One might conclude that affability, which seems to both visitors and natives a trait characteristic of Plodémet, could develop only as a result of a flourishing sociability linked in its turn to a flourishing culture which is politically and alcoholically red.

Of course, affability is more generally a Bigouden characteristic perhaps deeply rooted in ethnological and ecological conditions, and could not be said to constitute a distinct Plodémet "temperament." But the history of Bigoudennie—and in a particularly stimulating way, the history of Plodémet in the twentieth century—evidently transformed a latent characteristic into a dominant one, in sharp contrast to Menez-Ru, still isolated, still sullenly distrustful of visitors and even of neighbors.

Let it nevertheless be said that affability has not entirely overcome reserve and distrust in Plodémet. Although these characteristics are recessive at present, changing conditions and circumstances might reawaken them. This is yet another manifestation
of the commune's bipolarity; on the one hand, there is an open-
ness toward neighbor, stranger, and the world, and on the other,
a wall around family, village, and the genetic community.

THE METABOLISM OF PLODÉMET

Bigouden identity is deeply rooted in Plodémet. The commune
may not know that it embodies a microcosm of Bigoudennie, but
it knows and feels that it is a frontier. Here, as everywhere, the
country's heartbeat is strongest at its frontiers, and in 1962 the
red municipality erected on the cliff of Pors-Ensker, facing inland,
a proud statue of a young woman wearing the traditional Bigouden coiffe.

The identity of Bigoudennie, of Plodémet, of village or neighborhood, of family, all have the same roots. Identity is a sense
of genetic belonging which expands or contracts depending on
whether one is considering *his* family in relation to the village,
his village in relation to the commune, *his* commune in relation
to the other communes, *his* Bigoudennie in relation to Brittany,
and on a more superficial level, Brittany in relation to France.

Within the family, identity is equated with solidarity. On the
communal plane, the social structure of Plodémet is heterogeneous and fails to constitute a *de facto* community. Reds and whites
are opposed to each other in politics and religion; the miniature
identities of villages and neighborhoods result in miniature local
chauvinisms; isolationist Menez-Ru and outlying Lesnus do not
fully share in the feeling of communal belonging; tradesmen, seamen, peasants, townspeople, all form more or less self-enclosed
groups. Yet despite these heterogeneities, the identity of Plodémet
forms an extraordinarily forceful matrix.

In the most important occasions of life and death, the enact-
ments of Bigouden family sentiment are concentrated in Plodémet. All family ceremonies—weddings, baptisms, and funerals—
take place here, for the town with its church, cemetery, town
hall, and wedding halls is the center of identity for a dispersed
population. Reds and whites rediscover their common roots. The

reds do not attend church, yet they are baptized, married, and buried according to religious rites. These church ceremonies are also grand familial rites, reassembling parental lineages (in the Breton manner) and transforming the commune into a community for the day. Weddings and funerals are not private; on the contrary, they are open to the entire commune. Any resident can participate in the wedding banquet, if he pays for his meal, and join in the semipublic dance that is held afterwards in one of the wedding halls. Similarly, funerals are attended not by invitation but as a communal duty; until recently, everyone paid his fare in the bus that takes mourners to the cemetery. Wedding banquets and funeral processions draw two hundred to three hundred persons. At the funeral of the old tailor Le Moign, father of the dean at the Academy of Rennes, the procession consisted of more than a thousand persons.

Each great rite of life shakes the genealogical tree to its most distant branches and occasions a pilgrimage to the cemetery in Plodémet. Death is the deepest root of Plodémet's identity.

All Saints' Day, the ancient Celtic New Year's Day—holy day of the dead who live on, of their return among the living, of the visit the living pay them—is celebrated throughout Plodémet, although reds do not even observe the Fourteenth of July. Graves are cared for and decorated with flowers throughout the year, but on All Saints' Day they are bedecked with sumptuous floral displays. Busloads of young people come home from *lycées* and universities. Each year, more and more natives come from the cities of their residence; they seem to have become increasingly attached to their home town, and more and more of them have cars. The feast of the dead is the feast of the reassembling family, of the living reuniting with the dead. It represents a reconstitution of the *archē* and of the old Celtic beliefs, more or less overlaid by Christianity and secularization. All Saints' Day is the great feast day of genealogy and matrix, the common bedrock of life and death; it is also the most important day of the year for the commune when the identity of Plodémet finds its fullest expression.

The vitality of All Saints' Day is all the more remarkable when one considers that such quasi-pagan rites as midsummer bonfires and harvest festivals have declined in popularity, along with Bigouden arts and folklore. Plodémet has preserved only those elements of traditional culture that sustain the cult of family-Plodémet-Bigoudennie—that is, the sources of its identity.

Red republicanism has always sought to preserve all that is profoundly characteristic of Bigouden identity, but it has been indifferent to folklore and has repudiated any trend that might tend to encourage provincialism or autonomy. Attachment to the Bigouden motherland is completed, not contradicted, by attachment to the Republican fatherland. Red Plodémet is totally loyal to the great centralized nation, one and indivisible. Bigoudennie and the Republican State are both sovereign, each in its own way, each in its own sector. Such complementarity is based on the rejection of any regionalist or provincialist policy—a rejection that comes easily since Bigoudennie has never been a political or administrative unit. Plodémet citizenship is thus based on Republican nationality, not on community. This accounts for Plodémet's support for almost a century of a bourgeois family in the mayor's chair, although its members were strangers not only in origin but in class. In the same vein, the present mayor is not a native of Plodémet either.

The red citizen of Plodémet is wholly Bigouden and wholly French. The identity of Plodémet is firmly based on this dual foundation.

This bipolar identity enables one to understand Plodémet's bilingualism. Breton is not a provincial language but, with its own pronunciation, the language of Bigouden, or more precisely, with its local passwords, a dialect of the soil. It is preserved as the language of family life in the countryside and as the language of connivance and concealment in the town. Old people love teaching Breton to their grandchildren, and for the young it is the sentimental community language to be used with the old, for jokes among friends, and for mocking strangers. However, French is recognized by everyone as the necessary language, not only of commerce and education but also of thought and progress. Old peasants attribute their difficulties and backwardness directly to the Breton language: "If I spoke better French I could argue like the others." Some farmers in Menez-Ru told Paillard: "One can be understood only in French." It was inconceivable to them that Breton could be taught in school. Breton is not regarded as the same kind of language as French; it must be preserved as a dialect, not utilized as a language. French is the language of

ideas, of intelligence, associated with enlightenment and progress and with that aspect of Plodémet's identity which is enthusiastically national, while Breton is reserved for what is fervently
Bigouden. Conscious and voluntary bilingualism is an exact reflection of Plodémet's bipolarity.

The statue of the Bigouden woman at Pors-Ensker watches
over the commune. The foster mother of Albert Le Bail's children posed for the statue when she was young. The bust of
Georges Le Bail watches over the town hall. In this, again, Baillist
Bigouden principles blend together to share the identity of Plodémet. The Bigouden symbol is feminine; the republican symbol
is masculine. The maternal principle springs from the matrix of
archē, the paternal principle from the republican *polis*. For the
red majority, the two merge in the town hall, in the emanation
of native vitality and the republican system. The fullness of the
maternal-matrix element in Bigoudennie and the abundance of
the paternal-legislative spirit in Republican France fostered the
intimate union of the two principles, eliminating provincialism
and regionalism as well as any trend toward autonomy.

Crushed between Bigouden and national manifestations,
Breton identity has long been uncertain and secondary. The Bigouden was aware of the difference between himself and other
Bretons, but gradually, what with military service, two wars, and
increasing contact with the outside world, he began to recognize
himself as a Breton. He accepted the national cliché of the "stubborn Breton" and turned obstinacy into a virtue; the Breton is
hardy, he sees a job through, he is the foot soldier sent to the
front lines. He integrated it with Bigouden qualities—the Breton
likes his drink, he is gay and affable. Thus, he has been led to
accept his Bretonness more and more as a natural trait.

Breton awareness was definitely encouraged by the white element. Politically asphyxiated in red Plodémet, it was natural that
whites should tend to identify with interior-Catholic-landed-
separatist Brittany. I do not know whether the white party empha-
sized provincialist tendencies early in the century, but I am inclined to think that it identified more with Catholic, traditionalist
France than with federalist Brittany. The absence of any movement for Breton autonomy in Plodémet seems to indicate that
the white party viewed its political struggle more as a local
episode in a nation-wide conflict than as the resistance of an

autonomous region to a centralizing foreign state. Nevertheless, the new regionalist-provincialist tendencies that have begun to develop after 1965 (to which I make additional references in the final chapter) are reaching Plodémet through white channels, slowly infiltrating the thinking of red supporters. This represents a new awareness of the economic underdevelopment common to Bigoudennie and all of Brittany, requiring a specific program of remedial action. Thus the conception of Breton identity, once atrophied, is now evolving.

CONCLUSION

There exists, especially south of the Loire, a red France relatively unaffected by urbanization, industrialization, and efficient economic planning. During the Revolution the rural population sealed a grand alliance with the Republican State which brought integration with the nation, once France was identified with the Republic in a structural sense and not merely through the revolutionary struggle. Red France remained loyal to the Jacobin State which gave it the means of education and jobs in the civil service. It was rapidly secularized, even de-Christianized, and a century later turned, quite naturally, first to socialism, then to communism, which maintain and recapture the popular, egalitarian tradition of Jacobin radicalism.

The red native of Plodémet, fundamentally a peasant, seems to make Plodémet into a detached portion of southwest France. Yet he also belongs to Finistère, which means that he is conditioned by peninsular remoteness and Bigouden anachronisms, and has been integrated since the end of the last century with red coastal Brittany.

None of the elements that constitute the personality of Plodémet is unique to Bigoudennie, to Brittany, or to any part of France. What is unique is the singular combination of these elements, evolved through highly individual developments.

Under these circumstances, our problem was to determine the principle by which to grasp, assemble, order, hierarchize, and articulate traits that would eventually yield the profile of the personality of Plodémet.

The workable principle was found to consist in unearthing the foundations of ancient folk traditions, sustained by peninsular remoteness, Bigouden isolationism, and the French Revolution. The relationship between national and local development took the form of a remarkable interplay between social obsolescence and ideologically charged modernism, between economic backwardness and political avant-gardism—an interplay wherein obsolescence and backwardness were not residual forces but, on the contrary, components of avant-gardism and modernism. Escaping from its shaky feudal and religious framework, Plodémet found its orientation and its guidelines in the urban bourgeois Republic.

Far from abolishing the bipolarity, the era of development and diversification between 1880 and 1910 structuralized it for all intents and purposes. Bipolarity between Bigouden introversion and national Republican extraversion remained a fundamental factor. It set off new processes in that Plodémet opened up more and more toward French society, and with mobility and migration the communal substance seemed bound to be lost in the national melting pot. On the other hand, the little Bigouden commune remained ethnically almost self-enclosed, more than ever attached to its *archē*.

Thus the personality of Plodémet, a structural pattern stabilized during the first half of the twentieth century, is a historical phenomenon forged by a "metabolic" process which itself was constituted by historical forces at the end of the eighteenth century.

As this is being written, the personality of Plodémet is nevertheless once again in a process of transformation. Is it a new French Revolution that is beginning—without revolution?

4

The New Direction

> *Compared with the old days? There has been a
> change, certainly. What has changed? Everything
> . . . in every way.*
>
> (Conversation in Plodémet)

> *What has changed?
> As far as Plodémet is concerned? A lot of things
> have changed. Young people, for example, and cars
> —enormous changes there. Oh, I don't know what's
> changed—everything, I suppose. Besides, it's chang-
> ing at a devilish rate.*
>
> (Menguy, age 40, photographer)

When did the great change begin? It would be arbitrary to fix
one year as the turning point, yet the decade 1950–1960 may be
safely pinpointed for Plodémet.

The change was part of a nation-wide process that had begun
between 1948 and 1950, characterized, from an economic point
of view, by growth and expansion. It was concentrated in developed areas, while regions such as central and southwestern
France and Brittany—particularly Finistère—were in a state of
stagnation and decline. It was in effect their condition of "underdevelopment" that prompted the transformation process in these
areas.

In Finistère, underdevelopment had taken the form of a decline
in the traditional occupations of agriculture and fishing and in
the already atrophied industrial sector. Between 1954 and 1962,
the number of farmers fell by 25 percent and that of fishermen

by 20 percent. The canneries were jeopardized by large new industrial concentrations in northern France, and the newly initiated policy of decentralization had not been able to settle new industries around Quimper. The migration caused by population surplus and social mobility was now intensified because of the scarcity of jobs, resulting in the dire prospect of depopulation: 2,500 young people were leaving Sud-Finistère annually.

Yet the crisis in the production economy coincided with a growth in the consumer economy. The rural crisis coincided with the expansion of cities and towns, and with the irruption of urban civilization into the countryside. The demographic ebb coincided with the seasonal flow of summer visitors attracted to the coast of Cornouaille by its countryside, harbors, beaches, villages, and traditional coiffes.

MODERNISM THROUGH OBSOLESCENCE

Plodémet reached its demographic equilibrium at the beginning of the twentieth century. The slow decline in population from 1910 to 1940 had a beneficial rather than a detrimental effect on its economy. The symptoms of demographic imbalance began to appear after 1950. The declining ratio of young people in the total population compared unfavorably with the national average.

Young peasants deserted the land because smallholding could not solve modern production problems (mechanization, efficiency). Young fishermen deserted Pors-Ensker and settled in Audierne, where industrialized deep-sea fishing, now the only profitable kind, was being developed, while the old stayed and dabbled in shore fishing when the weather was good. Small merchants began to disappear, not only from the stagnant villages but also from the expanding town (33 grocery stores in 1962, as against 60 in 1930).

The two Azur canneries (one for fish, the other for vegetables and pork products) shut down in 1964 after a difficult period. They reopened in 1965, after being taken over by an outside industrial group. Only the furniture factory maintained the same output as in 1936, and now expects to expand.

The general crisis was basically a crisis of small business. It was caused not so much by competition from large-scale systems of production and distribution as by their inherent superiority. The decline of diversified smallholding was attributable to the scientific methods of vegetable production and cattle raising employed in the large-scale farming areas. The disappearance of millers resulted from the increase in large mills that could supply bakeries and farms dependably with consistent quality products. The local milk bottlers were replaced by large dairies. The small village stores had to compete against town stores, which were in competition themselves with stores in larger towns outside the commune. Three large chains established branches in the town, selling at cut-rate prices and delivering by truck in the countryside.

While the manufacturers abandoned family-type businesses in favor of corporate operations, the small enterprises resisted all change or restructuring based on modern criteria of profitability. Similarly, the smallholders resisted reorganization; less than one-third of the farmers belonged to the farmers' union and the majority rejected cooperative forms of production or distribution. Small stores kept large inventories but not strict accounts (90 percent of the merchants paid their income tax based solely on the tax inspector's estimate), and seldom made any attempt to display their goods to advantage. Although 95 percent of the craftsmen and tradesmen were members of their professional association, it met only once a year and did nothing to improve the situation. Outside observers saw in this rigidity a manifestation of traditionalism and custom. True enough, until 1965 most businesses were in the hands of the older generation, who were unable to adapt themselves to the new economic conditions. However, their habits stemmed not so much from traditionalism as from a fundamental attachment to individual enterprise that had been attained as the liberating reward of a century of political struggle. They were loyal, not to traditions, but to what was modern in 1900, and did not accept the fact that their modernity had become obsolete.

It was not so much the obsolescence of small business that struck the observer in 1965 as its long-standing chronicity. The whole social fabric maintained a will to live in the midst of decline, accounting for the survival of smallholdings of five, seven, and ten acres—nearly extinct elsewhere—and of small grocery stores with profits as small as their expenses.

Yet, for all that, small business has not seen its last days. It is the smallest of smallholdings, the most marginal of stores, and the most traditional of crafts (blacksmiths, millers, tailors) that are disappearing. On the other hand, small business has been able to make the transition in a number of areas from an economy based on need to an economy based on consumption. The extraordinary rigidity of customs coexists with an extraordinary flexibility deriving from what might be defined as polyactivity—the performance of a number of economic activities by the same person. The long-ingrained trait of polyactivity thus has become an instrument of adaptation to change.

Polyactivity was on the decline, though not in the process of disappearing, at the time the great change began. Some efforts were being made toward specialization in agriculture, but diversified farming remained the general rule. The fishermen indeed no longer collected seaweed, but they cultivated their plots of land, and the old women still had their cows. Village tradesmen still had their potato patches and cows, ran their stores, and did a little trading. Storekeepers in the town carried several different lines of merchandise, such as the bakery-café that sold fruit and carbon paper.

The changing times sustained and even revived polyactivity. Farmers now maintained diversified crops not merely to be self-sustaining but to protect themselves against the price fluctuations of an expanding market. Craftsmen and tradesmen carried on their business to the point of failure while making various attempts to get a start in other lines. Thus the miller continued to mill grain as he launched into poultry raising with 2,400 chickens. André, a grocer in Bravez, ran a taxi service; as more and more people began to have cars of their own, he went into knitwear; he is now grocer, bistro owner, taxi service, and dress-shop owner. Grocers and smallholders become contractors for combine harvesters. Menguy has two interconnected shops, one for photography, the other for hunting and fishing equipment. One enterprising schoolteacher runs a *bistro-crêperie* at the Pointe du Raz during the summer. The Café des Sports is also a tobacconist's shop, a storage place, and a stationery-bookstore. The owner is also an insurance agent, and what is more, gets up at four o'clock every morning to deliver newspapers on a fifty-seven-mile route. Hervé, a pork butcher, took over his father's business in 1962, installed a canned-foods section and a rôtisserie, sells milk, chickens, and since 1966, cooked foods.

The polyactivity of poverty provides the minimum necessities for survival, whereas dynamic polyactivity concentrates work with a view to attaining maximum income and thereby becomes a factor in economic expansion. Insufficient specialization—itself a condition created by an economy of poverty and stagnation—makes possible the polyactive dynamism of modernizing forces that are motivated not only by a desire for profit but also by an appetite for consumption, greater comfort, affluence, and so on.

It is difficult to estimate the extent of polyactivity in Plodémet, for the census lists only one profession for each person. Our impression is that it is a fundamental feature of the economy of Plodémet as well as of the new course of development. Although an economic relic, a characteristic of obsolescence, it has become at the same time an agent of growth and of adaptation to modernism. It has helped to effect transition without large numbers of people losing their livelihood.

The patronage of the small storekeepers' customers depended on good will, family loyalty, and neighborliness. The fewer the customers, the wider the range of products had to be. The national scheme of economic distribution represented no threat to this system as such; rather, it tended to turn the small store into a "drugstore," that is, to utilize it as a distributor for the products of large firms. The large chain stores certainly were a threat, but it was blunted by the small profit margins characteristic of thinly populated markets. In general large firms prefer to let small firms take the risks in areas where profits are uncertain and to use them as distributors, if not as dumping grounds. In any case, the profit margin of the small firm, low as it is, can become a component in the profit margin of the large firm, which acquires the additional benefit of an accumulation of local good will. Nevertheless, the long-standing network of good will has not always been broken through by modern distribution methods, at least not yet and not everywhere. In the case of sophisticated electrical appliances it showed its resistance by the fact that all television sets in Plodémet were bought from two local merchants and not at the impersonal department store in Quimper.

A mutually beneficial relationship can thus exist between the widespread confidence achieved by the brand-name products (through advertising) and the good will enjoyed by local trades-men (through personal contact), by providing a dual guarantee for the customer. Such a relationship preserves the small business and assures its future development. The pork butcher's own pâté and the pâté made in a large distant factory are sold in the same store, and their competition is to the advantage of both manufacturer and storekeeper.

Similar mutual benefits derive from a system of affiliation which protects the autonomy of a small business by integrating it with a large distribution network. Affiliation became virtually the rule in the grocery business beginning in 1960, as a result of external pressures (the establishment in Plodémet of branches of three large stores) and on the initiative of Le Kouign, a wholesale grocer. Le Kouign became affiliated with the national association of wholesalers (organized to resist the large chain stores), and having the necessary confidence and good will he arranged for the affiliation of most of the small grocery stores in the commune. Affiliation enables moribund small grocers to survive and expand; and they are now able to compete with the delivery trucks of the chain stores by cut-rate prices and trading stamps. Modern selling techniques are thereby introduced into the most backward stores, which nevertheless retain their former appearance (no show window, no attempt to display goods). The once obsolete food business has been totally modernized by affiliation.

The problem of affiliation became increasingly acute in the 1960's throughout the rural economy. Since 1966, farmers have been compelled to affiliate, either partially with manufacturers of agricultural products, or completely with the big Landernau cooperative, which operates throughout western Brittany.

Economic modernization in Plodémet thus advances principally by the subjection of small business. This process is gradually integrating the local economy with the industrial economy and with large-scale efficient commerce, without quickly or completely destroying small business. The compromises arrived at have made it possible to profitably juxtapose obsolescence and modernization. The new economic efficiency rescues some barely surviving businesses to its own advantage, while at the same time others are sustained or revived by the economic rationality. Such interactions encourage the flow of modernity into old molds, but they also consolidate (temporarily?) pockets of obsolescence and poverty. Moreover, as soon as a large firm takes over the initiative, the small stabilized business becomes "bureaucratized" within a large system and, manipulated from outside, tends to remain passive.

The inertia of the small business, whether still independent or already affiliated, is in the nature of passive resistance not only to change but also to having to disappear—in this respect, it is a will to survive. As a matter of fact, small business is still quite prevalent in Plodémet, with 350 farmers and 130 tradesmen. By the same token, economic passivity in Plodémet is much greater than in surrounding communes. Self-generated attempts at modernization or at responding to external competition, either cooperatively or individually, are rare and inadequate. There are but two cooperatives for agricultural supplies and a few farming partnerships between brothers-in-law. In the town, there is only one multicraft group (a carpenter, two plumbers, an electrician, two gangs of masons, and a roofer), who compete against outside contractors by offering prospective customers an all-inclusive price for building a house. Peasant and craftsman groups are generally organized by younger men who have taken over family businesses since 1960.

There are a few individuals who are animated by the spirit of private enterprise. In the countryside, for example, there are a few dynamic farmers who either work as contractors or employ efficient methods of production and marketing; in the town, a trucking contractor, three wholesalers (two in wines and spirits, one in groceries), and two forward-looking tradesmen who have committed themselves to modernization and to the utilization of profitable merchandising methods.

The two tradesmen, one an electrician, the other a pork butcher, are under forty; both modernized their stores with plate-glass windows and neon lighting in 1965; both are distributors of brand-name products; both practice individual skills. The dynamism of these tradesmen operates in the context of an interaction between polyactivism and modernism, between local confidence in them and the influence of brand names, and especially in their working in areas of economic growth.

Growth is concentrated in three sectors—food, home appliances, and trucking—where the demand is growing, though not enough to build sufficient local sales. For that there would have to be adequate interplay between the national economy and the local store. For example, in the clothing business the great increase in demand has benefitted outsiders—the monthly market held in the town—and the large stores in towns outside the commune which sell fashionable ready-to-wear clothes, all to the detriment of local tailors, whose decline is accelerating.

The growth of domestic consumption and of traffic favors not only the peak sectors of the commune's economy; it is also beginning to encourage almost everyone under forty to diversify and expand his activities. It is motivating young people to strive for something more than subsistence, for one no longer works merely to live but to improve one's life, to acquire furnishings for the home, more comfort, a car. It is this aspect of progress that is awakening and will continue to awaken, by a chain reaction, Plodémet's economic activity.

THE DOMESTIC REVOLUTION AND THE INCREASE IN CONSUMPTION

While Plodémet was going through an economic crisis between 1950 and 1965, and while old socioeconomic structures were in the process of disappearing, two hundred homes were being built (the grand total was just over a thousand), and the demand for household furnishings was causing something of a domestic revolution.

In 1950, the commune still lacked running water and, except for the town and its surroundings, electricity. Only a few privileged persons in the town enjoyed the luxury of some degree of comfort.

The installation of fuel-gas lines, begun before World War II, was completed finally between 1950 and 1955, and electrification of the entire commune was accomplished between 1951 and 1959. Nevertheless, with the chronic delay in providing a municipal water supply (now expected in 1967–1968), individuals have been installing water pumps on their own initiative since 1960.

The first wave of growth in domestic comfort (1950–1962) brought kitchen stoves, gas heaters, electric irons, coffee grinders, electric razors, small heating appliances, and radios.

A second wave (after 1962) brought indoor toilets, refrigerators, and washing machines. Central heating made small progress—it was first installed in a public place, the Ty-Koz café, in the winter of 1965. Television arrived in 1962; by 1965 there were sets in 221 of the 1,000 households.

The rural home has begun to imitate the urban home—kitchen-living room, dining room for special occasions, and bedroom. In both town and countryside there is more diversity in furnishings; the desire for comfort has been followed by the desire to decorate and ornament.

The use of domestic resources has become less parsimonious; interiors are still kept dark, but lights are turned on more and more often before nighttime. People are still hesitant about maintaining continuous heating, but fewer and fewer wait for really cold weather before turning on their radiators.

The home is no longer regarded as a citadel reserved for family life; it is gradually becoming the setting for the social activities of private life. It is breaking away from the rural model and adopting a suburban rather than a provincial pattern.

The advances of the domestic revolution are very uneven. Many rural households have not yet been affected by the changes that have invigorated the young families in the town and country, the merchant seamen, the merchants, and the retired townspeople, but the advance is powerful and continuous.

Eating habits are improving and meals have more variety. The *bouillie*, as we have seen, has been abandoned; pancakes are now regarded as a delicacy; potatoes are still the basic staple, but people are beginning to eat steaks, vegetables, desserts, and even cheese—formerly disdained as the object of some ancient food taboo; in addition to Hanff or Azur brand pâtés, other canned foods are gaining acceptance; canned ravioli and paella have appeared in the grocery stores. Concern about diet (generally female) and gastronomic aspirations (generally male) are emerging. The young avail themselves of a wider range of drinks —beer, mineral water, *muscadet* (a sweet white wine), whisky, apéritifs—yet at the same time alcoholism is declining.

The former neglect of body and clothing during working days has been replaced by a preoccupation with daily hygiene, health, and making a pleasing appearance. In contrast to the patriarch Toto Poullan, who boasts of the sturdiness of his fine black teeth never sullied by toothpaste (despite the attempts of a hospital nurse who wanted to take advantage of his unexpected confinement), clean teeth, feet, and nails have become the rule among young people, along with the use of shampoo. The women have abandoned traditional clothes for a variety of styles (dresses, suits, slacks), experiment with make-up and beauty products, and go to the hairdresser. The men too are moving toward more variety in clothes, though at a slower rate.

Consumption is stimulated by the practical, comfortable, new, and fashionable; the worn, unattractive, and out-of-date are thrown away and replaced. People are beginning to buy what is

attractive, decorative, pleasant, even useless. With few exceptions, they do not yet buy out of a desire for originality, or to
impress their neighbors, or for the sake of accumulating things
or gadgets. These motives appear only after the desire for the
useful and the pleasant has been satisfied.

The urge for consumer goods was still considered scandalous
in 1950. It was associated with the extravagance of seamen who
introduced what was once regarded as a life of luxury, later as a
life of comfort, and now—more and more by the young—as
ordinary life.

THE NEW ATTITUDE TOWARD MONEY

The growth in consumption has had a decisive effect on the
attitude toward money. For the older peasants, money is not yet
the universal agent and standard of economic relations. The
values of barter, service, and gift survive outside and in conjunction with monetary values. The real standard by which they judge
low-priced items is the pound of butter, the bottle and glass of
red wine, the packet of tobacco; the standard for major items is
the horse, the pig, or the tractor. Services are exchanged between
neighbors, and small units of some agricultural produce are used
as a means of exchange, or as gifts in kind.

The old attitude makes a clear distinction between the local
market where monetary relations are marked by confidence,
family loyalties, and neighborliness, and the external market
where one must defend one's interests ruthlessly in the inevitable
combat of bargaining against the big people—manufacturers,
agents, wholesalers, salesmen.

Desire for gain is absent both in the first case, where relations
based on personal trust exclude exploiting others, and in the
second, where it is much more a matter of protecting one's profit
than of increasing it.

Attempting to make the largest possible profit is regarded as
immoral when it is believed that value is inherent in the object
and not determined by the interplay of supply and demand. The
old peasants in Menez-Ru still do not understand that the price
of an object can change without a change in the object. "I don't
know why, but when there are a lot of carrots, the price is low.
It's strange, and it's the same for everything. When there's a lot

of something the price goes down, yet the thing is the same" (Duloch, age 53, farmer, Menez-Ru).

According to the old attitude, what is important is earning a living, not making money. Profit, like spending, is regarded as immoderation. Even today, there are tradesmen who remain completely untouched by the spirit of profit, as for example a hotel proprietor who disdains troublesome or disagreeable customers and neglects to ask for payment. In local situations, people insist on shrouding monetary relationships in some sort of human gesture from which any indication of the idea of profit is openly banished by an expression of trust, such as "There's no hurry," or "One of these days," or "It'll come out right in the end." People put off naming a price or demanding payment with an apparent lack of interest, feigning unconcern, as if extending a temporal credit intended to represent a spiritual one. They are wary about confronting outright economic relationships cold-bloodedly.

The elderly feel a need to humanize the act of collecting their pensions by slipping the postal clerk a small coin. The gesture is different from tipping in that it repels the abstract economic relationship by introducing a personal act of thanks.[1] The same ritual applies to bank checks and postal money orders, and is related to the distrust of the strange and unknown. For the same reason, summer reservations are made entirely through personal contact—never through agencies. The long-ingrained attitude is to put money into the circulation of trust, and trust into the circulation of money.

The same attitude condemns credit purchasing on two counts. It is immoral because one lives beyond one's means, and it is dishonorable because it entails indebtedness. Many people practice this "shameful" form of buying, but they mail their money orders in Quimper, so that nobody knows about it in Plodémet.

The introduction of the national price policy partially broke down the duality between local market and external market, as the established prices are neither those of friends nor those of enemies. The system has imposed a third market, anonymous and universal. Of course, local commerce resists it wherever possible; for example, a quart of milk costs 55 centimes in Menez-Ru but 64 centimes in the town. Nevertheless, the third market is gaining ground as the external economy progresses.

---

[1] For the older peasant, the post office is a kind of chapel of the god-State, to which one owes a small propitiatory offering.

Tourism too has disturbed old attitudes; the tourist is seen both as a stranger, someone belonging to the external market, and as a guest, someone who has a right to benefit from local favors.

When the tourist is regarded as a stranger, he is a new type of stranger nowadays, one who makes no attempt to get a rock-bottom price and accepts the highest price that can be asked. This creates a temptation to exploit the situation—as does one grocer who regularly cheats on weights and prices. When the tourist is a guest, he benefits from gifts and favors. In some cases tradesmen try to find a price somewhere between hospitality and exploitation, according to how well they like the customer's looks, or they arrive at a median price by reference to the national prices.

Essentially, the consumption ethic has brought the makings of a new attitude which is replacing hoarding with spending, while stimulating the profit motive that makes such spending possible.

The feeling that money is for spending has become widespread, even among some of the old people. Devaluation and the decline in the purchasing power of money have eroded the real value of savings, and retirement pensions and family allowances have encouraged the belief that money is easy to come by, that it can be obtained without immediate work and can therefore be spent without qualms. The new attitude has been directed not only at small household goods but also at those requiring large expenditures. Moreover, the enjoyment of possessions alone does not suffice to rationalize their acquisition; they represent well-being. "It's better to have things rather than a lot of money. If you don't spend money, you never have anything, you die without ever having had anything" (Mme. Gaelic, age 36, a farmer's wife from Menez-Ru). This woman, belonging to an intermediate generation, repeated "have" three times in justifying spending, in a sense that implied both pleasure and possession. She is approaching the stage where the pleasure of consumption justifies spending purely and simply.

In the case of household electrical appliances, often the more expensive of two equivalent articles is bought, not the cheaper one. When the consumer is unable to estimate quality, he places confidence in the pride. "People always buy what's more expensive. It's difficult to sell lower-priced articles even if they're good" (an electrician). On this point, the reversal of the old attitude appears to be total, even though the rejection of what is cheap may be construed as an expression of the old distrust. In the utilization of credit, the new attitude is making slower progress, because resistance lies not only in an old-fashioned attitude to economics but also in a basic feature of Plodémet psychology, "shame." Still, credit is being used more and more extensively by the young for household furnishings, implements, and construction. Also, young people make use of insurance policies and savings banks.

The old attitude survives almost intact among elderly peasants in more backward areas, and between the two extremes lie a series of intermediate positions determined by generation, occupation, and locality, with their numerous cross-currents.

Nevertheless, Plodémet is backward on the whole. Loans and bank accounts maintained at the Caisse de Bretagne in Pont-l'Abbé are generally lower than those in other communes. Still, the extraordinary fact is that the new direction has taken root despite the persistence, until as late as 1950, of a thoroughly unintegrated economic structure and collective attitude. The reasons for the change of direction must be sought in the simultaneous collapse of the many barriers that have isolated Plodémet from the outside world.

THE GROWTH OF COMMUNICATIONS

Evidently, the continuing growth of the French economy that began in 1948–1950 is widening the breach in the structure of Plodémet society.

The penetration effected by the external economy through chain stores and distribution affiliations was accompanied by a constant stream of inducements to consumption delivered by sales representatives, publicity, and advertising. The national economy joined forces with private capitalist economy in order to stimulate the revolution in domestic consumption by setting up model farms and organizing exhibitions devoted to housekeeping techniques. Schools too played a significant role; the CEG gave courses in home economics and hygiene, and what was perhaps more important, students from the external commune attending *lycées* were directly exposed to urban environments.

New long-distance communications with the outside world,

made possible by radio, television, and the increasing use of motor vehicles, provided many additional channels of penetration by urban civilization. Motorbikes—bicycles equipped with a small motor—became common in the countryside after 1950, at the same time as radios. The era of private cars began in 1953— mostly Citroën CV2 and CV4, Renault 4, and Citroën Ami6— and by 1965 teen-agers were beginning to acquire cars of their own. Three years after the establishment of a regional television station, one out of five homes had a set.

There are two constants in the area of communications: local-regional motor traffic and national-international telecommunication, the two being interrelated. Motor traffic facilitates relations between countryside and town, and breaks down the isolation of outlying farms and hamlets. Country people make frequent visits to the town, the women on motorbikes, even old women— one can see tall-coiffed riders putt-putting by on country lanes— and the men by car or truck, while at the same time delivery trucks from the town cover all parts of the countryside.

Also, the city is coming closer to Plodémet, and Plodémet is coming even closer to the city.

Quimper, the capital of Finistère, twenty miles from Plodémet, is turning into an attractive city with a population of over 40,000. Administrative ties and the increasing tendency of Plodémet businesses and associations to affiliate with region-wide organizations have led to closer contact with Quimper. Besides, Quimper is becoming Plodémet's supermarket; women and young people drive over to shop, or make shopping the excuse for the pleasure of going to Quimper. It is the shopping center for clothes, cosmetics, even for vegetables and goods that cannot be found in Plodémet. With its movie theaters and touring theatrical and cabaret companies, Quimper is also the center of entertainment.

Audierne is the hub and main market for seamen and the coastal population; in summer, its beaches and dance halls attract the young.

More and more natives of Pors-Ensker living and working in Audierne go back to their village only for weekends; more and more natives of Plodémet commute daily to jobs in Quimper. Plodémet is becoming not merely a bedroom suburb but a satellite suburb.

The people of Plodémet have taken to driving around the

region like tourists on Sundays. From the tourist's point of view, the region extends beyond Bigoudennie, comprising a large picturesque area reachable by car, staked out by the Pointe du Raz, the Ile de Sein, Douarnenez, and the Eckmühl lighthouse.

Thus, a new economic and tourist area has been created whose two centers, Quimper and Audierne, both lie outside Bigoudennie. The sense of belonging to all of Finistère is becoming pervasive in terms of a structured region administratively and economically centered on Quimper, as well as of a geographic individuality represented by the picturesque coast of Cornouaille.

The Return of the Migrants

Meanwhile, a more direct interchange is taking place between Plodémet and areas outside the commune with the seasonal return of natives who have moved away.

Prior to 1950, the migrants, or "transplants," came home only for weddings and funerals. Since 1950, owing to a steady rise in urban standards of living—which includes car ownership—people have begun to return for three additional reasons: All Saints' Day, summer vacation, and the permanent one of retirement.

Most of the summer visitors are migrants from the commune. In August 1965, 61 of the 83 summer visitors in Kéravrez (normal population 60) were migrants, and the rest workers on paid vacation or professional people shunning busier, more fashionable resorts.

Summer visitors stay in private homes, which in recent years have been installing such symbols of urban comfort as toilets. Migrants stay with their parents, whose homes they have equipped with gas heaters, television, and other urban amenities.

Tourists, migrants, and retired people all contribute to the domestic revolution by effecting changes in consumption, notably of food. In Kéravrez, for example, our colleagues Martineau and Stourm observed that the presence of summer guests has brought about a good many culinary changes. Foods previously unknown to the region, especially to the countryside, such as melons, cheeses, and oysters, have been introduced to the table. The single dish has been replaced by varied meals that include hors-d'oeuvres, fruits, salads, and desserts.

During the summer vacation, migrants and natives invite each other for meals, drinks, fishing expeditions, or to watch television. Their interaction is extensive; the migrants become reacquainted with the crêpes, *kouignes* (Breton cake), and rye bread they have known in childhood, and reassimilate, as it were, in Plodémet and Bigoudennie. The natives, on the other hand, want to be introduced to the customs and usages of urban civilization; although they reject the hectic, polluted, unhealthy metropolis, they want the comforts, security, pleasures, and paid vacations offered by urban civilization. The migrants pass on their acquired notions of the comfortable, practical, and attractive in everything from furnishings to table manners. Migrants are the active agents of the rapid and easy assimilation of urban civilization.

Urban habits are also brought back by the students who spend the school year in the *lycées* in Quimper, and even more by those studying in Rennes and Paris, who are virtually migrants already, and by young teachers, seamen, and technicians spending the summer with their families. What these young people introduce are new tastes, the habit of spending, and a liking for travel and entertainment.

By becoming a summer resort, Plodémet has become imbued with characteristics of urban civilization. The summer, representing a return to nature for city dwellers, is also the season of urbanization for Plodémet.

At the same time, the summer stimulates Plodémet's economy. For example, the pork butcher, the *crêperie*, and the hotels equal in two months their volume of business in the rest of the year. The modernization of stores is also hastened, and shop windows are designed to cater to the tourist trade—a hardware store will display pottery more or less in the Breton style, and the haberdasher's window will be filled with Breton dolls. Renting rooms brings additional income and has become a regular economic activity. The price of land is rising on the coast and in the town. While an abandoned house in Menez-Ru costs 2,000 francs, a *penty* on the coast might sell for 40,000 francs. In the summer of 1965, the influential women's page of the weekly magazine *L'Express* recommended the Breton *penty* to vacationers. Thus, summer vacations not only stimulate trade but also raise the value of land to unprecedented heights; the irony, uncomprehended by the peasants, lies in the fact that when land is diverted from its productive usage and given over to urban pleasures, its value increases.

PILOT GROUPS AND INTERMEDIARIES

The increase and intensification of contacts with the outside world amplifies internal change. By 1965, the domestic-consumer revolution was being propagated not only through individual avant-garde initiative but also through various native "pilot groups." They can be assigned to the following categories: (1) young people in contrast to the old, particularly married couples who furnish their homes with modern equipment and appliances; (2) women in contrast to men; (3) townspeople in contrast to country people, especially tradesmen, craftsmen, and retired people who had moved here from other regions.

In the countryside, the pilot groups are constituted of (1) merchant seamen in the coastal villages; (2) peasants' sons or husbands of peasants' daughters whose spending habits and standard of living set an example; (3) progressive farmers in white regions who are modernizing both their homes and farming methods.

Relatives and neighbors are the intermediaries who spread the example of the pilot groups, especially in the countryside. Marriages into modern-minded families and, most importantly—because they are becoming more and more common—marriages between farmers' daughters and tradesmen, craftsmen, civil servants, seamen, and clerks are widening the path of the new economic cause. The model farmer in Pors-en-Breval, for example, was converted to modernization by his father-in-law (a rare case of the old influencing the young); Donatien, an old farmer in Kéravrez, has only two and a half acres but lives comfortably because his daughter married a merchant seaman.

The multiplication of pilot groups in open-minded villages, such as Kéravrez,[2] has reversed the situation in that modernists are no longer regarded as eccentrics but as examples. Jealousy and shame, which had set up barriers against the new, now operate in favor of modernization as soon as it extends beyond the pilot groups.

[2] In Kéravrez the domestic revolution has been led by three families of merchant seamen, and by three women: one married to a driver-mechanic (Mme. Kéravrec), one a retired fabric-shop operator (Tante Thérèse), and one a schoolteacher in the *bourg* (Mme. Duraz).

With each innovation, the initiators have to confront, overcome, or sidetrack a barrier of jealousy and shame. In 1962, the
purchase of a television set was still inhibited, even in the *bourg,*
by the shame attached to asking for credit and by the fear of
jealousy. "When people see that somebody has bought something,
they wonder where he got the money" (Michel, mason, Menez-
Ru).

But as soon as a breakthrough has been accomplished, jealousy
turns into a desire to be like the others and to enjoy the same
advantages, while shame becomes self-reproach for being thought
backward and stupid. Having hindered innovation, shame and
jealousy now accelerate its spread. The mechanisms of imitation
now operate in favor of innovation, and the traditional disposition, which favored inertia, has come to encourage movement.

A conversation with old Gournet:

GOURNET. A car, what for?

J.-C. STOURM. To be more free . . .

GOURNET. Yes, that's true.

HIS WIFE. Oh, no . . . it's to do like others do . . . to be like
others . . .

GOURNET. Yes, there's a lot in that.

The process is still very uneven in Plodémet, but innate conformity has begun to operate in relation to the new as well.

THE HOW AND THE WHY

Despite obsolescence, stagnation, resistance to innovation, and
extraordinary unevenness of development, it seems that by 1965
the consumption breakthrough had been accomplished. How was
this possible in an underdeveloped, unproductive economy, and
where did the money come from?

It came, first of all, from those whose income was beginning to
reach urban standards, namely, tradesmen and craftsmen in the
growth sectors, wage earners (merchant seamen, clerks, full-time
workers), and civil servants.

Money also came from such sources as married couples with
both partners working, from multiple employment that often
meant overwork, from the summer income of tradesmen and
landladies, from fishermen and farmers who sold some of their
produce directly to housewives, from financial help received by

parents from migrant children, from credit utilized by the younger generations, from state-financed family allowances and retirement pensions, and from the conversion of hoarded capital into domestic investment.

Additional monies came from the savings of the growing ranks of retired people, especially former policemen, noncommissioned officers, and marines who had served in the colonies and received campaign bonuses and overseas allowances.[3]

At the same time, the survival of self-subsistence in the forms of a plot of land, chicken coops, or a cow, the advantage of paying low local prices for basic foods, and the ability to do odd jobs and repairs oneself all combined to avert wasteful spending of acquired surplus. In other words, the remnants of economic obsolescence made a paradoxical but almost indispensable contribution to the breakthrough of modernism.

Nevertheless it was obviously the pressure of external forces that had set Plodémet in motion, not the autonomous growth of the local economy, which was actually in a critical condition. Thus, the fundamental cause of Plodémet's transformation clearly emerges once again, it being the growth of the French economy beginning in 1948, and specifically, the penetration of its benefits into the commune.

THE NEW PERSONALITY

The economic crisis and the breakthrough of the consumer attitude are only the initial aspects of the transformation that may eventually alter the personality of the commune itself.

For half of the twentieth century Plodémet lived like an organism regulated by a stable metabolic process. Interaction with the outside world did not affect its cell structure but merely sustained it. Beginning in 1950, tides and ruptures have come to provoke cellular, even nuclear changes.

Rural life was withering away. The villages of Lesnus, Bravez, and Menez-Ru were being depopulated, their stores and *buvettes* barely subsisting; there were no games of ninepins, no clog dances on Sundays, and sometimes not even Sundays. The peasant's

[3] Moreover, men who retire at a relatively early age from the merchant navy (after twenty-five years of sea duty), the army, and the colonial police often begin a second career in Plodémet as factory workers, office workers, or tradesmen, which rapidly enables them to acquire domestic comforts and a car.

world was undergoing a crisis; its disappearance was imminent. Nevertheless, pockets of resistance—perhaps of revival—formed in the white regions, stimulating action by the farmers' union, cooperatives, and finally land redistribution.

The town diffused urbanization through the countryside, yet at the same time the deep-rooted plebeian homogeneity between town and country was disintegrating.

As the rural component of Plodémet's personality was manifesting decay, the commune was acquiring a dual function as residential area and summer resort. The town and the coast were becoming home bases for seamen whose work took them farther and farther away on lobster boats and oil tankers, for clerical workers who went to work in towns outside the commune in increasing numbers, and for retired people—some returned migrants, but also some not from Plodémet or even Brittany. The commune was becoming a center for the domestic life of people occupied elsewhere, its permanent population consisting more and more of old people.

It was during the early 1950's that Plodémet became, without any effort on its own part, a vacation spot. There is now a substantial influx of summer visitors, mainly "transplants" who favor the coast and the town. The flow of tourists will certainly increase when the projected coastal highway is built.

The summer vacation is a powerful economic stimulus for Plodémet; it also brings a breath of fresh air. Summer activities have radically changed the seasonal rhythm of Plodémet life. Summer used to be a time of hard work—feast days and weddings were held in the spring and autumn. While it is still the season for work in the fields and even brings extra work to the town, summer has also become a time for festivities; family celebrations, especially weddings, are held more frequently, owing to the presence of students and relatives spending the summer at home. Young people go to dances and sunbathe and swim at the beaches. Moreover, summer is the season of fellowship and communication. Plodémet's people communicate with the strangers in their midst, and its vacationing natives are reunited with their families. Through this grand reunion, combined with work, festivity, and communication, summer becomes the season that brings Plodémet to life fully and intensely.

In October, the buses take the last of the young people away.

The busy time is over; only odd jobs remain to be done. At the hardware store, the Breton pottery is replaced by chrysanthemums, and at the haberdashery, the Breton dolls give way to knitting wools. Half the houses on the coast will be shuttered, the shops empty, the countryside asleep. The summer is followed by a gloomy period of inactivity. The Plodémet winter is about to begin, grey, rainy, cold, gloomy, especially for those whose lives are at a standstill, for the lonely in need of company.

In 1965, Plodémet's industry faces many uncertainties. Will the canneries reopen? Will they attract and maintain a full-time labor force—in other words, a working class? Will the furniture factory —now being operated by young management—expand? Will new industries move in? Needless to say, these eventualities cannot but accelerate the transformation of Plodémet from a predominantly rural to a predominantly urban society.

With the death of Albert Le Bail in 1952, the Baillist dynasty came to an end. It might appear coincidental that the end came at a time when the Plodémet they had created was beginning to change; however, we have seen that the forces of political change had been already at work during the Occupation, and the post-Baillist coalition (Communist-Socialist-Radical) only confirmed the changes.

The economic and social changes since 1955, however, were not attributable to that coalition and remained outside its control. The municipality intervened in the process (for example, land redistribution) only later and to a limited degree; by the same token, although the white party was the originator of agricultural renewal, it was only a partial and inadequate response to the rural crisis.

The present transformation is primarily extrapolitical. It has been indifferent to the fortunes of the Fourth and Fifth Republics, as has been the national economy itself. It would seem that the detachment of economic and social processes from political activity has had an ossifying effect on the latter. The change from the Fourth to the Fifth Republic did not introduce the Gaullist party in Plodémet, nor did it alter the balance between the traditional parties. The Algerian war affected individuals and families, but left no mark on local history. The transformation is working its way at the foundations of the social structure, and its political implications, unlike those of the French Revolution, may become apparent only at its end, not at its beginning.

THE METAMORPHOSIS

Economic integration, the domestic revolution, the growth in consumption, and the process of suburbanization have brought urban civilization in their wake. The town is tending to become not a larger provincial town enclosed within itself but an agglomeration with the characteristics of a suburb.

At the same time, the economic, sociological, cultural, and psychological communication with the outside world (the large urban centers) appears to immerse the future of the commune in the future of the nation as a whole. Plodémet is now living in our time. Communication, which has played a generating role in the present transformation, is becoming inextricably linked with Plodémet's new personality.

So radical and varied a transformation has inevitably brought about a radical and varied crisis. Yet except for a few instances of peasant agitation, organized by the Finistère syndicalists, this crisis has not resulted in any manifestations of violence.

The transformation has avoided total disaster because the crisis was, and still is, linked with social advancement. This advancement, which has expanded and accelerated since the foundation of the CEG, is doing so even more during the crisis, and the crisis itself is expanding and accelerating (for it is causing nearly all parents to urge their children toward a secondary education). Moreover, the growth of the French economy provides an immediate outlet for the young, and for adults who are unable to find work in the commune. But advancement is not only external; it is taking place inside Plodémet, with the development of enterprises benefitting from the boom in consumption, housebuilding, and the tourist trade, and with the rise in the living standards of about half or two-thirds of the population at a time when the crisis is affecting perhaps two-thirds of the economic activities. Plodémet certainly does not feel that it is losing its former wealth. Even when viable, the old economy kept people poor. Life meant subsistence. Today, in spite of the crisis, Plodémet feels that it is moving toward progress.

The crisis shows how profound the change is. Advancement is

attenuating the gravity of the crisis. It is helping to bring about the transformation, which is made easier by the adaptability of the natives of Plodémet to multiple activities, a heritage from their economy of poverty.

In the case of the smallholding or small store, the sclerosis itself, although deepening the crisis in small business, has softened the impact of change until the advancement of the next generation is under way. The slowness of the decline has proved protective.

The extraordinary symbiosis between economic modernism and archaism, between external large-scale capitalism and the internal small business, has also, in a number of sectors, effected a gradual transition.

It is probably the prolonged survival of the small business (the basic acquisition of Republican Plodémet) which has done most to obviate the worst effects of change for the older generation.

At the same time, the domestic revolution is shifting the center of gravity of individual autonomy, formerly based on ownership of a business, to ownership of a house, household goods, and a car. It is beginning a transition toward a new concept of the salary, in which the loss of autonomy in work is compensated for by a new autonomy in private life.

Social advancement and improvement, the modernism-archaism symbioses, the slowness of the transition, the survival of economic ownership, and the expansion in domestic ownership not only attenuate the crisis but split it up into partial issues, either for the community or for the individual. These issues do not add up to a total controversy, but are dispersed and blunted in a total adhesion to the "modern," that is, to the great transformation.

Similarly, the depopulation and dilution that threaten the commune are offset. The threat of a massive exodus of young people is partially compensated for by the increase in new residents and the enormous influx of summer visitors. The genetic isolation is certainly being broken down: marriages are being made increasingly in the "region" which extends beyond Bigoudennie, and Bigoudennie is being partly dissolved in this region. But the native community is getting a second wind with the great periodic return of the young and the migrants and the final return of the retired people.

The inland population of Plodémet is being caught up in the

change; the young have been partially uprooted from their native soil. But the migrants, with their regular returns, are beginning to take partial root once more.

A new equilibrium is developing between native community and native soil on the one hand, and society at large and the spirit of the times on the other. A new personality, partly uprooted and partly replanted, is evolving.

The personality of Plodémet remains sharply etched even while undergoing transformation; in this sense there has been change. But the social structure is being subjected to more than change—is a revolution taking place under the guise of change? It is, in any event, a metamorphosis.

Transformation, evolution, revolution, metamorphosis—change is a perennial riddle, and the basic objective of our study. Everything in Plodémet is to be deciphered as a function of change.

Farming, business, houses, villages, behavior, attitudes, all must be categorized first of all in terms of backwardness, senescence, evolution, transformation, and renovation. Immobility cannot be a reference point, being a function of change itself.

Change is an ongoing process; it goes on under our eyes. In the short span of 1964–1965, the Azur canneries were closed, then reopened; land redistribution was completed; the production of green peas, the base of prosperity for the countryside, drastically declined; the pork butcher and the electrician modernized their stores; the first espresso machine (second-hand) was installed at the Café des Droits de l'Homme.

Is ongoing change simply a transition toward a new stage of stabilization, or is it becoming an inherent social form itself? How is such a multiple process to be grasped? How is one to distinguish between larva and chrysalis? How is one to tell whether death, change, or metamorphosis lies beneath the shell?

These difficulties are fascinating for the sociologist, because Plodémet, already a microcosm of Bigoudennie, is reflected through them as a microcosm of change in a region where time no longer stands still and clocks are being set to the time of France.

5

The Emerging Bourgeoisie

The village of Plodémet became a *bourg*, or small town, during the Baillist era, and its population is "bourgeois" in the literal meaning of the term, that is, not in relation to the working class but to rural people. But with Plodémet embarked on its new course, the word has come to imply a second differentiation, one between bourgeois and common townspeople—the plebeians. I will make frequent use of the ambivalence of the term "bourgeois" precisely because it includes differentiation both from the peasant class and from an inner core of the town's populace that is still steeped in rural culture, rustic and plebeian in values and outlook. This usage of an otherwise static term reveals a dynamic and complex process of urbanization and *embourgeoisement* which is eroding a rustic-plebeian value structure.

The process was extremely slow in Plodémet during the first half of the century, but since 1950 it has been accelerating, broadening, and acquiring new facets. Some rustic features have been effaced, others have become blurred but not yet disappeared; urban-bourgeois traits have become fixed here and there, but their development has been uneven. In 1965, we saw the beginnings of urbanization (actually, suburbanization) and *embourgeoisement* in a town where perhaps 50 percent of the inhabitants are children of peasants. We were witnessing the emergence of a bourgeoisie.

Unlike Poulzic, which produced its bourgeoisie from within, Plodémet evolved its internal bourgeoisie slowly and with difficulty, because migration and mobility have created a considerable external bourgeoisie. On the other hand, immigration to Plodémet has supplied the town with its administrators, its innovators, and some of its economically most productive citizens. The bourgeois development of Plodémet has been grafted on.

Most of the immigrants who settled in the town, usually through marriage, came from Bigoudennie and nearby regions of Finistère. There are only three non-Bretons, and they belong to the middle and upper social strata of the town.

After the Le Bails—who always remained partly outsiders, the mayorality passed temporarily to the industrialist Azur, a native of Plonéour, and is now held by the schoolteacher Maurice, a native of Plobannalec (as is the priest). Contrariwise, many of the secular schoolteachers—themselves graduates of the CEG—are natives of Plodémet.

Most of the energetic tradesmen are outsiders: the modernizing electrician and pork butcher, the proprietor of the Café des Sports, the plumber Robic, the salesman Goémon, the garage owner Kéravrec, the butcher Le Gouillou, one of the hairdressers, the owner of the movie theater, and the woman pharmacist; about half of them are from outside Bigoudennie (Quimper, Brest, Carhaix).

The upper stratum of the bourgeoisie (to whom I will refer sometimes as the "upper caste" and sometimes as the "well-to-do bourgeoisie," although they are not properly speaking a "caste," nor can their prosperousness be estimated by urban standards) consists of five wholesalers who have from five to ten employees each (one of the five is from outside Plodémet), two factory managers (one from Plonéour, the other from Audierne), the notary (from Concarneau), the dentist (from Normandy), and two doctors (one from Normandy, one from Paris).

In the representative population sample studied by our project, 20 percent were born outside the commune. Presumably, this percentage is higher for the town and rises with the social strata to reach 50 percent among the well-to-do bourgeoisie and 100 percent among the professionals.

Immigrants have been smoothly integrated into local life. Almost all play leading roles in the political, professional, social, or cultural life of the commune. Riou, who is now dead, organized the feast days, and the postman and the proprietor of the Café des Sports are vigorous supporters of the football club; Goémon is president of the association of former prisoners of war. Are they energetic because they are immigrants, or did they immigrate because they are energetic? In the first case, they might feel compelled to compensate for being strangers by extra participation in the community. Such overidentification sometimes conceals a latent underidentification; immigrants sometimes confide to visitors that the natives are passive and gregarious. The natives, on their part, sometimes give vent to aggressive outbursts: "What did he come here for? Why doesn't he go back where he came from?" or they declare bitterly, "To succeed here, you have to come from outside." Yet, confident in the knowledge that they have one of the best training grounds for university entrance in France, they do not feel at all inferior to the "successful" stranger —after all, their children and relatives are successful elsewhere.

Integration has been all the easier because in the majority of cases the immigrant has married a native and settled down permanently in the commune. By contrast, the non-Bigoudens of the upper caste remain on the fringes of the community, undoubtedly because they are strangers, both ethnically and socially.

THE "UPPER CASTE"

In the mid-nineteenth century, about ten rural families dominated the economy of the commune. A century later, about ten urbanized families dominate the town with their wealth. The town as a whole is just emerging from its rustic heritage, but the newly privileged, at least those under forty, are already completely bourgeois. They have money, they have a maid, they use and decorate their drawing rooms, they have begun to cultivate a style of dressing, manners, and social transactions; some have started collections of antique furniture, pictures, old firearms, precious stones (Dr. Lévi), and gadgets (the dentist).

The well-to-do oscillate between provincialism and a cult of Paris. Some feel a nostalgia for the provincial town, with its "honest people," rituals, visits, and decorum. For others, Paris is the ideal place, with its freedom, its absence of "what will the neighbors say?" its choice of friendships, the bustle of its streets, the shop windows, elegance, and sense of fashion. Mme. Teste yearns for Quimper and goes there as often as she can, while Mme. André, daughter of the rustic trucker Poullan, always smartly dressed as if for the city and driving her Citroën ID station wagon or her DS—for many in Plodémet the prototype of the modern woman—makes frequent visits to Paris, where she takes in the atmosphere of lights, shop windows, and theaters. The upper caste is already too urban in tastes and too bourgeois in habits to adapt itself completely to life in Plodémet.

The upper caste is not homogeneous; nothing unites families of geographically and socially varied origins but a few rarefied rituals of politeness.

People regard the well-to-do bourgeois as important individuals, not as a caste, because the caste is still only forming, presents no threat, and is not dominant. It has introduced a new social inequality, but its prosperousness is not power. Apart from the two industrialists, its members are well-to-do rather than "big." Political power is in the hands of schoolteachers and activists who, in turn, lack economic power. The industrialist Azur was the only one who ever tried to gain both economic and political power; he failed in business and was turned out of office. The upper caste has made no attempt (yet?) to conquer Plodémet. It turns away from it and gazes, in exile, upon cities.

THE CONVERGING PETITE BOURGEOISIE

Below the stratum of well-to-do bourgeoisie, a *petite bourgeoisie* is forming through a convergence in the direction of aspiring toward the same mode of life among tradesmen, craftsmen, teachers, clerks, and merchant seamen. Yet this homogeneity does not dissolve professional separations, especially among tradesmen, teachers, and merchant seamen.

The great impact of the external economy has shaken up the small tradesmen or forced them to shake themselves up; it has ruined some shops and revived others. This has put tradesmen on a somewhat reactionary path. Not only those who failed voice the obsession that they are being persecuted by the State; all denounce the State as the "big thief" that overwhelms them with taxes and irritating regulations and is even guilty of underhanded dealings. "The Leclerc stores are subsidized by the State, I'm sure of it," says Mme. Le Gouillou, the butcher's wife. Nevertheless, these reactionary trends do little to change traditional political loyalties, especially among Communist tradesmen; the long-standing claim of the party that it is the champion of small business keeps them within the red orbit.

The tradesmen have common complaints but no common solidarity. Although their association has a 95 percent membership, it meets but once a year and takes no collective action. Among other things, they cannot agree on measures of common interest such as closing stores during lunch, a weekly day off, or an annual vacation. The project for a "summer planning committee" was welcomed by the tradesmen,[1] and they made innumerable suggestions including, of course, the installation of a public lavatory for tourists. However, except for the photographer, no one intended to do anything in the common interest.

Tradesmen tend to occupy themselves with their individual business interests and their private lives, and it was precisely for the sake of their private lives that the younger generation eventually succeeded in agreeing on closing times for the shops.

The teachers reacted with repugnance to our suggestion that they join the tradesmen on the summer planning committee. In their eyes tradesmen are grasping and out for their own gain only. Teachers also tend to turn back to their professional interests and private lives; but they are alive to their professional responsibilities to the community, and despite a certain slackening they provide Plodémet with the framework and manpower for political activism.

THE HYBRID WORKER

The 1962 census listed 200 nonagricultural workers of whom 67 were factory workers, 24 driver-delivery men, 13 mechanics, 27 carpenters, 11 construction workers, 28 day laborers and municipal service workers. The factory-inspection report for the same year listed 60 workers at the cannery (40 of whom were women), and 32 at the furniture factory.

The category of factory workers is the least stable and the least in demand. Of the 60 workers at the cannery, only 22 worked

[1] We suggested this project with a view to increasing tourism. Both tradesmen and teachers would have taken part, the former by improvements in the appearance of the commune, arrangement of shop-window displays, and exhibitions of local produce, and the latter by devoting themselves to archaeological, aesthetic, and folkloric aspects.

full time. In fact, the cannery used mainly a seasonal labor force of women and retired people, for whom the work was a source of extra income.

The workers in the furniture factory and the small furniture workshops, as well as those in the small factory that makes clog straps, perform mainly semiskilled work, and some were no doubt entered as carpenters in the census.

Indeed, the category of factory worker conceals two hybrid categories, one of part-time workers, retired people, and women, the other of semiskilled workers (furniture). At Le Calvaire, dominated by the tall, now unused chimney of the COOP (Société Générale des Coopératives de Consommation), there was, of course, an initial concentration of workers, but the hundred who were laid off have been reabsorbed by their original economic sectors. The few full-time jobs there are too low-paid at present to attract young workers. The 450 to 500 francs a month (for a 48-hour week) are accepted either as a temporary expedient by girls or as additional income by retired people and housewives. These part-time workers exert no pressure for higher wages, and the boss can easily prohibit any union activity and maintain complete control. The part-time and seasonal workers scattered through the commune, unorganized and disparate in their work, do not constitute a class or even a social stratum.

The construction workers are either skilled workers' helpers or day laborers. They form another hybrid category, and an atrophied one at that. There is no longer a native unskilled labor force for heavy work. Contractors in Plonéour have been recruiting African workers, and in 1965 a black African was working on the site of the Jeanne d'Arc School in Plodémet, a forerunner perhaps of a new overseas proletariat.

The vast category of nonindustrial workers covers neither a definite work location (such workers are dispersed throughout the commune) nor a homogeneous class (they are variously or simultaneously helpers, shop assistants, clerks, or laborers); however, in Plodémet it describes people who are full-time wage earners and already benefit somewhat from the privileged status of the urban worker. It is to the extent that one becomes a full-time worker rather than a seasonal one that one will be assimilated into urban life, and therefore into the process of *embourgeoisement*. For them, as for all the population of Plodémet, the term "urban worker" signifies the wage-earning class, not the proletariat, upward mobility, not decline. "Nowadays the worker can compare himself with any man; I can't see much difference between him and the boss, I think" (Mme. Kéravrec of Kéravrez, wife of a driver-mechanic). In the opinion of farmers and most small tradesmen and craftsmen, the urban worker not only has a larger income than they do but also more leisure and security.

Thus, to be a worker means to belong to the urban wage-earning class, and in Plodémet that includes participation in the general *embourgeoisement* of the nonagricultural population. It is only in relation to the summit of the bourgeoisie that the urban worker is regarded as subordinated, both in his work and in his living conditions (the subsidized housing project). Even so, he is not looked upon with the disdain accorded to peasants.

Throughout the nineteenth century, a class struggle was being carried on between landowners and peasants in the countryside. No such antagonism exists in the town in the middle of the twentieth century. There is no urban proletariat, but a hybrid wage-earning stratum, part worker, part bourgeois, not only well on the way to becoming altogether middle class but sometimes even leading the way in that direction, as in the case of merchant seamen.

FROM SEA TO HOME

Unlike the fishermen, who are concentrated in Pors-Ensker and Gored, the 120 merchant seamen of Plodémet live along the coast, in the villages near the sea like Kéravrez, and in the town. Salaried seamen were first to introduce the domestic-consumer revolution into their homes. Their wages, increased by overtime and brought home almost intact, enabled them to build new houses or to install modern comforts in old ones; their travels opened their eyes to innovation, and the rotation in their lives made each return home a holiday. The young sailor was prodigally generous in dance halls, bars, restaurants, and pursuits of amusement.

Before 1950, the merchant seamen were a source of shock and scandal; since then they have become objects of imitation. But at the same time, they have grown more and more attached to their homes and less and less to the sea, unlike the fishermen, who have a deep, all-pervading love of the sea. Leclerc, a thirty-

five-year-old engineer on an oil tanker, left the sea in 1964 to
become a truck driver, because "it was too annoying being away
from my wife all the time." Domesticity wins out sometimes in
spite of the lure of early retirement and overtime pay. Because
the increasing automation of ships is reducing the number of
jobs, the seaman begins to look for work on land, near his home,
before his time at sea is up. The sea, then, is a roundabout route,
and a short cut, if not from land to city, then at least from peasant
to bourgeois. (Fifty percent of the seamen in Bourlière's sample
were the sons of peasants.) Merchant seamen are thus also joining
Plodémet's emergent bourgeoisie, and their sense of superiority
toward peasants is no longer the product of their belonging to
the sea but of their membership in bourgeois civilization.

THE BREAK WITH THE LAND

Interaction between country and town (shopping, medical
visits, bureaucratic formalities) and between town and country
(outings, tourism) is growing; there are more marriages between
country girls and town boys; the school is turning peasants' sons
into civil servants, teachers, and technicians. It seems probable
that a process of osmosis is about to begin, inevitably erasing the
old economic complementarity between town and country.

Plodémet was never the commune's center for the purchase of
agricultural products and equipment. The cattle fair is held at
Pont-Croix; the monthly market at Plodémet provides no outlet
for farm products. The recent changes have put an even greater
distance between the town and agricultural activities. The distributors of farm machinery are elsewhere, and there is not even
a repair shop for agricultural equipment.

Truck-farming produce is being shipped less and less through
Plodémet and more and more to Quimper. Vegetables for canning, formerly sent to the COOP or the Azur cannery, now go to
Poulzic, Plonéour, and Landernau. In the same vein, the trade
unions and farmers' organizations ignore the town in their organizational structures, which follow strict canton divisions.

From 1930 onward, municipal policy renounced agricultural
orientation in favor of solving peasant problems through the
educational advancement of the younger generation. Agriculture,
with only minority representation on the municipal council—

eight farmers in a body of twenty-three, although agriculture accounted for half the population—remained a minor question; since 1950, it has been becoming a major problem.

In 1965, the municipality admitted Le Kam, a leader of the farmers' union, to its council. The council decided on land redistribution, but more as a means for building new roads than as an end in itself. "The only way a commune can build the roads it needs is by land redistribution," the mayor stated in an interview in the newspaper *Ouest-France.* No municipal councilor attends the meeting of the farmers' union except Le Kam, who does so as a union official, not as a councilor. No subsidy has been granted, as in Landudec and Poulzic, to the agricultural information service, or to young farmers to take trips in Holland or Britain, or toward the cost of the public water supply installed cooperatively in the village of Kerminou. Evidently the municipality regards these activities as the work of political enemies, and in fact, the cooperative scheme, the farmers' union, and the information service are run by white activists. Nevertheless, in the absence of any red initiative they are the only attempts on behalf of peasant survival and revival; municipal policy is becoming, except for the upkeep of the CEG, exclusively a policy for the town. "All the money in the budget goes to the town!" This was said, not by a peasant, but by old Poullan—retired fisherman, deputy mayor, and Communist—during a council debate on whether an allocation should be made for two country roads or for a playground for the girls' school.

When the mayor was asked to name the basic problems of the commune, he put first the disappearance of the small tradesman, and then "the peasant business." Michel Loïc, tailor, municipal councilor, and Baillist activist, put the roads first, and made no mention of agriculture at all. When we brought it up, he said he was not well versed in those matters.

Generally speaking, the town effaces the country from its consciousness. For example, the youth club issued a pamphlet with the headline: "Students, apprentices, workers, join Youth and Leisure." Peninou asked a student why farmers were not mentioned. "Bah! They have been turned into workers," was the answer.

Moreover, the bourgeois strata keep aloof from problems regarding peasants; they look upon peasants as collectively "backward." This disdain is especially manifest among craftsmen and tradesmen who live in the villages in daily contact with peasants. The peasant is blamed for his own misfortune; he is too "stupid" to get himself organized; he "does not want" to make progress; he profited from the war and now pretends to be poor; he could live as well as other people but his "stupid avarice" impedes him. "They are stingy by nature, but they're not short of money." Contempt for frugality is all the stronger because consumer spending is so recent a phenomenon.

Here is Michel from Menez-Ru speaking of his new television set: "They'll say, 'So you've put one of those airplanes (antenna) on your chimney. You must be doing well. We peasants are too poor to afford television.' I haven't the money to buy a tractor—they have, though. They could buy a television and a tractor; they could buy a lot of things, but they won't let go of their precious money . . . They wouldn't spend money on a piece of steak. They've got hens; when the hens lay eggs, they sell them and then complain about the price they get."

Stories about the hidden wealth of peasants used to be popular among townspeople. They have now been adopted by those aspiring for membership in the *petite bourgeoisie* as a means to assert their superiority, for they are still incompletely divorced from rural habits and therefore strive to differentiate themselves all the more markedly.

They prefer to ignore the economic gulf that exists between bourgeois and rural incomes (excepting small tradesmen doomed to extinction or bare subsistence, and conversely, a few modern farmers who have attained bourgeois income levels) because they want to bring about a sociological gulf. The nonpeasant plebeian element abandons the peasantry during its ascent into the *petite bourgeoisie*, and the contempt it develops for the peasant is a psychological stage in the progression toward urban status. The gross image of the peasant is the external projection of an internal repudiation. As it exorcises its all too recent rural past, the new rising class props up its satisfaction with its own mobility by disdain for a lower class, in this case, the peasantry.

The rupture is a repudiation, not a divorce by mutual consent. The peasants themselves aspire to the advantages and the security of the urban worker. It is toward the bourgeois life—away from the land—that they direct their children.

SUMMARY

If one wishes to sort out the reality of Plodémet in terms of the idea of class, and sort out the idea of class in terms of the reality of Plodémet, one cannot avoid the split between bourgeoisie and peasantry. Although there is in a general sense total dominance by one over the other, there is no exploitation in a strict sense, for the two economies are separate. Class struggle is either diverted into the channels of the long-standing political struggle between whites and reds, or more effectively, muted by the movement of the younger generations of all social classes toward urban careers.

The emerging bourgeoisie is extremely heterogeneous in composition, containing as it does special interests and orientations, both old and new. It bears within itself the seeds of differentiation and conflict, but because it is still in the process of emerging, these seeds are in the process of sprouting, not yet uprooting the idea of bourgeoisie.

In describing the *embourgeoisement* of Plodémet, the word "bourgeois" must not be assigned too precise, too restrictive a meaning. (Imprecise formulation suits imprecise reality best, if it gives the precise position of that reality in the total picture.) The meaning must leave room for some rural touches; it must remind one that half the people of Plodémet have a peasant for a father; it must note that "plebeian" traits still abound, disappearing very slowly. "Here in Plodémet, everyone belongs to the people," said the principal of the Jeanne d'Arc school as late as 1965. True, manners are free and easy, the *buvettes* are earthy, few men wear ties or hats, and jealousy is feared all the more because status symbols are not visible. But it must be remembered that bourgeois characteristics are seeping in on all sides, what with the growing importance of home life, the fixation on the car, the devotion to the rituals of etiquette, the brushstrokes of provincialism being relieved by a touch or two of Paris. Lastly, but always, due prominence must be given to surburbanism, which dominates and engulfs both provincialism and cosmopolitanism; linked to and nourished by the big cities, it opens at the same time toward the peace of sky, land, and sea and wraps serene evenings around peaceful homes.

6

The Wretched
of the Earth[1]

*Perhaps there won't be any peasants any more. Still,
you'll always need peasants to feed the cities; farming is the basis of everything. There wouldn't be
anything without peasants. But perhaps they'll no
longer be peasants.*

(Duloch, farmer, Menez-Ru)

Our first impression of the Plodémet countryside was that of a
landscape of small valleys, gentle slopes descending to the sea,
low walls, sunken roads, rustic and timeless peace. Then Paillard
in Menez-Ru, Le Bolloch in Bravez, and Martineau in Kéravrez
brought back their findings of obsolescence and backwardness;
then, we discovered the modernized farms and the hamlet of
Kerminou . . . We had to accumulate a mass of information
gathered in people's homes, in chance encounters, in meetings
with activists, and finally in interviews with forty-five farmers
before we were able to form a full picture of the anguish, the
struggles, and the transformation hidden by the pleasant landscape.

As one drama is beginning, another is drawing to a close: the
agricultural proletariat is becoming extinct. In 1962, there were

[1] This chapter is based on a more detailed report, submitted by Jean-Louis
Peninou to the Délégation Générale à la Recherche Scientifique et Technique.
The report utilizes more fully the economic, statistical, and historical data
that have been gathered; it deals in particular with land redistribution, trade-
union activities, and the processes of market organization.

but thirty-five agricultural workers and day laborers left in the commune, unable to find other employment because they were old or alcoholic, and managing to get work on the land only because of the chronic manpower shortage. Poverty is less acute than it used to be: "The landowners have to behave themselves now, we were nothing but slaves before." Yet this proletariat, residual though it is, still suffers from the worst griefs of the past. There is the case of the aging spinster who became pregnant (having previously given birth to an abnormal child), abandoned the newborn baby on a dunghill, and was found guilty of murder. Another elderly unmarried woman is the mother of two children, does not speak French, and makes a living from menial jobs. One man, between two attacks of illness and two periods in the hospital, found work on a farm while his wife, herself one of a family of nineteen, hired herself out in order to feed their eight children. Another man cannot count to ten, wets his bed, earns three francs a day and spends it on wine. A third man cannot keep a job more than three months, but always finds work at harvest time; he drinks, steals, and frightens the villagers—who once had to call for the police. One old couple lives in a house without electricity; the man alternates between inexplicable weeping and bouts of blind rage. Their son is a fisherman, and once after a good catch he bought his mother a gas stove.

Help from a son, sacrifice from a wife, or a pension sustains the last of a dying proletariat, being supplanted by the machine and the overwork of the smallholder—whose own tragedy is just beginning.

Disintegration

Plodémet was caught on the wrong foot by the crisis. The average size of holdings had been decreasing, until in 1950 it stood at 12.6 acres (when the national average was 24.7), just as it suddenly became vitally important to increase land size. Conservative diversified farming, so lucrative between 1940 and 1947 when the cities were at the mercy of the countryside, abruptly turned into an obsolescent activity pointing to poverty.

This great reversal was less the result of the return to a peacetime economy than of advances in the mechanization and efficiency of large-scale agriculture. Each of Plodémet's agricultural products—pork, milk, cereals, potatoes, and vegetables, primarily green peas—was strangled by poor distribution and uncompetitive prices. Specialization in the Oise region in the cultivation and canning of green peas was a severe blow to the agriculture of Finistère: in 1956, Finistère produced 31 percent of the country's green peas, but by 1962 its share had fallen to 22 percent. Peas were the mainstay of agricultural prosperity in Plodémet, and the decline came at the same time that the weakest link in the Bigouden canning industry (the Azur factory) broke.

Meanwhile, truck-farm produce from Plodémet now had to compete with produce from the environs of Quimper, consequently arriving in the Quimper market under a disadvantage.

On every front, the Plodémet smallholder could not meet the new prices without reducing his profit margin and thereby his capability to modernize. Moreover, he was now subjected to the effects of sudden fluctuations in the market where the speculation of the middlemen and the vagaries of the weather were no longer the only adversities. The confused, disorganized response of the local producers to the crisis in effect intensified it. Thus, Finistère's energetic efforts at export production were for a time profitable, but within two or three years the avalanche of artichokes, cauliflowers, pigs, and chickens toppled prices. The inertia of the Plodémet peasant, depriving him of the rewards of initiative, also saved him from these disasters, but could not protect him from either the sudden jolts or the permanent uncertainty of the market.

The need to increase productivity, that is, to modernize equipment and methods, and the need for a production policy forced themselves on Plodémet agriculture with equally vital urgency.

THE MULTIDIMENSIONAL CRISIS

The hour of modernization struck at a time when the electrification of the countryside was just beginning and there was still no running water on the farms; the peasant had to go almost without a pause from oil lamp to tractor, from well or cistern to electric pump.

The scattered location of water sources, which had been instrumental in creating the extreme dispersion of settlements in the region and had delayed the installation of running water, was now causing a water shortage. Supply was short, not only in the coastal region where the rainfall is not absorbed and in the dusty area in the north, but everywhere else where livestock rearing, truck farming, and the needs of the household have increased. While waiting for running water (planned for 1967–1968), Plo-démet countrymen must solve by individual efforts a problem that many other country districts had solved by community action before 1950. Even electric pumps could be installed only by the most advanced farmers.

According to the Centre d'Économie Rurale in Finistère, the minimum size for a profitable farm is fifty acres in the mediocre land of the north and twenty-five elsewhere.

The marketing system is antiquated. The truck farmer has to be merchant as well, without deriving any profit from it; he has to ship his vegetables to Quimper but then surrender them to the wholesaler. The farmer has to operate through the broker, who is the middleman between producer and cannery. The broker is often the village grocer, and he always takes his cut although his role is often merely parasitical. A tight network of brokers covers the countryside, often intertwined with networks of mutual obli-gations and family relationships. It would be very difficult for the producer to bypass a relative, or the grocer, who often has great influence in the village. It would mean tearing the fabric of tra-ditional and human relationships, without even so much as estab-lishing direct contact with the buyer—the cannery owner.

Obsolescent production and marketing are faced with a fluid and uncertain market, and each season the Plodémet producer must revaluate the prospects of his produce. Mass-produced car-rots, 20 to 25 francs a kilo in 1964, fell to 10 francs in 1965, and canned beans from 60 francs to 50 francs. Pork was 170 francs a half kilo in 1962, and 125 francs in 1965. Plodémet, which used to produce 600 to 700 tons of green peas a year, was hesitant about continuing production in 1965. The canneries, reeling under the blows of rough competition from the Oise region, guarantee nei-ther a floor price nor even purchase.

There is a fundamental incompatibility between the situation of the general farmer who is compelled by the necessity of sur-vival to make decisions on a day-to-day basis, and the overall situation which demands long-term investment in modernization, that is, specialization in a single crop or livestock. This incompatibility is implicit in a crisis whose dimensions—price, distribution, production, size of holding, modernization—are interconnected. Each particular problem raises the overall problem, and the overall problem sires a host of particular ones.

Pork, for example, is a profitable staple only if it is of uniformly high quality, produced in large quantities. The farmer has to buy piglets that are uniform in weight and age, which is not possible in the ordinary market in Pont-Croix; they must be uniformly fed, which requires either the purchase of prepared feed or modernization of the farm's fodder production and the installation of a mixer. Product uniformity requires large-scale breeding, which requires a modern pig farm with automatic feeding and cleaning equipment, which in turn requires an enormous investment in capital and massive rebuilding, all without the security of guaranteed prices.

The overall problem compels either retrenchment to the methods of subsistence economy, which is no longer possible, or an infeasible economic revolution that would destroy the present structure of farming. The agriculture of the whole of Finistère is in the no man's land between the old and the new. The past weighs particularly heavy on the peasantry of Plodémet, and the future is scarcely glimpsed.

The overall problem is also a human problem. Economic and technical change requires a transformation of the peasant personality. It is not enough to acquire the new attitude to money, which regards credit as the condition of progress, not as a family dishonor, and expresses all transactions in terms of money. It is also necessary to have an aptitude for bookkeeping and to be able to understand productivity and think, not in terms of financial viability—income—but of economic viability—overhead, current prices, and amortization. (Pautard estimates that 75 percent of the farms in Finistère have chronic deficits; the figure for Plodémet is certain to be even higher.)

The farmers had neither prior experience nor available information for estimating the profitability of modern machinery, and the relative overequipment in tractors in recent years has come about apparently as much as a result of ignorance as of the smallness of the holdings. It is easier to adapt to the economy of the machine than to the machinery of economics. Beyond a certain point, modernization requires a combination of financial, economic, and technical aptitudes, together with the managerial ability to organize work efficiently and judge the prospects of the market.

Above all, the peasant must be able to break the habits of a lifetime, to turn away from his style of life. The modernization-mechanization-efficiency spiral, both unavoidable and impossible, both desirable and destructive economically, creates a psychological spiral ending in a personality change that will catapult the young farmer away from the land toward the city.

The peasant personality is developing very gradually from generation to generation, obsessed with problems of the farm, but the peasant woman is evolving more rapidly in a direction away from these problems. The woman—the all-purpose servant of the farm with special responsibility for the livestock—is rebelling against what she now regards as the filth of manure, against subjection to chickens and cows. Increasingly, she aspires to a clean, comfortable, pleasant home, and while her husband is being assailed by the technical revolution, she presses the claims of the domestic revolution. While the man thinks and talks about crops, cattle, and machines, she thinks and talks about the house, about adding a story to it, about installing a toilet, a shower, a stove.

Two kinds of modernization that ought to be joined together are forced into opposition. For the woman, modernization means the home, for the man it means farm equipment. Meanwhile, inasmuch as both aspirations are frustrated and as they frustrate each other, the young are deserting farming in large numbers.

Until the 1950's, a son or a daughter was always willing to continue running the farm. Today, there is a general exodus. The boys go into other trades via the school. The girls either continue with their education, or marry men who take them away from the land. The farmers can no longer find wives in Plodémet, and only with difficulty even in the most rustic communes. Not a single bridegroom of the seven who held weddings in Plodémet in June 1965 was a farmer; of the eight in September and October 1965, only one—and he married a girl from outside the commune. The lack of opportunity to marry discourages even those otherwise willing to remain home. The mothers encourage the exodus; the fathers waive the tradition of obligatory succession and accept the inevitable, urging their children toward the escape route from all local problems and miseries: the school. Then, with the help of the school, the children discover another world.

Here is a portion of a conversation that took place in the home of Leclerc, a farmer:

MOTHER. What do you want to be when you grow up? A farmer like your father?

CHILD (age 7). No, not that.

AUNT. He always says no to that!

INTERVIEWER. And why don't you want to be a farmer?

MOTHER. The work's too hard, eh?

CHILD. Yes.

AUNT. You don't even know whether it's hard or not!

CHILD. It's dirty.

The father said nothing.

No farm that is smaller than twelve acres seems to have a prospective successor. In Bravez and Menez-Ru, only two boys under twenty are intending to work on the land. In Kéravrez, only one young man is working on his father's farm, and he does not plan to return to it after military service. Here and there, a few young men are still undecided or waiting (sick parents, a sister's marriage, failed examinations).

In 1962, 63 percent of the farmers were over fifty years old; as few as 5 to 10 percent of the young men under twenty have decided to follow in their footsteps. Worse still, the young, who are reformers and innovators by nature, are digging the grave of modernization by abandoning the farms to the old, for the old are all the less motivated to modernize when they have no successors. Thus, the crisis of succession is implicit in the crisis of technical, economic, and psychological backwardness underlying the overall crisis in the structure of farming. The interaction of these crises is deepening and widening into one involving the entire fabric of peasant life, threatening to bring about the disintegration of the peasantry itself.

The same problems that exist in various regions of France are compounded in a most acute fashion in outlying isolated Finistère and critically concentrated in the commune of Plodémet—the microcosm of a national transformation.

The Meanest of Vocations

The peasant cannot help constantly comparing his life with the life led by relatives who have moved to cities, by vacationers in his village, by tradesmen, teachers, and wage earners. His vocation appears to him as the lowest of the low, his class as the disinherited of the earth.

The earnings of peasants are the lowest in France. An urban worker's monthly 700 francs seems a princely sum to them, not merely because it is large but because it is regular. The newspaper of the farmers' union published a study of farm income in the canton of Plogastel which estimated that 160 francs a month was the average per capita income from the smallholding of less than 25 acres, 350 francs from the holding of between 25 and 38 acres, and 250 to 340 francs from truck farms. The usual counterargument that other vocational groups have higher expenses for housing, food, and transportation is turned aside by reference to the disparity in standards of living. In the words of a young man from Bravez, "We work one hundred hours a week while he [a young teacher] works forty, but he can buy himself a car and a house in five or six years."

The peasant regards himself as a slave to the hardest of all work. He has to be outside in every kind of weather when others are indoors; others have fixed hours of work, which the peasant sees not as confining but as liberating. The various chores at home, which are a form of relaxation for the urban worker, are a continuation of work for the peasant. Even his sleep can be threatened by a calving cow.

The old farmer, with little or no mechanized equipment, with no help from his children, sometimes must work even on Sundays. His protest against the excess of work expresses his exhaustion. The young man is eager to dissociate his work from his home life and thinks mostly about his weekends and his vacation. The old man thinks about his retirement, which is welcome but late at sixty-five; his work will be useless then, and he sees seamen and policemen retiring at fifty. A seaman son can retire almost before his peasant father. ("My sons-in-law retired before I did and their wives never had to work.")

Then there is constant insecurity resulting not simply from the fluctuations of prices but from the nature of the work, vulnerable as it is to caprices of the weather, to diseases of crops and livestock, and to all sorts of mishaps. "A worker doesn't take any risks, but on the farm a pig might die just when it is ready for the market." The old peasant regards insurance on livestock or buildings not as a form of security but as an excessive expenditure, although he views the insurance premium deducted from the worker's salary entirely as a benefit. The hard work, the anxieties, the insecurity, and the meager rewards conspire to deprive the peasant's life of sense. In some cases, old farmers are so exhausted by work that they have no energy left for a little Sunday recreation. Old Cloerec in Kerlaeron, for example, had no desire to go into the town, which makes him dizzy, or to see a movie, which hurts his eyes, or to listen to the radio, which tires him. He forces himself to read the Sunday newspaper so as "not to live like the animals"—which sleep near him in the other room.

Yet neither he nor others (except a few former big landowners) look back to the past with nostalgia. It is with the life of today's urban classes that the peasant makes his comparisons. "This is no life" means that the peasant—especially if he is young, even though he works less and earns more—feels deprived of what he thinks of as life: a private life separate from work, and work protected by security. Security and independence, which once seemed guaranteed in perpetuity by landed property, have become properties of the urban salary. The wage-earning class is becoming the ideal symbol of emancipation. To the young, a farm means disowning one's freedom and therefore one's future. Only the modernizers and big farmers hope to reap the advantage of both wage earner and employer. One man alone wants to take a step further still—the biggest landowner in the commune, Goémon from Kerminou: He wants to build a house in the town and become "a bourgeois peasant."

The progress of urban civilization and the contemporaneous development of the crisis besetting the core of the rural world make the peasant conscious of his wretched situation. He knows that he is regarded as backward, and while he does not deny being indeed backward, he attributes it to—and blames it on—having been left behind. He feels scorned and struggles against a nagging sense of inferiority. When asked by an interviewer why he has remained on the farm young Le Corre replied, "It must be because I was too stupid to do anything else," and we do not know whether he guessed what the questioner had in mind or was expressing his considered opinion.

A lot of farmers think they were stupid to stay instead of becoming seamen, policemen, or teachers. Those who tried but failed their examinations cannot free themselves of a feeling of personal failure, which coincides all too unfortunately with the collective feeling of decline. Nevertheless, at the same time they all protest against their situation. Why should society disdain the people who feed it?

"People should realize whenever they sit down to eat that all the food comes from the soil, and that someone had to extract it from the soil. The peasant isn't stupider than anyone else. The president himself comes from the peasant class, the first man himself was a peasant. So why are peasants looked down on?" (old Le Calvez from Bravez).

No one speaks of it, but the men undoubtedly endure sexual frustration in addition to the economic and social frustration.[2] The young peasant at a dance knows that he cannot pick up girls from the town, so he takes refuge at the bar and gets drunk; he can no longer find a servant girl who will wait for him at night in the potato fields, and even girls of his own class spurn any suggestion of marriage. ("They'll go with anyone but a peasant. They'll go for the first policeman they see.") The daughter of the biggest landowner married a worker from Nantes, demonstrating that the lowest townsman is better than the richest peasant.

The peasants speak about the dearth of matrimonial opportunities in what is almost a tone of ghetto humor and self-deprecation. Menguy the photographer cited the following exchange as an example of banter circulating currently:

"By the way, I heard the other day that a convoy of Dutch girls is coming."

"Who said so?"

"The farmers."

"Why Dutch girls?"

"Because they also have to be good workers."

The inordinate proliferation of tractors in Plodémet is perhaps a compensatory reaction to suffocating frustrations. Sitting high up in his tractor—an imaginary tank dominating roads and bourgeois cars with its rumbling mass—the peasant can let himself feel like a conqueror of technology, a master of nature. The tractor is his noblest acquisition, not only because it alleviates his adversity but chiefly because it helps him forget it.

[2] The use of sleeping pills is one of the reliable indices of frustration. According to Bourlière's study, peasants as a group use more sleeping pills than any other group in Plodémet.

The peasant also regards himself as one exploited by brokers, wholesalers, factory owners, and retailers. He sees his products being sold at up to four times the price that he was paid for them; he has put in all the work, others get all the profit.

He feels abandoned by everyone in every respect. The young abandon the old, the girls abandon the boys, the big abandon the small, the town abandons the countryside, the government abandons the peasants. The State's neglect is felt particularly deeply. Recent legislation on loans and retirement pensions is viewed by the peasant not as a solution but as a palliative measure. The Provident State ought to guarantee his prosperity and security as it does that of other classes! The red smallholder points his accusing finger not only at the Provident State but also at the Republican Father-State who has emancipated him only to abandon and betray him.

Nevertheless, deep down, the peasant retains the conviction that the State cannot abandon him completely, because in any event the land will have to be cultivated in order to feed the towns. In our conversations with the peasants of Plodémet they repeatedly and spontaneously brought up the idea of the future nationalization of the land, not to reject it but to consider it as a last resort.

With or without land nationalization, the peasant class is rapidly disappearing. Everyone, including the most active exponents of modernization and the most ardent unionists, is aware of living through the last days of peasantry. Kerzinou, the spokesman of the most progressive cooperative, says, "Everyone agrees that this is the end." Most see the end not in the form of a slow decline but as some sort of fatal hour when the clock of destiny will stop; some say in ten years, others in twenty. Still, in addition to guessing that the land will be nationalized, the peasant tries to apprehend the future. Young Le Neur thinks that "the age of the big landowner will come back," and he is not alone in that belief, while Le Kouign speculates that "the *pieds-noirs* [former colonists from Algeria] will buy up everything."

The awareness of death pangs is shrouded in a sense of total resignation, as if the inevitability of the end had erased all possibilities of revolt. Resignation to the approaching end is also reinforced by the changes in the peasants' attitude toward land and property. Although attached to the land, they experience less and less the unique symbiosis between man and the nurturing soil. They struck us as being more devoted to their animals than to their land, and this seemed to be true not only of the old men who weep when a horse dies and the old women who talk to their cow as to a friend, but also of the young. The relative detachment from the land is a development parallel to the continuing decline in the value of landed property in relation to salaried work.

Of course, peasants would willingly accept the farmer-bourgeois solution if it were within their reach. In their present adversity, they would almost resign themselves to conditions that were unanimously rejected fifty years ago, namely, to become peasant wage-earners, provided that the State was the employer, for there can never be a return to a system based on the dependence of agricultural worker on landed peasant.

This is why the peasantry is psychologically ready for nationalization. Le Braz from Kéringard, the last representative of a once great white family, is completely in favor of it. Old Joseph Autrez of Kéravrec says, "It will be good for the farmer for the State to take over." Another old peasant, Le Neur: "Of course, it will be like the kolkhozes; we'll be slaves like factory workers, and maybe happier than we are now"—voicing the idea of the happy slave while expressing the peasant's ambivalence in regard to property and wages.

Finally, beyond all these there is keen awareness of a future when the peasant class will have disappeared, but when the individual family will have been transplanted into bourgeois society. It is a fundamental point that a disconnection, even a contradiction, has already come about between the fate of the class and the fate of the family. Already the older sons are advancing themselves through education, which will be the way up for the younger ones as well as collective salvation for the family. The smallholding may continue to subsist just long enough for the children to complete their education.

The contrast between despair of the class and the hope of the family is a decisive factor in the identity of the Plodémet peasant today. It produces sufficient lucidity to neutralize the extremes of both despair and hope.

The Division Among the Peasantry

The peasantry of Plodémet is unanimous in its acceptance of the values of modern urban-bourgeois civilization, but a difference is apparent between those who take up the challenge of modernization and those who are simply waiting for the end to come. The line of separation follows the long-standing cleavage between reds and whites, but in this case the whites are on the offensive, the reds on the defensive, and the enemy common to both. The red-white separation may be defined roughly as that between smallholding and medium-size farm, or that between holdings incapable of modernization and those capable.[3] The whites—almost all with medium-sized or large farms—are inclined to modernize all the more because the Church, which has encouraged them to stay on the land, has formed a corps of trained activists to direct the struggle for renewal. Conversely, the reds are less motivated to meet the challenge, because their families and peers are already committed to upward mobility and migration.

In addition to the economic, ideological, and political divisions, there is the cleavage between old and young. Smallholdings, deserted by the young during the last twenty to thirty years, are now almost entirely in the hands of old men, while almost half of the medium-sized and big farms are run by men thirty-five and forty-five and have available manpower even in the twenty-five to thirty-five age group.

All in all, old men run the vast majority of smallholdings and almost half of all larger farms. Out of 330 farmers, perhaps 80 are

[3] The correlation between medium-sized farms and young farmers on the one hand and smallholdings and old farmers on the other seems more significant than the criterion of the white-red cleavage. The sons are less tempted to stay on and run the farm when its size makes it uneconomical. Historically, it is true enough that red Baillism was strongest among smallholders, but in present-day Plodémet political antagonism between smallholders and big farmers is more a historical datum than an actual division. The three oppositions, small-big, red-white, and old-young, commingle to form small-red-old and big-white-young—useful basically as poles of reference. The process by which these configurations evolve today is different from processes that operated fifty years ago. In the past, one became red because one was a smallholder; today, the head of a farm is young because the farm is big enough to survive. [Note by J.-L. Peninou]

young enough to modernize—a figure that matches the estimate of the Centre d'Économie Rurale Finistérien, which found that approximately 80 farms were in a viable condition. Between these 80 farms and the 150 smallholdings there are about a hundred surviving in a state between mere subsistence and semiagricultural polyactivity. The truck farmers complicate the picture in that they earn as much or more than middle-range farmers, yet they are smallholders in terms of acreage, age, and inability to take collective action. They too can be subdivided into a passive majority who continue to take their chances each Saturday in the Quimper market, and a resourceful minority who are open to experiments and work on building their own market contacts.

The old smallholders are waiting for retirement. They have retrenched so as to cover most of their needs with minimal outlay. They eat their own potatoes and vegetables, use the milk from their cow, and the eggs from their hens; they keep a few pigs and feed the animals on waste and fodder; they exchange services with other farmers. Their houses are decrepit if they have no children, but may be well equipped and well furnished if they have a son or daughter married away from the commune. They accept the fluctuations of the market as if they represented the weather charts of destiny, neither understanding nor trying to oppose them. They do not belong to the union. They submitted to land redistribution as they submit to everything else, with distressed resignation. They are incapable of sharing a tractor. They cannot conceive of cooperative agriculture, of sharing the machines that alone could save them; the collective farm, so attractive to young Catholic farmers with twenty-five acres, is regarded with horror by old Communists with only five. They are resigned to the fact that when they go their holdings will be left derelict.

The medium-sized farm provides the best impetus for modernization. It has been stimulated from outside the commune—by union activists from Plonéour or Quimper, by farmers who have come in through marriage from Poulzic, Plovan, and Landudec. During the 1950's, the appearance of electric pumps and tractors marked the beginning of the power revolution. Mechanization was introduced unsystematically, always on the larger farms, in the form of tractors, power-driven cultivators, plows, planters, and threshers; the combine harvesters were bought by contractors. Mechanization was followed in the 1960's by the introduction, on a smaller scale, of efficiency techniques on the farm and modernization in the home. At the same time, the farmers' union undertook a number of modernization projects, such as land redistribution, green-pea-planting improvements, an information service, and the groundwork of a cooperative.

Modernization is a cause of dissension between generations even on medium-sized farms. There is conflict between young modernizers and old conservatives, and between old modernizers (who want more machinery) and new modernizers (who favor efficient reorganization). Impatience is all the greater and modernization all the more hampered because a son may have to wait until he is thirty-five to forty before he can succeed his father.[4]

Although the modernization of the medium-sized farm has proceeded in a rather uneven manner, it has done so sufficiently to distinguish it clearly from the smallholding. This has produced a new inequality, annulling the democratic virtues of the technological revolution of the late nineteenth century, which had benefitted everyone and the smallholder in particular—what with new fertilizers, crops, tools, and implements. On the other hand, the technological revolution of the 1950's has spread its benefits in direct proportion to acreage. (This is attested to by the lists of buyers of agricultural machinery, which show that all own less than eighteen acres.) Clearly, technology favors those who are able to combine mechanization with efficiency and adapt to market fluctuations.

The new inequality does not result in the servitude of smallholders to big landowners, as it did in the nineteenth century, because modernization does not require a larger labor force but more machinery. Modernizers would certainly take over smallholdings if they could, but the peasants hang on to the end and even beyond, for their children who live in the towns keep the land for vacations and eventual retirement. Some have even converted the farmhouses into "suburban" homes, commuting to jobs in Quimper. Thus peasantry and urban mobility combine once again to prevent the development of the land and the expansion of the large and medium-sized farm.

[4] The law conferring a lifetime annuity on the head of a farm holding upon retirement did not come into force until 1964 and has not affected any holding in Plodémet as of this writing.

The smallholder is conscious of the new inequality and of the divergence of interests, and consequently rejects collective activities such as the union and the cooperative, preventing the formation of a united front of the peasant class. The middle-range farm operator ignores the death throes of the peasant who has no productive use to him; sometimes he even seeks to accelerate the peasant's demise because the smallholding handicaps his operations and objectives.

Reintegration

THE STRUGGLE OF THE UNION

The Plodémet chapter of the farmers' union was founded in 1924, but until 1955 it was primarily a branch of the white party. The transformation of agricultural unionism in Finistère during the 1950's has been well documented elsewhere by Serge Mallet.[5] Essentially, the old union of rural notables was transformed during that period into a union of activists, manned mainly from the ranks of the middle peasantry, championing the cause of modernization and militating for reforms in all agricultural functions, ranging from the organization of cooperatives to marketing techniques. The union led a series of protests that were either based on the industrial model (mass meetings) or were of an entirely new type (road blocks, marches on the towns). The regional sections soon began to specialize (artichokes, cauliflowers, potatoes, pigs, poultry), and consequently each region became extraordinarily vulnerable to the decline in prices. They risked ruin by their modernization policies and constituted in every way the spearhead of Finistère unionism. Plodémet, with its fragmented general farming, its backwardness and passivity, took some part in the movement but left leadership to the activists of Quimper and Plonéour.

Since 1955, however, the Plodémet chapter of the union has been under the control of a group of middle-range farmers in the twenty-five to thirty-five age group, all former activists of the JAC (Jeunesse Agricole Chrétienne, or Young Christian Farmers). The takeover by the new generation has brought about

[5] In *Les Paysans contre le passé* (Paris, Éditions du Seuil, 1962).

radical changes in aims and methods, and signaled the beginnings of a countercurrent in Plodémet society that is linking itself to a similar shift in Finistère as a whole and to the national progression toward modernization. Ten years of activity, skirmishes, battles, and half victories have produced the most important events in Plodémet since 1880-1900.

The first reform consisted in the democratization of the union organization, which made it possible to replace the local notables by freely elected activists. The commune was divided into seventeen districts; the district leaders, who are elected by secret ballot, constitute the executive committee of the commune chapter, and they elect the chapter's president, secretary, and treasurer. The first president, Kermélec from Kerminou, was the Moses of the union movement; the second president, Le Kam from Le Calvaire, established a link between the union and the town hall, and was elected to the town council of the red electoral list in 1965. The fact that the current president, Demet, is from Kervelen proves the success of union activity in the white countryside of the southeast.

Between 1959 and 1963, the union had between 115 and 130 members—over one-third of the farmers in Plodémet—most with large or medium-sized holdings and nearly all whites. The truck farmers and the traditionally red villages of Bravez, Kéravrez, and Menez-Ru remained outside the union. Membership and the greatest activity were concentrated in the white regions of Kerlaeron, Merros, Queldrec, Lesnus, and Kerminou.

During the years 1959-1962 there was a great upsurge of union activity. An intercommunal committee (Plovan, Poulzic, Plodémet) was set up in 1959, and this gave birth in 1962 to the three communal information groups. The union persuaded its own members, and subsequently Plodémet peasantry and the municipality—which saw it as an opportunity to build its roads more cheaply—to accept the principle of land redistribution (1960-1966.) The crucial year was 1962 when the union succeeded in persuading both red and white peasants to take part in the demonstrations that were sweeping Finistère, got them together in the pea producers' association to fight the canneries, and started the first equipment cooperative. With backing from Quimper and Plonéour, the union leaders in Plodémet tried to coordinate a sweeping reform of attitudes—by means of technical information and propaganda in favor of the cooperative system; of the methods of production—by means of land redistribution, the equipment cooperative, and group agriculture; and of distribution methods and prices.

INFORMATION

The union distributes to its members the newspaper *Paysan Breton,* which devotes more of its space to economic and technical information than to union news. It urges young farmers to attend agricultural schools and take study trips both in France and abroad. It worked continuously on setting up the intercommunal committee and the information groups.

The Plodémet information group, organized by union activists from Plonéour, meets once a month, except in the summer, at the farms of each of its twenty members in turn. The meeting lasts all afternoon and takes up practical work problems, experiments with methods and materials, and reports followed by discussion.

The group consists mainly of union leaders under forty, and we were told that average attendance is between ten and twenty; however, at the meeting of October 12, 1965, only three members were present. The host himself was absent, trying to sell a cow that had just been killed in an accident, and the meeting was postponed until Sunday two weeks later, at which time six members were present.

COOPERATION

The farmers' cooperative through collective investment in and use of a minimum of machinery (CUMA, or the Coopérative d'Utilisation du Matériel Agricole) on the maximum number of farms (GAEC, or the Groupe Agricole d'Exploitation Collective) is the most original innovation of the union movement in Brittany. In a sense, cooperation is the answer to the need to modernize farm work over large acreages, and in a larger sense, it is a social idea that is capable of creating a new peasant solidarity and breaking down the old proprietary individualism. For some, it is a communal idea—perhaps of Christian Socialist inspiration with a touch of the *kibbutz* and the collective farm—providing a foundation for cooperative socialism, that potential utopia the peasant class so badly needs.

When the idea of cooperation first surfaced in Plodémet and

then crystallized into the CUMA, the ancient custom of exchanging services was still firmly embedded. Although machinery had done much to end the day of harvest when farmers banded together to bring in each other's crops, other forms of exchange of labor and equipment still survived. This type of mutual aid is based on private ownership of the horse or tractor which is lent; it does not derive from a sense of community but from family relationships or friendships. One gets help from a relative who may be living miles away, rather than from a neighbor. One might turn to one particular neighbor, but not to just any neighbor. One is far away from a close neighbor but close to a faraway relative. The boundary of property is a frontier, whereas relationship is an open road. The relative, however distant, is always an ally by nature, whereas the neighbor, however close, is first of all the nearest rival. Characteristically, when a member of the cooperative was asked, "Do you ever have trouble in the CUMA?" the reply was, "No. There are only two farms nearby."

The Plodémet peasants' opposition to the CUMA is expressed in terms of "human nature" but in fact reveals their own attitudes. A machine can be looked after properly only by its owner, they claim, and anything owned jointly is neglected. Yvon Le Braz from Kéringard, a long-time union activist, made an agreement with neighbors to share in the purchase of equipment with each retaining ownership of one particular item and lending it to the others. "This way everyone will take care of his own property; in the CUMA you have to have someone in charge and often no one pays any attention to him."

The ingrained proprietary spirit and distrust of neighbors make it extremely difficult to establish a cooperative. Those who are disposed to cooperate will not hear of doing so with their neighbor, and even those who are on good terms with their neighbor will not go so far as to form a cooperative with him. Only family relationships can turn mutual assistance into new forms of cooperation.

It was under these difficult conditions that the first CUMA was set up in 1962, remaining the only one until 1966. It was formed by thirteen farmers for the purpose of buying equipment; what had been acquired by each member prior to joining together remained his personal property, and each could continue to buy equipment for his own use only. The scope of cooperation was thus considerably reduced. The CUMA covers an area of 383 acres, drawing together farms ranging from twenty to forty-three acres, and one of twelve. All thirteen farmers were under thirty-five in 1962, and belonged to the union's information group. Decisions are taken collectively, and expenses are divided in proportion to the acreage of each farm and the duration of equipment usage. Each is assigned the care and responsibility of a member machine. The CUMA is continually buying new equipment and owns plowing machines, one manure spreader, one manure fork-lift, and small equipment. Despite the urging of the more dynamic members, no heavy machinery such as large tractors and combine harvesters has yet been bought, although some individual members do own large tractors. Also, a proposal by Kermélec to organize work teams—a step forward in cooperation—was not accepted. Nevertheless, within its limited framework the CUMA functions to the satisfaction of its members.

Neither the prestige acquired by the CUMA through its success among the middle peasantry nor the active propaganda of the parish magazine has turned its example into a model; a second attempt to found a CUMA failed. However, a new experiment was begun in 1966 by a group of livestock producers which included a few big landowners. The group was outside the framework of the union, and based itself on joint distribution rather than on cooperative production.

The GAEC set up by three brothers-in-law on January 1, 1965, was the advance guard of cooperation in Plodémet. Kermélec and his two brothers-in-law, themselves activists, joined their farms together in a partnership that owns the land and allocates each member a fixed salary (in 1965 it was 600 francs a month with profits to be proportionately divided at the end of the year). It was agreed at the outset that each of the original farms would specialize in a predetermined crop.

The experiment, which receives favorable tax treatment and other assistance from the Chamber of Agriculture, is not only the first cooperative integration of individual farms in Plodémet but also a vigorous effort at technical modernization. It has turned the three brothers-in-law into manager-technicians and put them in effect into a new profession that embodies the peasant's long-frustrated ambition of becoming both employer and wage earner.

Will a project with so many advantages inspire imitation? The skepticism we found was directed not at economic viability but at the psychological feasibility of an enterprise with three bosses.

Cooperation in Plodémet in the form of CUMA and GAEC has taken root only when a set of conditions limiting any possible expansion have coexisted. These are age (under forty-five and over twenty-five), acreage (medium-sized farms only), tradition (Catholic), and above all, long-standing solidarity either with the union or with family.

Family is an omnipresent factor, not only in the CUMA, where the three brothers-in-law of the GAEC are joined by two other brothers-in-law and two brothers, but also in small cooperative partnerships of two relatives formed for buying a tractor to be owned jointly. The family is the easiest means of modernization— an archaic structure serving as the foundation and scaffolding for a modern construction.

Family relationship is not entirely advantageous; the farms in the partnership may be far apart, and the forging of family links across the commune from one village to another is breaking up the village when it ought to be united, preventing the establishment of an organic solidarity with one's neighbor. Such is the case at Kerminou, the most progressive hamlet, where despite the cooperatively installed water supply, each of the five larger farms is linked, on the basis of mutual assistance or of cooperation, to distant brothers-in-law.

The cooperative movement is based on the most ancient institution of society—the family—but draws its strength from the unionist spirit. Some members justify the enterprise primarily on grounds of necessity and utility, but to the union activists cooperation is the very purpose of life. They implant union solidarity in economic activity. These activists are far ahead of the other union members. As the secretary of the information group remarked, "The CUMA works only when its members are all of the same kind." In terms of placement conditions "the same kind" means a total membership of twenty to thirty in all forms of cooperative venture, out of 120 union members and 330 farmers.

LAND REDISTRIBUTION

The peasantry of Plodémet is hostile to the CUMA, which does not even threaten the farm unit as such, yet it accepted the radical surgery of land redistribution. The apparent paradox dissolves when one realizes that the CUMA profoundly alters the concept of property, whereas redistribution merely touches its surface.

Very few communes in Finistère had undertaken land redistribution at the time a general assembly of the farmers of Plodémet accepted the principle of redistribution (1960), with the agreement of the municipality. How did such a relatively progressive act come about? Because of an agreement between whites and reds on a move that facilitated the building of roads and also helped the local economy? Because of excessively fragmented land? Because of the confidence placed by the middle-range farmers in the new union leadership? Because of the general confidence in the supervision to be exercised by the municipal and administrative authorities? All these factors must have played a part, and in any event, redistribution was confidently decided upon and concluded amid disputes.

The classification of the land proved to be a particularly delicate process in a region so fragmented and diversified; in the truck-farming areas, for example, the slightest difference of gradient and exposure to sun results in variations of up to eight days in the maturation of early vegetables and hence in substantial differences in price.

Redistribution reactivated dormant distrusts and brought cunning to the fore. Everyone undervalued land he expected to keep and overvalued land he expected to give up. Since the trickery was practiced by nearly all, this method of valuation came to be regarded by the surveyor as the most satisfactory. However, when the allocations were made, many farmers began to believe their own deception and complained of losing their best land. Moreover, everyone filed at least one reclamation against the initial plan, either out of dissatisfaction or to camouflage satisfaction, and some filed two or three formal reclamations as bargaining points to gain justification for one. The potential benefits of redistribution as well as people's hopes were dissipated in the process. Of 129 reclamations, 17 percent were wholly satisfied, 38 percent partially. We may estimate that less than one-third of the farmers felt themselves wronged, but even among those who did not, there were many broken relationships, and in practically every case one's neighbor once again became one's rival. Be that as it may, redistribution cannot now be defined as having been anything else but a competition between neighbors. The competition was all the more bitter when it involved a struggle for survival, when a smallholder hoped to gain the extra bit of land that would keep him going, or when a middle-range farmer hoped to get over the threshold of secure profitability.

Discontent spilled over into quarrels throughout the commune; some blamed the surveyor, others the mayor and the teachers, some the white farmers on the commission, but most of the discontent was the result of the policy of redistribution itself, not of its political residues. In the end, resentment fastened on the union leaders who had initiated the redistribution and, being modernizing farmers, benefitted from it. In 1964-1965, this resentment coupled with defeat in the "battle of the peas" (see below) and caused a reduction in the active membership of the union.

September 29—Saint Michael's Day—was awaited with apprehension in 1965: land redistribution was to go into effect. Peasants had been declaring throughout the commune that they would not give up their allocated plots. Here and there blows had been exchanged. One man had lost a finger in a fight. Pitchforks had been brandished. One farmer had rented a plow to break up the field he was leaving. Two neighbors chopped down the pine woods they were to exchange. But these scorched-earth tactics meant only that opposition was crumbling. On the 29th, everything was quiet: no one dared go out to his new land or return to the old. After a few days, the cows were put out to graze on the new land, but the plots were not plowed for two more weeks; then people started making plans for leveling hillocks and knocking down boundary walls. Only a few old men went back to look at their old land.

By February 1966, the association responsible for the financial aspects of redistribution was able to summarize its activities without difficulties. According to the surveyor (harbinger of anger, tears, and progress), it would take from three to four years for feelings to settle down and for the advantages of redistribution to be appreciated. Despite its extreme complexity, the redistribution in Plodémet was one of the least dramatic he had supervised. It was one of the most important ones in Finistère in terms of the reduction of the number of holdings and the extent of road construction. It reduced the number of holdings by 71 percent, from 8,260 to 2,390. It made possible the construction of nearly twenty miles of rural roads and over fifty miles of asphalted farm roads capable of accommodating combine harvesters.

Redistribution favored those who were already better off and increased the inequality between them and smallholders, between the obsolescent and the modern. The Rural Engineering Commission will not maintain roadways of "farms with no future." When the whole terrifying business was over, the small farmer discovered that redistribution was a means of accelerating his own decline to the profit of others. "Redistribution came ten years too soon or ten years too late," said Demet. It came too late for a new beginning and too early for a sharing of the spoils.

THE BATTLE OF THE PEAS

Green peas were the main vegetable crop in Plodémet—produced in quantities of six to seven hundred tons a year—and most farmers devoted some of their land to pea growing. The tough competition from the Oise region was a matter not only of price but of quality, inasmuch as city consumers in greater and greater numbers began to favor the small-sized pea at the expense of the large pea produced in Finistère.

Hostilities were triggered by the installation of a sorting machine and the calibration of prices according to pea size by Hanff, the largest cannery in the area.

It was the year (1962) in which the farmers' union in Finistère pushed the middlemen out and began to offer their cauliflower directly to the consumer. It was the year in which the long-neglected peasants of western France suddenly discovered their Herculean strength, and in waging a wave of protest, attacked prefectures, descended on Paris in fleets of trucks, and set up road blocks. At the initiative of the union and under its leadership, an association of pea producers was founded in the four coastal communes of Plonéour, Plovan, Poulzic, and Plodémet, receiving general support from the outset. Ignoring the brokers (who continued to take their 10 percent for services amounting to little more than nothing), the association addressed itself to the cannery in order to obtain a guaranteed minimum price—preferably at planting time—control over size sorting (rightly or wrongly, the cannery was suspected of cheating), and payment on delivery (producers sometimes had to wait six months). The association was an autonomous body representing the producers who were trying through collective action to force the cannery to share in the risks that had been borne solely by themselves. At the same time, they established a system to replace individual brokerage.

Hanff refused to recognize the association, preferring to maintain his brokers. An old-style right-wing boss, a sort of despotic squire in Poulzic, he would not accept the slightest challenge to his omnipotence. Moreover, he thought that the dependence of so many peasant families on the cannery, with wives and daughters working there, the old bonds between peasants and brokers, and the slight difference between his terms and those of his competitors, would soon crush the association. But the canneries backed down before the peasants did. Raphalen's cannery in Plonéour agreed to negotiate with the association, which had to abandon several of its conditions but preserved what was most important—its existence. However, Hanff then weakened the producers' front by offering a few extra francs per kilo to those who dealt with his brokers, and a bonus to the most efficient brokers. He paid the farmers as early as the end of August, although the association had won an agreement to be paid in three installments spread over the autumn. By the end of the year, half the producers in Plodémet had returned to the Hanff cannery and the old system.

The association survived until 1964 when the canneries agreed among themselves to divide the market. This time the militant pea producers did not return to Hanff, but went to Landernau.

The association did not fail completely. Even Hanff has by now partially abandoned the brokerage system and established direct contacts—although these are individual ones with each farmer. The militants were completely demoralized both by the attitude of the canneries and by the defection of the "yellows," who, having benefitted from the action of the association, now obtained better prices than the militants themselves.

Thus, land redistribution and the pea producers' association both created still more dissension among the Plodémet peasantry, the first by its success, the second by its failure. The divisions were made manifest in the decline of union membership, but still more in a general feeling of powerlessness. Not only the smallholders but the whole farming community lost the hope of being able to control events and create a future by collective action.

CROSSING THE THRESHOLD

The years 1964 and 1965 were a time of disappointment, discontent, and divisions. Union membership fell to 50 in 1964, then rose in desperate straits to 60 by the end of 1965. The union was hoping for its second wind, but apart from isolated protest demonstrations, it failed to rally either the reds or the smallholders.

There were conflicting tendencies toward mass protest or action for organizational change. Of course, the demonstration of 1961-1962 against what were regarded as flagrant excesses implied a desire for radical change; but the revolt was too superficially formulated and too vague in scope to be anything more than an appeal to the Father-State to intervene on its behalf.

On the other hand, the information group, the land redistribution, and cooperatives, and the pea producers' association contained sufficient fundamental force to have formed a new basis for local agriculture to effect efficiency and coordinated production, control distribution, and eventually formulate an overall policy for fulfilling its needs.

It was not possible to initiate organizational action immediately. The years 1964-1965 showed the union incapable of playing a transforming-integrating role in the agriculture of Plodémet. This was partly the result of the nature and number of smallholdings, of backwardness, of diversity, and of ideological divisions, all of which atrophy or destroy any policy; and partly it was the result of the fact that the problem of transformation-integration goes beyond the framework of commune and canton.

This is also the conclusion reached by the union activists, who now envisage integration in the form of a powerful regional cooperative system, because it is the only practicable form.

During the last five years, a gulf has been widening between the activists and the regular membership of the union. As members of cooperatives, the activists have become organizers and/or ideologists; they have adhered to the modernization process which turned them into technical managers; they attend meetings and seminars, keep files, take notes, talk about productivity, profitability, organization, and structure, and devise projects, legislative proposals, and reforms. Without being aware of it, they have the makings of a new caste.

THE CONTRACTOR SYSTEM

A few people under thirty have joined the CDJA (Centre des Jeunes Agriculteurs, or Young Farmers' Group), which has recently opened a branch in the canton. Is it a new spurt of activism or a more technically oriented base? Will the CDJA assume control of the feeble new movement that seems to be placing its hopes in individual innovation and in the spirit of enterprise as the means of attaining a peasant-bourgeois state?

The reluctance of the smallholders and even of the CUMA to acquire heavy equipment collectively has left the field open to a small-scale rural capitalism that has all the costly machinery, notably combine harvesters. Eleven firms dealing in agricultural machinery have been set up and their services are in increasing demand, to increase still further with the effects of redistribution.

The firms are regarded favorably by the union activists because they contribute to modernization. However, they dispossess the farmer of an essential means of production, which demonstrates that it is economically impossible for Plodémet farming and sociologically impossible for Plodémet peasantry to solve the problem of modern equipment by themselves.

Except for Hanff, the largest of them, the machinery contractors are of peasant origin: Goémon, a big landowner and livestock breeder, "bourgeois-peasant"-to-be; Fanch Gaelic, who abandoned farming for contracting in agricultural machinery, brokerage, and bondstone manufacture; Le Braz, who was encouraged and helped by his son-in-law, a former merchant seaman, and now supplements the income from his twenty-five acres with that from contracting; and above all, Gaelic, who has a model farm in Pors-en-Breval and is reputed to be the richest and most modern farmer in Plodémet. He also has his own truck-farming operation and built up his own marketing system; he attends to production, distribution, and management, working from 6 A.M. to 10 P.M. and already suffering from managerial insomnia. Gaelic is the only man in the commune who combines the cooperative spirit (with his brother-in-law Goémon) and the spirit of enterprise (he is planning to open a camping site for tourists on the coast) in the dual objective—systematically and intelligently pursued—of modernizing and getting rich.

These contractors are a transitional phenomenon between the old brokerage system and the new agricultural capitalism, between the rural and the bourgeois worlds. They have acquired a vestige of power over peasants who want to be on good terms with their contractor in order to be able to harvest early. Also, since 1965, four contractors have been elected to the municipal council, which now has eleven members, making them the best-represented professional group.

Like the cooperatives, the contractors are focal points in the modernist trend. But whereas cooperatives want the peasants to acquire the key machinery of modern production, contractors are contributing to the dispossession of the peasantry.

BEFORE THE TRANSFORMATION

Fifteen years after the beginning of the crisis that mortally wounded the Plodémet peasantry, the observer is struck by the stubborn survival of the smallholding.

Evidently, the disappearance of the smallholding and a substantial increase in the size of the average farm will not happen overnight. The 131 acres freed by deaths between 1954 and 1963 have not all been redistributed for agricultural use. The process of freeing land will progress very slowly. At the beginning, the smallholdings vanish but without increasing the area of medium-sized farms, because the heirs tend to turn them into summer vacation spots. A reduction of 40 percent in the number of farms raises the average size of the Plodémet farm to only twenty-one acres. Other things being equal, the migration of the young will have its cumulative effect only at the end of a gradual extinction process lasting approximately thirty years.

General farming has proved that it possesses the strongest survival traits as a method of small-scale farming. Only the biggest farmer, Goémon, tends to specialize (in cattle raising). The GAEC itself has three specialties, which is to say it is still general. True, Plodémet's natural diversity is not easily adaptable to specialty farming; still, specialization is eminently conceivable—in vegetables or livestock, pigs, for example. But the usual Plodémet delay, rigidity, and uncertainty kept on postponing such moves even when specialization was already widespread in Nord-Finistère. The crisis that later struck specialized producers of artichokes, potatoes, pigs, and poultry in the north, and the similar fate of Plodémet peas, confirmed the idea that it was more prudent and intelligent to wait. Even the union activists and young farmers opted for a wait-and-see policy of continued general farming, even though it retarded modernization and weakened their bargaining position.

Caught between crises in vegetable canning and in the pig market, and unable to go in for milk production—which requires large-scale operations to make it profitable in the face of the fixed price—Plodémet farming is holding on to a formula of general farming and livestock, adaptable to changing market conditions.

In effect, the farmer plans for the coming year on the random example of the market during the previous year, reducing his pea acreage, adding beans, and buying more or fewer piglets. At the last moment, guided by the prices of that moment, he decides whether to sell his grain and potatoes or feed them to his pigs. Only price stabilization could make the farmers give up this method and specialize instead in livestock or vegetables, according to the quality of their soil and the needs of the market.

The endurance of general farming may also be attributed to the inactivity of some and the activism of others. By failing in its main aims, union activity, includng the cooperative movement, has become a factor in helping the medium-size farm to survive. Similarly, the old age of smallholders and the wait-and-see policy of middle-range farmers have given a new lease on life to farms under fifty acres.

Is this a momentary reprieve? Everyone thinks it is. Yet it is by no means impossible to envision a future revival of the small farms on the basis of a return to "natural" and "earthy" food products, already apparent in the big cities. Though a minor one, this trend could become an adjunct to the industrial mass production of food, and create a new type of rural "craftsman" who would benefit from higher prices. Conditions are favorable in Plodémet for this particular economic activity. Farmers could utilize seaweed as a fertilizer, raise pigs on forage, use the moors or salt meadows for sheep grazing, and even revive pea podding by hand for high-quality canning. (The mechanically podded pea is punctured first and therefore deteriorates slightly before cooking.) A return to quality would benefit the small farmer and

enhance general farming. The long-term prospects are unpredictable, and this is precisely the reason why it is not a certainty that
specialization and large-scale production are universal solutions
to the problems of agriculture.

In any case, the present hiatus has enabled the Landernau
cooperative to penetrate Plodémet. Landernau made enormous
progress during 1964–1965. In 1964, it became the largest diversified cooperative in France with an annual turnover of 300 million
francs, 83,500 members, and offices in most of the communes of
Finistère (including Plodémet) and Côtes-du-Nord. During
1964–1965 it underwent radical reorganization. Its four associated
cooperatives were split into fourteen specialized sections, thus
benefitting from laws favoring producers' associations in food
production and forestry. In December 1965, Landernau offered
farmers three options: (1) the farmer gets only his supplies from
the cooperative, without tying himself to it, but incurring an
obligation to subscribe to shares in a sum of not less than fifty
francs; (2) the farmer provides the cooperative with his total
output of one product and obtains all his raw materials for this
product from the cooperative; (3) the farmer supplies the cooperative with several of his products and obtains only 50 percent
of the raw materials for these products from the cooperative.

Landernau is in effect in a position to absorb the whole production of Plodémet, to provide security of sale and a guaranteed
minimum price; however, the farmer has to obtain his supplies
from the cooperative, which moreover reserves the right to impose its own production norms and quality controls, and even to
assess penalties for their infringement.

In the farmers' eyes, Landernau is not a cooperative, something
organized by peasants, but a huge enterprise that takes a brokerage commission higher than that charged by the association and
pays almost bottom prices for peas. In brief, it acts in the manner
of the capitalist industrialist. At the general meeting of the
Plodémet chapter of the union on December 7, 1965, someone
shouted from the floor, "The farmer is asked to trust the cooperative, but the cooperative never trusts the farmer," and no one
contradicted him. Paradoxically, Hanff, the old-style boss, is a
more comfortable figure to the farmers, who know his moods, his
faults, and his good qualities, whereas Landernau is like an unknown monster.

The union leadership is already stirring. Kermélec, who has

been in the forefront of every progressive movement, is in favor
of joining up with Landernau. Le Kam declares, "We'll be integrated in one way or another, so it might as well be by Landernau." Being Plodémet farmers themselves, union leaders who
have been dreaming about local integration controlled by local
producers are not enthusiastic about Landernau; they are moving
very cautiously in that direction, product by product. But being
union activists, they feel they are in their own territory and hope
to establish a dialogue with the Landernau leaders, who are, after
all, activists themselves.

Events will show whether the big cooperative machine is different from the big capitalist machine. They will show to what
extent small farmers will be able to make their voices heard in an
organization where 80 percent of the shares are held and 80 percent of the turnover produced by a third of its membership.

They will show whether Landernau will make a success of its
integrated operations, whether it will encounter competition from
industrial concerns–French, European, or even American.

It remains to be seen whether Landernau will break the small
capitalist-contractor by setting up stations for heavy machinery
and combine harvesters, or whether it will cooperate with him
and perhaps integrate his orientation. It also remains to be seen
whether Landernau will develop production cooperatives like
CUMA and GAEC, which would be parts of the big cooperative.
In any event, the dominant tendency is toward the vassalization
of the individual farms, and it is this vassalization that may
guarantee the survival even of small ones.

Such arrangements will function in the manner of making the
farmer a link in a great chain, standardizing both the quality and
the quantity of his output. The central organization will supply
raw materials of uniform quality, whether seed, fertilizer, piglets,
calves, or fodder, and the farmer will raise the crops and livestock
to maturity according to prearranged specifications and norms.
Advances in technology and efficiency will be passed on by the
cooperative and/or incorporated in the raw materials. When the
product is ready for market, it will be delivered to the cooperative
for a guaranteed minimum price.

It seems likely that the agriculture of Plodémet will develop
along these lines. It is quite possible, of course, that a small number of flexible, individualistic farmers will continue to survive.

The grave crisis of the peasant world in Plodémet reveals two contradictory and ultimately insoluble aspects, namely that the small general farm is in the throes of extinction yet is surviving almost unchanged. In fact, it is the condition of peasantry that is disappearing, which in turn sustains the small farm still longer, which in its turn contributes to the disappearance of that farm in its old form. In the process of interlinked, self-propagating extinction and survival, both farm and farmer are being transformed.

The transformation is taking place partly through the development of individualistic "neo-peasant" enterprises, and on a larger scale through the integration of the farm into an industrially oriented chain operated by a large, diversified central body within an organized, even planned, regional economy. This slow transformation from the outside is accompanied by internal transformation begun mainly by union activists.

Those who work on the land will no longer be the same, or rather, they will no longer be peasants. They will be akin to the craftsman who applies his art to the transformation of a raw material; they will be partly the technician who is being integrated into increasingly scientific work; they will be almost the wage-earner through the discipline of work, the guarantee of minimum income, and the increase in security; to some extent, they will also be their own boss, the legal owners of their land; they will be almost bourgeois in domestic ways of life and certain advantages of urban civilization.

This farmer-craftsman-technician, almost a wage earner, almost bourgeois, will be the new farmer, and in his way he will rejoin his countrymen who have moved into the urban strata. Fundamentally, the disintegration of the peasantry is paving the way for a new integration.

7

The Old and the Young

The Old

We'll have seen it all, from the bicycle to the moon.
(Caradec, age 80, carpenter, town of Plodémet)

I regret growing old, but I got used to it here.
(Mme. Mascoler, age 57, storekeeper, town of Plodémet)

THE OLD RUSTICS

Those over seventy in Plodémet are of an ancient mold. A few last survivors have never emerged from it; they have been unaffected by the changes that have swept through Plodémet during the past sixty years. They can neither read nor write, and live without running water, gas, and electricity, either because the landlord would not install them or because they could not or would not install them for themselves. Louis in Kéravrez is "afraid of fire" and feels safer with candles and oil lamps, while old Catherine does not know that the earth is round and moves around the sun. They are of the remnant of day laborers and tenant farmers.

There are some among the very old who are different, even a rustic Diogenes or two, Alain Autrez of Kéravrez, a former tailor, introduced communism to the village, then turned his back on it when Stalin—"a true Breton"—was betrayed by his own people. He scorns electricity although the lines pass by his thatched roof, or running water although the cistern is only three hundred yards away. "What do I want water and electricity for?" he says.

"They're not of our age." In effect they do live in another age, and lacking even the rudimentary comforts of modern civilization they do not feel deprived of things they regard as disturbing or unnecessary.

Most of the patriarchs never cease to be amazed at how much they have seen. "We'll have seen it all!" exclaims Caradec. They preserve the awe they were seized by when they saw the first machines. Kerdan in Menez-Ru evokes vividly at seventy his surprise and terror on seeing a car for the first time. "The noise! And it had two eyes in front and one in the back!" Alain Autrez is still astounded by the 75-millimeter gun. Eighty-year-old Thérèse in Kéravrez is still dumbfounded that machines "heavier than air" can fly. Even wheat bread, coffee, and red wine remain novelties for octogenarian Kérourédan in Bravez.

Household machinery causes less astonishment, but delight in pushbutton and thermostatic controls is lasting. "This oil heat is wonderful, you go to bed, you feel cold, and it lights automatically," said an old lady who felt direct telecommunication between her body and the furnace. At first, the old people were bewildered by television, and even as it becomes accepted as almost natural, it retains some magic. "In the beginning my father didn't understand, he didn't dare get too close to the set, but he likes it now and even turns it on himself when we're not there," Mme. Kéravrec observed. Even the dead, who are very much present in Brittany, especially for the old, are made to share in the general astonishment: "I'd like to see the people who died fifty years ago come back and see the progress" (Menguy). "If the old people came back to Kéravrez they'd be dumbfounded" (Thérèse).

The memories of the old reach back to the nineteenth century, and their amazement is not only the reaction of simple people but also a constant comparison with the past. In isolated villages more than in other areas, the past is synonymous with barbarity. "A hundred years ago this was a country of savages. People weren't civilized. They were always fighting each other. A lot of them were thieves. And they were always trying to sleep with their neighbors' wives. They weren't educated, and couldn't even read or write; there was no school. Now people are civilized and at least they can read and write. People used to live in misery. They're well off now" (Kerdan).

The essential element of modern civilization, from the point of view of the old, is the elimination of the poverty of the past. This is proclaimed with approval by the two Communist patriarchs, Michel Poullan of Pors-Ensker ("There are no poor people any more") and Menguy of Menez-Ru ("Oh yes, modern life means people are better off. I'm delighted to see the improvement in that area"). The few old day laborers who are still active also feel the difference. "We've been able to fix up the house and scrape together a few francs," said Charles Autrez of Kéravrez.

Optimistic Thérèse sees money in every pocket. "Nobody's really badly off. The old people get their pension money and the young get money when they have children. The children can grow up properly and stay in school until they're eighteen or twenty, and then at the university they get scholarships. If they get married and their wife doesn't work, they get money. And so it goes until they get old and get *their* pension money."

Old people most of all appreciate the activity of the State in the field of welfare. For them retirement is a deliverance, the beginning of an independent life.

Most of them have some additional source of income, either from odd jobs or regular allowances from their children; they get presents, such as a kitchen range, a television set, and other things that make the old house more comfortable. These new-found comforts are all the more enjoyed because the needs of the old have never kept pace with their means. Absence of unsatisfied desires, real economic security, and the unconcern of old age with the preoccupations, anxieties, and conflicts of active life all contribute to create an oasis of contentment. They live for the day, without yearning for the past or anxiety about the future.

Thérèse is a special case but also a symbol in a way. She was once the village haberdasher, and she is still active, being the last skilled presser of the traditional Bigouden coiffe in the commune. She has also taken up knitting again, and the Parisian women researchers of our project were her first customers. Thérèse has discovered the pleasures of personal comfort, and she laughs at the "unfortunates" who "keep their money in old stockings." She watches all the programs on television with fascination, then recounts them to other old people. She weeps when she sees the hungry children in underdeveloped countries or the straw huts of Vietnamese peasants going up in flames. She loves to talk about everything with everyone, and brings out a bottle of red wine for visitors. Fond of the imaginary and the real, active with hands and mind, gay and childlike, octogenarian Thérèse is thriving in the soil of this modern age.

In contrast, there are those afflicted with personal misfortune, like Brezec of Menez-Ru, who lives with the memory of his son killed in the war and of his wife who died of grief; those who are infirm, sick, abandoned, and handicapped, feeling "hardly good enough to guard the house like a dog."

Old age inevitably brings decline to everyone, but for the "happy" old—and they are numerous enough not to be exceptional or even the minority—decline is compensated for by the improved standard of living. While old people generally feel that times are changing for the worse and that the world is going to the dogs, this feeling is neutralized here to an extent by an awareness of fundamental progress. The flimsiness of modern objects when compared to old ones is compensated for by the ease of their purchase; the decline of the small farmer, craftsman, and tradesman—experienced dramatically by those now in their fifties and sixties—is compensated for by the increase in security.

The only nostalgia indulged in by the old and also by the not-so-old who remember them, is for the grand old days of festivities, weddings, and dances. It is no use praising the charms of the old ways—the hoe and the spade, seaweed as fertilizer, the delights of rye bread and sour milk, the poetry of thatched roofs—to the old. One of our Parisian colleagues tried to tell old Poullan that young people with all their machines and radars don't know what a *real* peach tastes like, only to be rebuffed angrily: technical progress was not to be equated with regression, as far as he was concerned.

The respect once accorded to old people is waning. The Old Man is no longer listened to, obeyed, and venerated as a patriarch. He is no longer the source of wisdom and experience to his children or grandchildren. Even the old tailors who played such a legendary role in the old days are no longer listened to and are left out of political activity. Yet they too are content in their retirement.

The old represent the remnant of village life: they *are* the village. Ancient Bigoudennie, dying rustic civilization, lives on in their speech, their customs, their mental attitudes.

In Kéravrez, there are sixteen people over sixty-five—a quarter of the total population—seven living with their children, three married couples, and three widowed or unmarried. The unmarried include the most modern-spirited (Thérèse) and the most old-fashioned (Alain Autrez). Most of the old accept the amenities of modern life but retain the traditional velvet, the women in their bonnets and skirts, the men in their vests. They speak Breton among themselves. They like to meet and talk or simply sit in the sun. Many drop in to see Thérèse, glance at the television, and leave after a few words. A group of four or five meet in the Fombeurs' henhouse, and the only one among them who can read—she attended school for five years—reads to the others from old copies of *Paris-Match* and other magazines. In this way they catch up with events several months and sometimes years after they take place. Still, this sometimes gives rise to lively arguments.

The retired fishermen in Pors-Ensker, approximately twenty of them, are virtually a tribe. They look back on past difficulties greater than those of the farmers, but they have attained a higher standard of living. They can depend more on their children, who have moved to Audierne for the lobster fishing and have climbed up the social scale in every respect. The old men still do some shore fishing in good weather and sell their catch to the tourists at a good price. They regard themselves as strong and virile, and it is said that many continue to have spirited sexual relations with their wives. They are very interested in politics. They meet in the harbor to mend their nets, and drink round after round at the bar of the Rendez-vous des Pêcheurs. They observe the summer tourists with amusement and add to their already rich experiences that of ethnographers of the behavior of vacationers.

There is a definite difference between the old and those in their fifties and sixties. The old are witnesses of both the old world and the new whereas the others have grown up in a world that was in the process of progress and lived in a society that possessed economic balance without yet being affluent. They, not the old, are the real victims of the great crisis of 1950–1965; they, not the old, benefit least from the revolution in domestic consumption. While most of the old people have acquired at least some of the advantages of progress, the middle-aged have been left behind by the technical advances in the world of work; in the town, many long-employed workers have been considered incapable of adapting to changed techniques and new young bosses. (In 1965, an old cook in the state school was replaced after a new stove was installed.)

The distress of old age is felt more acutely by this age group than by the old. Overwhelmed by problems and anxieties, they feel hopeless and abandoned, while the old gain a new lease on life. Yvon Le Braz, a farmer in Kéringard, only fifty-five years old and the last of a long line of farmers, feels not only lonely but deserted: "How many parents have been deserted by their children?" He is afraid of old age but even more of becoming ill: "What worries me is that one day I'll be all by myself here. One shouldn't have to end his days in a hospital because there's no one to look after him." He has lost all ambition and sees his life's work as meaningless: "To have spent your whole life building something up and then to find that there's no one to take it over . . ."

THE RETIRED

All the old people who have lived out their lives in Plodémet are rustic by nature. Even in the town, *embourgeoisement* has affected only their lives, not their personalities.

The people who have come to Plodémet to retire are in a different category. Most of them are natives of the commune who returned after having worked in the cities, the civil service, the colonies, or the army, and brought urban civilization with them. Between these two categories are the schoolteachers who have made their career in the town and a few prosperous bourgeois under sixty.

A great difference between the two main groups lies in the age of retirement. Those from the outside world retire at an age when the local people still have many years of work ahead of them. The official retirement age for farmers is sixty-five; outsiders retire between fifty and sixty—sailors, for example, at fifty-five with even earlier retirement for policemen and soldiers, whose time of service spent in battle duty, as prisoners of war, or in the colonies counts double. One of the Le Talvecs, a noncommissioned officer in the army, retired at forty-two, after having been a prisoner in Germany and in active service in Vietnam and Algeria.

Those who retire young often take up new careers as workers, clerks, and tradesmen, which enables them to realize their aspirations more fully. When they retire from their second career, they putter about in workshop or garden, or build additions to their houses. Retirement by stages allows them to gain leisure without being catapulted into inactivity, and eventually to combine leisure and activity with their hobbies. Of course, it also helps them earn money and reduce expenditures.

They prefer the town to the seashore and countryside, and many of them settle in a district of new houses some three hundred yards from the stores in the center of town. Their houses have a porch, an upper story, and an attic, with steps leading up to the front door, and fussy little decorative details; their suburban fantasies are limited, however, by local regulations that make certain Breton stylistic features obligatory. The gardens combine the meticulous geometry of shaped hedges, symmetrical beds of geraniums, artificial rocks, stone statuettes, and china figures of dogs and/or Walt Disney characters. The gardens are objects of pride, obsession, and delight; they are endlessly tended, adapted to the seasons, altered, and improved. They embody so much care, work, and imagination that when one was displayed to us by its proud owner, we felt vaguely respectful, as if we were viewing the mausoleum of one of those people who lavish all their efforts on the residence of their dead.

The houses are new, none older than ten years. They have central heating, refrigerators, television, and many gadgets. These pioneers of the revolution in domestic consumption are also pioneers, if rather more timid ones, of bourgeois epicurism, having somewhat broadened their gastronomic tastes during their travels abroad. They are often pioneers of tourism as well—except the former colonials and sailors, who have had enough traveling. Mlle. Luc (a retired schoolteacher) goes on organized tours to Spain and Italy. The mayor, also a retired teacher, "did" Italy by trailer in 1965.

The Mascolers are a significant if not a typical couple. The husband returned to Plodémet before he was sixty, after twenty-five years in the colonies. The wife opened a novelty store and every Christmas spends a week or two in Paris, combining calls on suppliers with a vacation. He is always correctly dressed, with a decoration in his buttonhole; he chooses his words carefully (he is not from Plodémet, but from a town in Finistère); he gardens, reads the paper, meets friends here and there, and visits the store.

On Sundays they make gastronomic forays. When we first met him, he was getting ready to fly to the Balearic Islands, seemingly as fascinated by the prospect of flying in a jet as by the islands themselves.

Thus, as a result of careful planning and parsimony over thirty years, together with earnings from postretirement jobs, men and women are at last achieving independence, leisure, and pleasure, and giving life to the clichè of the "second blooming."

The comparison between the late retirement of local people and the early retirement of outsiders casts still another light on the totally unjustifiable inequalities between the urban and rustic ways of life.

With all that, the old rustics have one sentiment in common with the retired people from outside: contentment resulting from the improvement in their standards of living. Growing old may not produce contentment; growing old *in this way* does.

"I regret growing old, but I got used to it here," says Mme. Mascoler.

The Teen-agers

JOHANNE. *What recent events affected you most?*
TEEN-AGE GIRL. *The death of Kennedy and . . . the marriage of Johnny Halliday.*
SECOND GIRL. *That's not an event.*
FIRST GIRL. *Not for you perhaps, but it's an event all the same.*
THIRD GIRL. *And there are all those launchings of rockets, and the man who walked outside the capsule . . .*
(Interview with three seventeen-year-old girls from the town)

Parents seem to have forgotten that they were young themselves once and that things have progressed since then.
(Maryvonne, age 17, Kéravrez)

In the old days, children weren't as smart as they are now, and it's better this way, but they're too fresh now, and one has to scold them. It's not good to be too shy, but it's no better to be too fresh.
(Mme. Michel, mason's wife, age 40, Menez-Ru)

Each October 1, three Poullan buses filled with teen-agers leave Plodémet for the *lycées* of Quimper. Others go off to technical schools in other parts of Finistère. The rest pile into the three schools of the town (two state CEG's for boys and girls, and one Catholic CEG for girls). The CEG's take in many more girls than boys; boys go in increasing numbers to *lycées* and their place is taken by students from the more backward inland communes. Of the 250 to 300 boys and girls between fourteen and nineteen,[1] 85 to 90 percent are receiving a secondary education, and only 10 percent work, mostly as apprentices or wage earners outside the commune. A few, about twelve to fifteen in all, work on the family farm.

Throughout the day, no young people are to be seen in the villages and the town. In the late afternoon, a few pupils from the CEG's, then a few apprentices, meet in small groups or go to the Café des Droits de l'Homme. The proprietress of the cafe, Marie, is a handsome woman of fifty-five who wears the Bigouden coiffe. The café was decorated recently with neon lighting, fishnets, and sea shells. The teen-agers play the jukebox and the pinball-type machine games.

On Saturdays, the eve of holidays, All Saints' Day, school vacations at Christmas and Easter, and above all, at the beginning of summer, the mass of students returns. Plodémet comes alive and then sinks again into a deathly quiet, according to the rhythm set up by the young people who alternate their summer lives between work in Quimper and entertainment at home. These regular journeys in and out of the commune are rehearsals for their grand departure, the mass migration to the cities.

Our problem was to get hold of these young people if we were going to learn about them. During the Easter vacation in 1965, they frequented the Café des Droits de l'Homme at all hours of the day. Romain Denis and Peninou went in and were soon captivated by the miniature football and the jukebox. Johanne and I wandered in casually. While Johanne was discussing with three girls—whom we came to call our "three flowers of the moors"—the relative merits of two pop singers, and while Peninou was being beaten at miniature football, one of the most fascinating chapters of our project had begun.

[1] The official census excludes boarders outside the commune and includes those at the CEG from outside the commune. The project research team corrected the figures of the 1962 census and estimated 175 girls and 114 boys between fourteen and nineteen for that year.

THE YOUTH CLUB

We invited the regulars of the Droits de l'Homme to a get-together, and on April 20 about twenty boys and girls gathered around a table with beers and cokes, as inhibited as Romain Denis to whom, out of cowardice, I had handed the task of opening the discussion. Romain, disdaining any "directive" intervention, declared in a little speech delivered in a monotone that in a society where everybody talked about youth it was up to the young to make their views known. Silence—and embarrassment. Johanne then tried to get them to talk about pop songs, about their personal aspirations. Georges Lapassade, whom fate had brought to Plodémet that day between two conferences and two bouts of hepatitis, then suggested the applications of the secret weapon of group psychology, the Philips 66 tape recorder. The meeting was then divided into two groups that would decide for themselves what subjects were to be discussed.

Both groups expressed a unanimous desire for a youth center. We asked them to describe such a center, and they envisioned a dance hall with a record player, a game room with a ping-pong table and mechanical games, television, and a reading corner. The girls also added organized songfests and excursions.

As a result of this meeting, an organizing group was formed with the objective of founding a Plodémet youth club. It was to join with young wage earners who were invited to a second get-together that evening. The second meeting was attended by twenty to twenty-five boys (girls are not allowed to go out evenings during the week) and turned itself into a constituent assembly. The next evening a general assembly was held, bringing together most of the boys in the town. Everyone wanted a youth center that would be independent of adult society. But what sort of independence? A young Catholic teacher who was attending the meeting, having been alerted no doubt by traditionalist adults, said that it was necessary to have an adult in charge. The assembly seemed paralyzed: would it approve or not? Lapassade, in a vigorous "nondirective" speech, succeeded in delaying any decision. "I am intervening," he explained, "only to point out to you that the selection of a president is a serious matter. A group may become identified with the views of its president and cut itself off from the allegiance and support of people with different views." For my part, I wanted to show the young people that they could finance their center themselves by organizing a film show or a dance with a live band, and I offered to obtain films and the services of a pop singer.

Next day, a delegation from the new club came to see me to work out a program for the film shows and the dance. A few hours later, the buses took the students back to Quimper, as Easter vacation was over, but the club had a plan of action. The election of a president was left pending.

On May 1, fifty-four teen-agers elected a steering committee of five boys and five girls, who immediately set to work. The president and treasurer did not enter the scene until early July; they were twenty-one-year-old students who seem to have been discreetly and indirectly backed by the religious authorities. The approach of summer vacation increased the activities of the committee; it drew up the charter of the club, asked the town hall for help, canvassed for membership, and scheduled the film shows for June 24 and the dance for July 24.

The state and religious schools were invited to the afternoon performance of the film, and the evening performance was reserved for adults. The state school sent a few classes, while a nun took her flock on a field trip to the woods in Le Calvaire. The evening show was a complete failure as far as the adults were concerned. The profit from both shows—owing to the disinterestedness of the owner of the cinema—came to thirteen francs. The difficulties were beginning.

Nevertheless, by July the club was beginning to grow. Caradec offered the use of the hall in his hotel. The club, now constituted legally as an association under the name of "Jeunesse et Loisir"—Youth and Leisure—decorated it with pop-record jackets, installed ping-pong tables and other games, and on July 16 the first "party," with a small band that was vacationing in the area, launched a series of weekly dances that was to continue throughout the summer.

The dance on July 24—led by Charly Bennet's band, brought in at considerable expense from Lorient, but without the pop singer, whose fee was too high—drew a paid attendance of 350. At the beginning of August, the club had 180 members, including 30 vacationers from outside the commune. The average age was seventeen to eighteen, with no one over twenty. The town youth joined in full force (with the exception of the schoolteachers' sons), providing a contingent of 116, as against 67 from the country. The influence of the club extended over the countryside surrounding the town, stopping at Pors-Ensker, where young people favor Audierne for entertainment. It did not penetrate the red fortress of Menez-Ru, or the Catholic countryside in the east, or distant hamlets.

The club committee was fairly representative of the teen-age population: 80 percent of its members attended *lycées* or the CEG, their social background was varied, though 30 percent were farmers' children.

While the club itself expanded rapidly, its leadership was in grave difficulties. From the beginning, Alain the president and Marcel the treasurer had created a certain disequilibrium. They were older than the membership and wanted to bring some order to the club's bustling activities. The first conflict arose in early July. Marcel and Jacqueline, who were both of prosperous bourgeois families, suggested that the volleyball equipment be stored near the ball field in the house of Dr. Aujourd'hui's sons, two "aristos" disliked by the committee members. It seemed also that Marcel and Jacqueline had discussed a revision of the club's charter with young Francis Aujourd'hui. Jean-François, a garage apprentice, led the fight against the proposal in particular and the Aujourd'huis in general, and he was supported at first by a majority of the committee. But he soon found himself alone when an agreement was reached to regard and treat everyone, including the Aujourd'huis, as equals. Jean-François thereupon attacked the president and demanded that the committee be subject to removal at any time by the general assembly of the club. He was defeated at a general meeting held on July 31 by a majority that regarded him as a troublemaker; he was supported only by the worker members and subsequently resigned.

The club continued as a recreation center but ceased to be the focal point of a Plodémet youth movement. The weekly dances went on throughout August, and a group excursion was organized to Plomeur-Bodou, but the club was being operated under the "presidential dictatorship" of Alain and Marcel, who administered its activities but derailed its democratic processes.

On September 6, after a raucous dance, Caradec threw the club out of his hall; it became a wandering body with no home of its own. A television set sent by the Ministry for Youth did not

reach its addressee, was refused by the town hall, and went back
to Paris. The parish magazine issued a warning to young people
that life was not an endless party. The mayor sermonized to a
delegation from the club, but promised to provide a home by
spring if young people listened to the advice of their educators.
The club's last meetings were very poorly attended, and when
the students went off in their buses on October 1, it virtually came
to an end. On All Saints' Day, the committee made a vague decision to organize an evening of entertainment at the end of the
year with a program of folklore, theatrical sketches, etc., that
would reconcile them with the adult world. No one displayed a
real desire to actually do anything about such an event, however,
and the project petered out.

We discovered later that ours was not the first attempt of its
kind in the region. In the summer of 1965 there had been apparently a profusion of youth clubs and centers throughout the
west of France, including Finistère and especially in Audierne.

Unwittingly, our project unleashed the antagonism of the
Church and the town hall that had previously prevented the
formation of any unified movement among the young. The failure
of two earlier attempts—one under the aegis of the Church, the
other associated with the state school—was due not only to their
factional character but also to the dislike of young people for
adult supervision. As for myself, I was neither a moralizer nor a
pedagogue nor an organizer; I liked these young people and I had
no wish to influence them to take any particular direction. I was
accompanied by young research workers who were as close to
them as they were to me, and I was sufficiently unlike their idea
of an adult to win their confidence. Moreover, I had the advantage
of university connections, which gave an air of respectability to
the youth club from the point of view of the adults. All these
factors enabled it to develop internal contradictions, and led to
its eventual confrontation with the adult world.

The success of the club was as remarkable as its failure. For
the first time in Plodémet history, teen-agers joined together in an
attempt to define themselves as a community in relation both to
themselves and to adult society.

Failure was not the result of the beginning of the school year,
which could have meant simply a normal period of hibernation,
nor of the lack of help from the adults who refused the only thing

asked of them—material help—and whose original neutrality turned increasingly grudging and critical. It was due more to internal crises and tensions. The young people resembled each other sufficiently to want to assemble, but their semblance was not strong enough to keep them together. There was common identity, but not community.

TEEN-AGE SOCIETY

At the outset, we had the impression that the club was a gathering together of individuals. In fact, it came about because a number of teen-age bands had decided to get together, and the club committee members were representatives of these groups. For teen-age society of Plodémet is made up of bands—a band being a group somewhere between a cluster of friends and a clan.

The depopulation of the villages and the scholastic dispersal brought to an end the old bands which used to admit all teenagers of the same approximate age and the same sex within a given territory. They were perpetually at war with other bands in the neighboring districts. Yet despite their turbulence, the bands were in effect homogeneous aggregations of peers within the boundaries of traditional society. Today the segregation of the sexes disappears at sixteen or seventeen—except in Menez-Ru, where boys and girls still meet in secret—and there are many mixed bands of two or three boys and two or three girls. Comradeship precedes boy-girl attachments, which generally appear at eighteen or nineteen. The youth-club committee exemplified the new relationship between the sexes by composing itself of five boys and five girls.

The neighborhood of the home is no longer the automatically cohesive factor in the formation of a band of solidarity, except in Menez-Ru and Pors-Ensker. Nowadays it is the schools— especially in the *lycées*, where strong solidarity is formed among boys boarding together away from home—that determine the new attractions that counterbalance the gravitational force of the home village or district. Even in the commune, the increased mobility brought by the motorbike, and in some cases the car, makes possible daily meetings of band members and of groups of friends who are geographically distant.

Thus there is a fairly wide field wherein personal relationships can develop, disregarding the neighborhood of origin, the division between peasants and bourgeois, and professional differences between parents. Relationships based on neighborhood, school, and random affinities cut across the loose ties of the bands, clearing the way for them to cooperate in the youth club.

The new dynamics of segregation emanate from the school, which breaks down the social differentiation of parents but creates others, notably one between *lycée* and CEG. Also from the same source, two new spheres of segregation have formed on the periphery of teen-age society: those who come from the prosperous bourgeois families—the "aristos"—and those who are not able or willing to pursue a secondary education—the "proles".

The "proles" form a number of small bands in the town; the "aristos" are a fairly loose group recruited exclusively from the local upper stratum and selected vacationers, centered around the sons of Dr. Aujourd'hui.

The proles and the aristos are subjected to teen-age segregation to a much greater extent than the rest of Plodémet youth, while at the same time they represent the opposite poles of its society and culture.

The proles wear black imitation-leather jackets and pointed shoes, but after they reach seventeen they begin to go to dances dressed up in suit and tie. The aristos alternate between the latest fashions and the casual wear of the hippie–Saint-Tropez type. Francis Aujourd'hui turned up at a dance in Pont-l'Abbé barefoot, wearing jeans and a faded pullover, and with a three days' growth of beard. Many of the girls, innocent in the ways of supreme chic, refused to dance with him, and the young man exclaimed, "Oh, these young ladies! They must have their suits and ties!" In this way, a sort of turnabout has taken place, with the proles trying to adopt bourgeois tastes in dress and the upper middle class seeking to express refinement in an extreme casualness. The proles rev up their motorbikes as if they were motorcycles, but seldom venture outside the town. The aristos travel around the entire region. The proles gather in the Café des Droits de l'Homme or the Café des Voyageurs. The aristos, who are in Plodémet only during vacations, frequent the Saint-Tropez-type places in Audierne. The aristos have more money, more leisure, and more liberty. United by a sense of caste which their parents have not developed, they are intent on differentiating themselves from the bulk of Plodémet youth. In contrast, the proles feel they are an integral part of it, despite their different social origin, and yet at the same time have an almost proletarian class feeling against "aristocratic" intrusion. This alliance split up after that incident, and the original conflict was replaced by one between the more educated (students) and the less educated (wage earners). In the end, the centrist position of the middle group, which rejected domination by both extremes, had to accept the "presidential dictatorship." Unaware of the social conflict that had been played out, yet coherent in its social reaction, the teen-age middle group acted exactly as a middle class, to which it belonged in effect, by virtue of its secondary education.

These incidents reveal that the structure of teen-age society by no means reflects that of adult society; it does not follow demarcations established by the adults, except in the case of the aristos, but obeys new ones created by the system of education. Thus, the sons of farmers are integrated at once into the bourgeois stratum from which their parents are excluded. Similarly, a young man assumes a working-class identity if he becomes an apprentice after failing his school examinations.

Only at the summit of the social hierarchy of Plodémet does education cease to be a determining factor. The aristos base their superiority on social privilege precisely because they do not have an educational one. But even there, it is not simply a reflection of adult society, for the young of that stratum, unlike their parents, accentuate and even create the cleavage between the prosperous bourgeois and the rest of society.

Teen-age society partially contradicts adult society because it is already ascending toward the next stage of *embourgeoisement* while at the same time signaling the emergence of new differentiations within bourgeois society.

Because teen-age society is already more of the future than of the present, the youth club could easily surmount or even ignore the political conflicts of adult society. Neither the nomination of two young men from white families to the key posts of president and treasurer, nor the wariness of the sons of the state schoolteachers, nor the clash between Alain, a Catholic student, and Jean-François, son of a red activist, tipped the balance too far in the direction of the whites. The original committee members were equally divided as to white and red background, and they were elected without reference to such criteria because the structure of the bands that elected them excludes the use of such criteria— a factor that also made possible the subsequent election of Alain and Marcel.

The committee meetings were always held on Sunday morning, at the hour of the high mass, in the presence of a left-wing state schoolteacher, Jean-Claude, who recorded the discussions for our research project without ever incurring the slightest objection. It mattered little to committee members that their president was a white and that there was a red witness in their midst, because these categories did not imply adult interference. It never occurred to them that politics or religion could have anything to do with their affairs, and it was in full consciousness of wishing to express its nonpolitical character that the committee invited the state and religious schools to the same film show—to the extreme astonishment of the adults.

As long as the club flourished, the adult red and white interests were neutralized by the independence of the teen-age movement. When the political antagonisms were reactivated during the period of the club's disintegration, they acquired no influence over the process. The club went under because of social antagonisms alone. It was a specific class struggle that eventually destroyed the communal impetus of the teen-age society.

DIVERSIONS

The first overt signs of a new teen-age identity appeared between 1955 and 1960. The girls of the town—aided, it is said, by an extraordinarily rough winter—dared to wear slacks. This breakthrough spread from village to village and eventually reached even Menez-Ru. Girls over thirteen, including those living in the countryside, wear the usual teen-age uniform—slacks, flat shoes, sweater. Except for the proles and aristos—as we have seen—most of the boys alternate between Italian-style casual wear of slacks and light-colored pullovers and the American T-shirt. Boys and girls have abandoned the well-worn, oft-mended country clothes for work along with the stiff, solemn Sunday dress for an everyday modishness.

At the same time, teen-agers have been acquiring the two chief means of gaining relative independence from the adult world and of withdrawing into their own. First, for most, the motorbike, and for some (and not exclusively for the aristos) the small used car, presented by parents to reward success or console for failure in the *baccalauréat*. Second, audio equipment: the personal transistor radio; the portable record player, more portable than musical but spreading rapidly; the tape recorder, which has so far appeared only among the prosperous. The guitar made its appearance in a different context, completing a cycle that began with undifferentiated sound consumption (radio), continued with selective sound consumption (records), and led to personal sound interpretation, even to a neotroubadourism.

The teen-agers of Plodémet have now attained the same subculture as urban youth. They follow the same fashions, and although these arrive later than in Saint-Germain-des-Prés, the mainstream sweeps through here as it does through the whole country and the whole Western world. During the summer of 1965, in the field of the pop song, for example, the teen-agers of Plodémet, like the majority of French youth, preferred French versions of British and American songs. The teen-agers of Plodémet are acquiring the same independence of the adult world as urban youth, mainly in and through leisure activities.

This "*yéyé*" subculture unites in an appropriately vague manner a style of life, a sort of embryonic or already atrophied ideology, a complex of tastes and attitudes, a particular musical beat, all revolving around the axis of diversion. The rhythm-dance, song-tune symbiosis fills the hours of solitude and links the young together in a network constituting a culture of diversion. The movies are also a form of diversion, but they do not exert anything like the influence of pop music; television is too closely linked to the home, although it is appreciated in youth centers; football (soccer) attracts groups of supporters from the commune to the matches of "La Plome"; beach volleyball, ping-pong, and card games have their fans.

In this small town, with its lack of recreational facilities, its movie shows two or three times a week, its Café des Droits de l'Homme, the youth club expressed a need for permanent, varied, and autonomous diversion, particularly for those who were not free to escape the confines of the town and commune. Nor was it disdained by others, to which it offered additional facilities of recreation.

The thirst of the young for diversion has expanded to such an unprecedented degree in the last ten years that it is incomprehensible to the Plodémet adults. The summer vacation is less and less the season when the young help in the fields, and more and more a time of ceaseless diversion-seeking.

With their new music the teen-agers have transformed the old rustic dances, which are now much more numerous. Though overequipped with three large dance halls Plodémet lacked occasions for dances, for which there is an almost permanent demand during the summer. Neither the increase in wedding dances during the summer—open to all—nor the youth club's weekly dance satisfied the demand. Yet the region as a whole—and it is now accessible to most people—provided at least one dance each night during the summer. The teen-agers in Plodémet would pile into a friend's car or share a taxi and go dancing in Plonéour or elsewhere in the area, even as far afield as the clubs in Audierne, Loctudy, or Douarnenez. The clubs along the coast are frequented more by those between twenty and twenty-five, but the dances in the town are exclusively teen-age affairs. They attract youths from surrounding communes, and sometimes as many as five hundred tickets are sold. The bands come from Quimper, Lorient, or Brest, and they are not a bit like the poor rural groups of the past. Radio and records have made teen-agers' ears very demanding, and the bands come equipped with amplifiers, electric guitars, and organ.

In dancing, as in everything else, Plodémet youth is following fashion, if not the avant-garde. In 1965, the Twist was obviously widely known and the Surf had its elite, but the Jerk, still restricted to the inner circles of Paris and Saint-Tropez, was unknown. The girls wore slacks or dresses and little make-up; the boys either the latest in suits, light striped shirts, and narrow ties, casual clothes. The younger country boys all wore old suits and the proles under seventeen imitation-leather jackets. The boys without girls, most of them from the country, gather at the dancehall bar; they drink until they are slightly drunk and confident enough to go after girls. There are bolder spirits among the eighteen- and nineteen-year-olds, and they are usually the most urbanized. Girls sit on the benches doing needlework; some girls dance with each other. Some couples kiss while they dance. One sees hands in unexpected places. Gradually, with the noise, the movement, and the drinks, the dance warms up, but it has to end at 2 A.M., when the euphoria is dissipated and all that remains is a few broken glasses and litter.

The dance is not only an occasion for collective drunkenness but also a marriage fair, since the rules of kinship and family interest have ceased to regulate marriages. The dance is a traditional mold into which new ingredients have been poured, a melting pot wherein rustic-plebeian culture blends with urban culture; it is a key institution in teen-age society—a stage in personal development, an ecstatic moment of collective communion.

The components of the dance are to be found again in the diversions of the summer. Those more prosperous, better educated, and older (eighteen to nineteen) follow the example of those over twenty (who all work outside the commune) and throw themselves into a sort of minor *dolce vita,* an endless round of pleasures consisting mainly of dancing, drinking, and girls. This is a recent development and as yet not widespread, but already the magnetic pole of aspirations for the eighteen- and nineteen-year-olds of the less privileged groups. This *dolce vita* is no longer confined to attending one dance a night, but takes the form of traveling from one to another, then going still farther afield to dances that continue far into the night and end up at dawn in a club in Douarnenez or Audierne.

As the teen-ager gets older and has more money, the club tends to replace the dance hall. The clubs on the coast are decorated either as Parisian *caves,* or as fishermen's bistros. Dress is quite casual, even hippie style. Dancing is to records. As in the dance halls, there is a preponderance of slow, amorous dances.

The private party is a recent innovation, not welcomed by parents. It is often clandestine and relatively exclusive, attended by teen-agers of the upper caste, summer visitors, and young people over twenty. It is held in a discreet location—a house with the parents absent, a converted barn. "Original" decorations are put up and "amusing" things served (*fondue,* barbecues, buffet, cocktails, whisky and *sangría,* most recently introduced by the aristo pace-setter). The music is predominantly jazz (Sidney Bechet, Miles Davis, Ray Charles) and the latest pop. Dancing takes place by candlelight or in darkness and is frankly erotic. Sometimes a couple disappears and returns some time later. The party, which may go on into the early hours of the morning, is an invitation to love-making, whereas the public dance is an invitation to flirting.

This ever-expanding *dolce vita* is extending the area of diversions well beyond the commune, and will soon exclude the town of Plodémet altogether. In 1965, there were two focal points, a communal and a regional one. The former was centered on the Café des Droits de l'Homme and the Gored and Menhir beaches. The aristos ignore these centers almost entirely while the others, at eighteen, begin moving gradually between the communal and the regional. The regional center for daytime activities is Audierne, with its bars, clubs, possibilities for meeting a wider range of people, and Parisian vacationers; the nocturnal centers of attraction are Douarnenez, Loctudy, Le Guilvinec, and Quimper.

The car, necessary for frequent trips even within the small area of the commune, becomes indispensable for excursions to new, shifting, and far-flung centers of diversion, lying within a thirty-five-mile radius. The Plodémet advance guard are far behind those of Douarnenez, however, who think nothing of traveling up to sixty-five miles for a dance or party.

The car is not only a machine for constricting space. It brings with it an intoxication with speed, competition, risk, and virility. The young proles rev up their motorbikes and ride them at their maximum speed of thirty-five miles an hour. Car owners take their driving seriously, as a sport. Pierre-Jean of Bravez, nineteen, races around in his secondhand Renault CV4, which is painted red with a checkered border. He relates his dramatic exploits over meals, to the anxious sighs of his mother.

The elite of the *dolce vita* set out on their nocturnal expeditions in groups of two or three cars. The drivers race each other on the road leading to the coast. They don't like being passed and they don't mind frightening the girls. The car has revealed or aroused a miniature James Dean complex in Plodémet. It has also revealed or aroused a great restlessness. In allowing for wide choice of diversions it has provoked uncertainty in choosing. The young go from dance to dance, wandering restlessly, perhaps in search of an unreachable archetypal dance, and in the end they find themselves traveling for the sake of traveling, aimless, seeking excuses for moving on, hoping to find what, whom? At a party, a group goes off, calls at a wedding dance, comes back, and goes off again. It would appear that this restlessness conceals a certain desperation, as if the tireless pursuit of diversion were a flight from a state of original boredom lurking inside the diversions themselves.

There is an original state of boredom. In the town, throughout the year, despite the Café des Droits de l'Homme and the transistor radios, the teen-agers are bored. The boredom is dissipated in the endless round of activity in August. From September on, it returns. On a return visit in mid-September, we were greeted everywhere with variations of the same dirge: "We're bored."

In Menez-Ru the teen-agers have no cars and remain isolated even during vacations. Boredom, individual and collective, is permanent. "When young people get together in Menez-Ru it is to get bored together," notes Paillard. They are bored at home, they are bored when they are together. The old pleasures and games are boring, and the new pleasures and games of love have not yet arrived in Menez-Ru. There is a no man's land between the abandonment of childhood play and the sustained inhibition of sexuality. The transistor radio and the record player may alleviate boredom but they do not dispel it. Menez-Ru reveals the immense void that can exist in the lives of teen-agers when the old culture has disappeared and the new has not yet arrived.

Emptiness and boredom are thus apparent, among those saturated with diversions (the elite) as well as among those deprived of them (the young in Menez-Ru). Is it the period of adolescent hiatus when adult values have not yet replaced the outgrown values of childhood? Is it the hidden nihilism of a civilization where values are reduced to individual pleasure? Is it both?

It seems to us that two contradictory but not easily separable sides are discernible in the adolescent cult of diversion. In certain respects it is an antidote to boredom, in others a search for pleasure, expressing futile flight but also an aspiration to joy, which was stifled in the past by material needs, taboos, constraints, and rules.

Is it possible to decipher the full meaning of the message contained in the teen-agers' desire for a recreation center?

THE DOUBTFUL CONFLICT

The teen-agers' desire for an *autonomous* recreation center, and the reservations of the adults with regard to this double aspect of the enterprise, reveal the key problem in the relations between them as that of the autonomous tendency of a teen-age "class."

The data that we have gathered indicate superficial disagree-
ments alternating with radical conflict, because a given problem
changes according to the point of view. There is mutual ignorance
between teen-agers and adults, a conflict of authority, a conflict
of values, and also a community of values.

First of all, there is a lack of interest on the part of parents in
the interests of teen-agers, and vice versa. Not two generations
but two worlds are living together with barely a common language. Parents complain of absence that is both physical and
moral: "Claude is never in the house. Even when he comes back
to Plodémet, he's always out with his friends." In fact, the teen-
ager leads his real life outside the home and regards it as a secret
domain even if it is not clandestine.

Most of the youth-club activists left their parents in ignorance
of their activities. They preferred us to write to them *poste
restante,* or at school, rather than at home. The parents, for their
part, were as disinterested in the youth club as in any of their
children's other activities.

The teen-agers of today have some independence of time,
movement, and consumption. Holidays and vacations are free of
work for those from the town, but in the country it is difficult to
avoid being requisitioned for summer work on the farm. Boys are
allowed out after dinner, but girls only on Saturday night, as a
rule. Even in Menez-Ru where liberalization spreads more slowly,
parents cannot always prevent their children from going out at
night and have to content themselves with retributive action after
the event. "Perhaps I'll find the door locked like the last time.
They locked it so that I had to wake them, and they could see
what time it was . . . Tomorrow they'll wake me at seven o'clock
and I'll have to get up. They'll say, 'If you can go out at night
you can't be tired, so you can work harder,' " reported an eighteen-
year-old girl.

Generally, boys and girls get a fixed weekly allowance that they
spend on entertainment, records, and dress. Those who work keep
part of their wages; those who help in the fields often get a small
allowance. They could all earn extra money by working part of
their summer vacation, but they refuse to work to earn their
leisure.

Neither semiliberalism nor liberty at home satisfies the teen-agers, who want free time, unrestricted mobility, and more money. They resent all restrictions. The parents refuse to give in on the question of their authority, but the teen-agers want recognition of their freedom as well as freedom to exercise it. It is an autonomist movement that does not know where to set the limits of its demands yet regards itself as limited even in making its demands.

The mayor, the parish priest, the principal of the state school, and the headmistress of the religious school expressed in virtually identical terms the view that young people should be guided and supervised. Both the mayor and the parish priest saw the failure of the club as a just punishment for its claim to independence.

The teen-agers believe, both individually and collectively, that their needs are unsatisfied because they are not understood. The adults, on the other hand, feel that teen-agers enjoy privileges that are not only unprecedented but exorbitant.

It is at this point that the conflict of authority becomes a conflict between work values and diversion values.

The parents began to work with their hands between the ages of nine and fourteen, and with the exception of the teachers, still do not have vacations. To them, young people "don't want to do anything—all they think about is amusing themselves."

The youth club wanted to extend its dance of July 24 to 4 A.M., in order to attract young people in the area who leave other dances at 2 A.M. The mayor refused permission, and his decision was approved by every parent we spoke with. When I was explaining to Menguy that the club needed the money to buy equipment, he exclaimed, "They want money! Then they should go out and gather seaweed, peas, and scrap iron!"

The adults do not condemn all diversions, only those not earned by work. Moreover, they deplore not only the loss of the sense of work but also the nonsense of the diversions of today's teen-agers.

When I asked the new principal of the state school to interview me, he in turn immediately posed the question that concerned him most: "I should like to know what you think about young people today!"

"In what sense?"

"Take those youngsters who go to bed at midnight and get up at ten in the morning!"

To him, as to nearly everyone else in Plodémet—whether town

or countryside—a life not conducted in accordance with the sun is unnatural. It is preposterous to amuse oneself at night. The nocturnal excursions in cars and the expense involved ("astounding sums of money") are a source of scandal.

Let it be said, though, that condemnation of hedonism is not unanimous. The old people either condemn the parents—their own children—for not being able to bring up their families properly, or salute the good luck of today's youths and approve of their easy-going ways.

"Good for them! They're quite right! They were born at a good time!" (Gaelic).

Mme. Luc, seventy-five years old, wanted to give the young people the use of the Maison Kérizit.

"For dancing?"

"Of course! Let them dance!"

A few parents have actually been won over to pop music. "The teen-agers, I admire them! I don't criticize the girls who go dancing. I like pop music, too. I found it hard to understand the songs at first, but I've got used to them now" (Mme. Kéravrec).

The unionists are not all hostile. Michel Loïc criticizes the young only for their indifference to politics. Pierrot Le Kam, a union leader and member of the municipal council as well, thinks that young people have a right to amuse themselves: "After all, they do work." La Talvec takes a sociological view: "The young are the same as us, but conditions have changed."

Contrariwise, teen-age diversions are regarded as libertinism by many puritanical activists and teachers who have devoted their lives to public service. To them, it is a matter of civic spirit versus selfishness—reason and unreason. The principal of the CEG sees in the tragic death of young Le Kam, killed while driving a car at night after breaking out of his army barracks in the summer of 1965, the symbol of the present generation. The town clerk exclaims, "It's no longer a gap between the generations but a gulf!"

The mayor perceives that the gulf separates not only two stages in time but two *Zeitgeists*, two philosophies of life: "The young are impatient . . . people nowadays want a fast life and I think it's a bad thing . . . It seems to me that the young want to live, and live intensely. They may succeed materially, but not intellectually."

What seems abnormal to adults appears quite normal to teen-agers, who regard themselves as fully modern. At our first meeting with them one of our first questions was, "What does 'modern' mean?"

The answer came at once: "A certain freedom."

Someone else added: "For parents, too much freedom."

The parents are not encumbered by past experiences, but they are incapable of assimilating present experience. What is bad to them is so natural to the teen-agers that the parents, regarded as a homogeneous mass ("they're all the same"), seem not only old-fashioned or backward to their children but incapable of understanding life. In this sense, the children feel that their tastes, their interests, and above all their very being are called in question.

Considering the conflict of authority in the light of the experience of the youth club, it is evident that the questioning spirit of the teen-agers is not unlimited. On several occasions, the assembly was ready to accept the tutelage of an adult and even seemed to want adult protection. But as they acquired the knack of administrative function they became more and more uncertain about the possible role of an adult.

In any case, our encouragement and guidance were determining factors in launching the club and remained sources of reassurance to the teen-agers on the committee throughout its existence. We were rather more avuncular than paternalistic, and refrained from directing discussions. We personified the model of the "acceptable" adult: one who does not criticize, does not judge, understands enjoyment, and knows how to enjoy himself. It would appear that cooperation was possible between these particular teen-agers and these particular adults, even on the terrain where they most felt the need for autonomy.

The charter drawn up by the committee declared that "the aim of the association is to establish an educational center and to organize leisure activities (physical education, sports, theater, cinema, music, lectures, excursions) . . ." Their adherence to traditional, standard phrases that emphasize educational aspects, although they were interested only in diversions, is proof of the duplicity underlying their relations with adult society, which indicates moderation rather than aggressiveness and rebellion.

In any case, Plodémet has no antisocial "gangs" engaged in hostile acts against adult society or aggressive on the level of delinquency. We found repeatedly that no one has even dreamed of rebellion. In a discussion following a showing of the famous Marlon Brando film *The Wild Ones,* as well as in later conversations, we were able to find only a germ of solidarity with the heroes of the film in the teen-age spectators. One of our young workers held out a bait: "Which side are you on, the side of the bourgeois or the side of the young gang?" The replies were mild, uncertain. Topalov made the following note in his diary: "They are basically on the side of the teen-agers, but they do not approve of their idleness, the absurdity of their diversions, or their taste for violence. They disapprove of the honest bourgeois for taking the law into their own hands, and think they should have left it to the police to deal with Marlon Brando and his gang." They failed to grasp the basic conflict, although in a sense it was the same one they were involved in. They missed it because it was carried to such extremes in the film. Alain Le Calvec put his finger on the matter afterward: "We didn't understand everything. For example, why they were against the adults and why the adults organized against them . . ."

It is evident that the teen-agers' pursuit of freedom is not a general libertarian demand in Plodémet, even less an open rebellion. They respect society, so long as it does not create obstacles to their aspirations; they do not want adults to intrude in their activities, but they accept adult authority.

The real conflict seems to be a feeble one, and the discrepancy of values has been overemphasized owing to the special circumstances of the confrontation. Adults and teen-agers are physically closest to each other just when the psychological distance between them is the greatest—in the summer. The adult world is working harder and longer (harvests for the farmers and tourism for the tradespeople) while the teen-age world devotes itself to diversions. Conversely, in the winter when the adults are working only part-time, the teen-agers are working hard in their *lycées* and schools, out of the parents' view.

The percentage of Plodémet youth receiving secondary and university education is higher than the national average. This fact would imply a seriousness of purpose in sharp contrast to the pleasure-seeking of the summer, were it not in effect but complementing it—a phenomenon that enables us to grasp the dual nature of teen-age society.

Serious study is not to be taken at face value, as a *Ding an sich,* but as preparation for a career and as aspiration to the bourgeois life. There is fundamental agreement between parents and teenagers on this point and on related matters, including the abandonment of the family business and the establishment of a new life away from Plodémet. Moreover, parents readily accept the psychological evolution that has made the young much more self-confident than they are themselves, much less in the grip of rustic timidity and gaucherie—another aspect of *embourgeoisement*. The young envisage protected careers in the civil service or teaching, with boys increasingly gravitating toward technical specialties. Desire to roam and travel is kept well within the conventional notions of vacation activities. Indeed, the theme of home, wife, and children emerged spontaneously time and again in replies to the question: "How do you see yourself at the age of thirty?"

The bourgeois life to which the teenagers aspire is also the ideal of the adults of Plodémet. In both town and country, there is a new demand for holidays, a new desire for amusement. As they grow older, the teen-agers will integrate their cult of pleasure into that of a career and a home.

Is it then merely a misunderstanding that is separating the two generations?

The answer must be no, because not comprehending is always more than misunderstanding; values held in common do not preclude either antagonistic differentiations or authority conflicts, and in the final analysis, the aspirations of the young for independence, even if they remain latent, constitute the keystone of contention.

There is an ambiguous conflict that should be viewed not only in the context of the fundamental ambiguity existing between the future adult and the former teen-ager, but also as part of the uneven process by which Plodémet is attaining the norms of urban life. The adults are still half submerged in rustic-plebeian traditions and values, whereas the teen-agers are already integrated into the modern world. The processes whereby the young are integrated into modern society and segregated from adult society have the same source, which itself increases the distance between them and their parents and attenuates their conflict. Teen-agers at present identify their local cause as that of modern society at large, challenging not adult society as such but only when they consider its manifestations of local backwardness.

We must not locate the problem in the decade 1955–1965 alone. It is possible that at a later stage teen-agers will evolve more radical qualities and move toward greater alienation. At present, we detect the seeds of a libertarian and communal spirit, a certain spontaneity and nonconformism, a verve for pleasure, and an unfocused ferment. All these latent energies might become virulent and impel the teen-agers either toward delinquency or hippie life-styles, or hedonism, or revolutionary activity, according to the dialectics of world-wide processes that have increasing influence over local ones.

The Old and the Young

> *"We'd like to modernize, but the old people are always in the way."*
> (Pouldrenzic, age 28, roofer, town of Plodémet)

> *"They talk about things we've never heard of, they want to pass us by."*
> (A sixty-year-old in a Bravez *buvette*)

> *"You young people can't understand what we old ones are saying; even if you're intelligent and educated you can't understand."*
> (Le Grevez, age 67, farmer, Menez-Ru)

There is no practical conflict between parents and teen-agers who are going to leave both home and the family occupation. On the other hand, a cruel conflict exists between young men and fathers who live and work together.

A great break occurred during the 1950's between those who matured during the interwar period of stability-stagnation and those who had grown up since World War II. It was during the great transformation that a "new wave," aged between twenty-five and thirty-five, who were eager to modernize the farm or business came into conflict with their fathers, who were in their fifties. The fathers suddenly saw their own sons questioning the knowledge and experience they had acquired over thirty years.

The son has to accept paternal reign and wait until he is thirty or thirty-five before taking over. The conflict sharpens for ten long years. Living with one's parents, once considered customary, becomes a heavy constraint and an additional fuel to conflict. The old couple and the young find agreement only in front of the television set. The young are impatient to throw off the tutelage of the old and change everything. We have heard a young peasant couple discussing the idea of a retirement home for old farmers with an evident desire to send their own parents to such a place.

The decisive battle of the two generations, dispersed in a multitude of single combats over a period of ten to fifteen years, is coming to an end, bringing discomfiture for those in their fifties and sixties. As soon as the younger men assume control, they reorganize, buy new equipment, fire the old farmhands, and generally uproot the traditions and methods of their fathers. In about five years, they start thinking about rebuilding the house or demolishing it to build another.

The conflict of the generations has become general only in agriculture, since the new wave of 1955 took control of the farmers' union. But this new wave has not yet produced militants who aspire to running municipal affairs. Although in 1965 the holidays committee came under the control of craftsmen and tradesmen between twenty-five and thirty, it was only at the repeated request and because of the eventual resignation of Menguy, a man whose age placed him between the two generations. The municipal council remains a bastion of the old, but red sons show no sign of wanting to take over from their fathers.

Between these two generations, that is, between the modernists and the conservatives, is the generation now in their forties. Their leaders, who came of age under the Occupation, especially members of the Resistance and repatriated prisoners, wanted but were unable in their time to transform existing structures. They could not readapt themselves fully to the old world they found on their return, and either resigned themselves to it or were broken by it. They are less estranged from their parents than are those of the next generation and will be in turn less estranged from their own sons than the old of today.

There is thus a gradation of generations[2] and a diversity of

[2] The new relations and conflicts between the generations accelerate the decline of the omnipotence of the father. He is no longer a patriarch-guide but an old man and therefore unadapted to the modern world. (This includes forty-year-old fathers to their fifteen-to-eighteen-year-old sons.) Yet the father is not openly challenged. The principle of paternal authority is not questioned, provided it does not interfere in the emancipation of diversions (for teen-agers) or of the family business (for those between twenty-five and thirty-five). Both the most oppressed and the most emancipated sons would disapprove of the idea of a world devoid of the presence and authority of the father.

problems, with tragic prospects for those between fifty and sixty who have been rendered obsolete either by the great transformation or by their own sons. The generations at the extreme poles, the really old and the emancipated teen-agers, are the ones most satisfied with the *Zeitgeist*. Both already have one foot in another world, and they can indulge in their separate dreams and thoughts.

8

Women, the Secret Agents of Modernity

They don't like dirty fingernails, they want to wear nail polish.

(Yves Michel, 55, farmer, Menez-Ru)

In Plodémet, the women place flowers on the graves throughout the year. They are guardians of the age-old cult of the dead; they preserve the greatest and most solemn tradition of Celtic prehistory and are the natural protectors of primeval values in a world of change.

In the process of change, women always seem to be one step behind men. The old women speak only Breton and have never been outside the commune, whereas the old men know French and have been elsewhere while in the army. Most women over fifty wear the Bigouden coiffe, but only the old men in remote rural districts still wear the round hat. The women have remained more religious than the men, and even the freethinkers in Pors-Ensker keep a religious picture over the fireplace. The women do not frequent *buvettes* and other public forums, and therefore take little part in the discussion of public affairs. In short, at first glance, women appear to be still immersed in an archaic world.

The abandonment of the Bigouden coiffe by women under fifty is indicative of a hesitant evolution. However, if the coiffe does provide a sign of a break with the past, it is not a conclusive one, any more than its presence is synonymous with archaism.

The coiffe is not a sentinel against all innovation. It is perfectly compatible with motorbikes and television, and is seen in cars leaning on the shoulder of the son at the steering wheel. It hovers above the miniature football machine, the jukebox, and the brand new espresso machine in the Café des Droits de l'Homme. It is not a boundary line between two separate, irreconcilable worlds. The abandonment of the hat is the spectacular sign of a small change in a chain of changes, whereby the evolution of women, like the evolution of Plodémet society, manifests tropism in the direction of urban-bourgeois civilization. Rather than attempting to label the innumerable fragments of a jigsaw puzzle, I shall try to determine the factors in an uneven transformation according to social groups and generations.

The Manumission of the Peasant Woman

When one enters the home of an old peasant couple, one finds an ancillary wife. She stands while her husband sits, serves the wine without drinking herself, speaks only when her husband asks her a question, and never contradicts him.

One may well wonder whether such subordination serves to conceal the actual power behind the throne. True enough, the peasant woman is in effect a servant who cleans the house, does the cooking, looks after the animals, and helps in the fields. But she is also the matron in charge of the money, the children, and the house. The ambivalence of her status will sometimes tilt it in the direction of servitude and sometimes—for example, when the husband has sunk into alcoholism—toward responsibility.

The women who have long endured such responsibility and servitude are now over sixty. Their fine old faces are engraved with wrinkles and create an impression of wisdom, rather than of faded beauty. They are from an age that regarded the beauty of old faces as the true beauty and young faces as unfinished, in contrast to modern bourgeois civilization that recognizes beauty only in the young.

All around them, peasant women see the domestic revolution advancing; even in the countryside, the houses of the craftsmen, tradesmen, and seamen are being turned into autonomous domestic kingdoms. In 1965, women under fifty were being caught up in a ground swell that was sweeping away their subordinate role, and transforming servant-matrons into housewives.

The old *penty* consisted of a single room, with its hearth, table, benches, dresser, cupboard, bed, and religious pictures; by 1950, the separation between sleeping and living areas had become fairly general, but not yet that between cooking and eating spaces.

The peasant woman is far from wanting to transform her home into a salon, but she is gradually opening the door to products of the domestic revolution. Overworked as she is, her first aim is to alleviate household chores. She replaces the fireplace with a stove, then with a gas range, thus destroying the ancient polarization around the hearth. The washing machine is much higher on her scale of priorities than the icebox. Gradually, her demands become more sophisticated, and she moves on to electrical appliances. The first, and the cheapest, is the electric mixer, which has become the vanguard and symbol of a new pushbutton world in the home. Such modern infiltrations are no longer motivated by utility only; they also create new desires for new comforts, all of which crystallize in a newly found pride in the home.

The house itself is in sharp contrast to its sordid, dirty surroundings. A new developed horror of dirt is directed at the cow dung in the stable, the urine in the farmyard, the dirt and smells brought into the house from outside. This aesthetic refinement is an expression of a domestic ideal, which culminates in the repugnance felt by most peasant girls toward the peasant condition generally.

For the peasant woman between thirty and fifty, this factor will become the motivating force for wanting to modernize the stable, asphalt the farmyard, and above all, get running water installed in the house for washing up, for the laundry, and for hygiene. Supported by the young generation, the women are also demanding toilets and showers.

Cleanliness leads to an interest in decoration. First come curtains, tablecloths, pictures, potted plants, and knick-knacks—other than the shell from the Franco-Prussian War or the statue of Saint Bernadette. Then comes television. The home ceases to be a place of labor and becomes a place for relaxation, the promised kingdom to the woman who succeeds in freeing herself from the servitude of farm work.

So far, the kingdom has been restricted to the living room. The bedroom is still a dormitory. The dining room, among the middle-range farmers who have one, is a sanctuary where money, jewelry, family photographs, and of late, antique furniture and objects are kept, as well as a ceremonial room for receiving visitors.

Women have had to battle for each new attainment, and they are now in constant battle for recognition of their new status as housewives. When the husband is engaged in modernizing his work, he neglects the home because investment in the household is bound to have a retarding effect on him. At first, he regards the time devoted by his wife to the home as wasted, and household equipment as luxury apart from the installation of gas and a cooking range. The Le Menez brothers, three bachelors who are among the most technically advanced farmers in Menez-Ru, still use the fireplace for heating and have no modern amenities in their shack other than a transistor radio and a washing machine they no longer use.

The younger he is, the less the husband resists the wife's demands and the attractions of the home. Nevertheless, antagonism between the two processes of modernization—those inside and those outside the home—remains acute.

Pierre Gaelic, age forty-three, with eighteen acres in Menez-Ru, and his wife, age forty:

SHE. When one has got one thing, one always wants something else . . . Now it's a television set.

HE. Bah!

(She laughs.)

HE. I'd rather see two horses in my stable.

SHE. And then a car.

HE. A car's secondary . . . too many accidents.

SHE. In the winter, when we finish work early, it would be nice to sit in a warm room and watch television.

M. and Mme. Kerfuric, aged twenty-five and twenty-one, from Menez-Ru:

HE. At the moment, we've got to improve the farm equipment. The house comes afterwards.

She says nothing. Later, he says that he would like to modernize the house to please his wife. She is inhibited by the interviewer and still says nothing. He adds: "It's not my job to look after the house; it's my wife's."

Young, modern-minded farmers recognize the legitimacy of their wives' demands for domestic modernization, but try to reconcile it with the development of the farm and envisage a redistribution of chores; although they completely accept their wives' vocation as housewives, they cannot feel completely pleased about it.

Young couple, both twenty-six, with forty-two acres in Kervoeret:

SHE. The wife should be able to stay at home. There isn't enough time to do the housework...

HE. She should spend most of her time at home, but she should take an interest in the way the farm is being run.

Le Neur, twenty-six years old, with twenty acres in Kérongard-Divisquin, intends to install running water and a washing machine: "I'd like my wife to stay at home, if possible."

KERFURIC (quoted above). "The husband in the fields and the wife at home, but unfortunately [the wife sighs] she has to help in the fields too."

Le Neur's "if possible," Kerfuric's "unfortunately," and the Kervoeret farmer's "should . . . but" indicate the limits imposed on the wife's acknowledged status. There can be only compromise or break.

THE DOMESTIC REVOLUTION: THE RED AND THE BLACK

The dissatisfaction of the women is playing a major role not only in the development of rural life but also in the progress of the farm itself. In order to acquire the means for modernizing his home, the farmer must modernize his business. The young, modern farmer is seeking a solution that will enable his wife to acquire all the amenities of domestic life and exchange her vestiges of servitude for an administrative role in the business (accounts, secretarial work, supervision). But progressive farms have a long way to go before they can achieve both modernizations, hence the abandonment of the farm by most marriageable girls and, consequently, by the young men.

It is not only the farm that cannot satisfy feminine needs, but also the men whose transformation is slower, less far-reaching, and less deep-seated than that of the women. The man who modernizes his equipment is primarily responding to an economic challenge; the woman who modernizes her home is adopting a new ethos, that of a better life. The woman is transformed into a bourgeoise in her house while the farmer remains a peasant on his farm.

By modernizing herself domestically the woman is modernizing herself psychologically. With her home, she conquers and tames the interior no man's land; it is the beginning of a process toward autonomy, an expansion of her personality. The interior change will rapidly surpass the domestic change. The slacks worn by women under forty testify that they no longer accept an inferior status and their polished fingernails signify that they want to accentuate their femininity.

The domestic revolution was the beginning of an interior revolution; the aspiration to live in a decent house has led to the aspiration to live in the world. By turning its back on the land, the house has opened itself to the world. Girls now set their sights not only on the life of a bourgeoise but also on independence and a job in the town. This is why women between twenty-five and thirty who have stayed on the farm are stifled by their domestic life and by life in general.

Everything condemns peasant life: the work, the lack of comforts, the dirt, the isolation, the lack of diversions, living with one's parents, or worse, with one's in-laws. The conflict between the new feminine personality and the peasant condition is insurmountable.

"Why are so many people leaving?" we asked an old peasant. Before he had time to answer, his sixteen-year-old granddaughter interjected, "To be free."

There is no longer a middle course when the alternatives are servitude or freedom. The former exodus by necessity of country girls has become an exodus by aspiration, including even girls from larger farms. The girls are unanimous in their desire to leave; some boys do remain, and more would if they did not see themselves condemned to celibacy. Some girls seize upon merchant seamen, who are regarded as ideal husbands; others, and they are more and more numerous, get a job in town first as nurses, schoolteachers, or post office clerks, and many do not hesitate to work in a factory in order to leave the land.

The last four Catholic farmers' daughters to leave the Jeanne d'Arc school to marry farmers did so in 1957–1958. Since then only a few girls have been compelled to stay home for other reasons, as for example the only daughter of a widower. In 1965, the headmistress of Jeanne d'Arc told us, "I don't think you'll find a single girl who has stayed at home on the farm."

The Modern Woman

The personality of the townswoman is changing along a broad front of generations that includes all women under fifty, some older, and all strata of the emergent bourgeoisie.

The townswoman, whether or not she has a job, is already a housewife. Since 1950, she has been the leading spirit of the domestic revolution, supported, not thwarted, by her husband. Young wives and the newly retired "suburbanized" wives are the vanguard of the movement which has accelerated since 1960. They complain impatiently when progress is held up: "Ah! If only I had a bathroom!" One necessity leads to another, and they all lead to a villa with every modern comfort.

The movement transforming the home is also transforming marriage itself, which remains the center of women's lives and aspirations. The old system of marriage, an arranged alliance between two families, was already disappearing in the country by 1950. An evolutionary process that had begun early in the twentieth century gradually opened up new possibilities of matrimonial self-determination to young people, and the social and economic transformations of the 1950's lifted the last prohibitions, the last of the family imperatives. Girls benefit more from the new freedom of choice. Whereas the boys want a good, pleasant, level-headed wife, the girls pose a wide range of qualifying conditions that include amorous considerations, good prospects, recognition of their authority in the home, and a suitable house. The demand for love is profound but domesticated. Of course, now as ever, couples are brought together by love at first sight, but even when passionate, love is not blind, which explains why parents are not unduly worried by their children's freedom. Mme. Goémon talked to us calmly about her daughters' freedom (one of them married a worker in Nantes). "Perhaps they'll go to work in Brest, Rennes, or Paris, and get married there. I wouldn't want one of them to marry a North African, but if they were really happy we'd be happy too."

The desire of young married couples to live away from their parents existed long before 1950, but it could be realized only by moving to one of the larger towns outside the commune. After 1950, with the women leading the domestic revolution, they succeeded in getting the house enlarged, making it possible to relegate the old people to their own quarters with a separate kitchen; meanwhile, they are pressing for a new house to be built that would definitely separate the generations.

The new mother, who now always has her baby in a hospital, follows the urban practice of devoting a great deal of attention to the hygiene and diet of her children. When they go to school, she takes an interest in their lessons and homework, takes pride in their successes, envies those of the neighbor's children, and sometimes even complains to the teachers. The mothers urge both boys and girls to go on to secondary school and do not take kindly to any objections. Disdaining political repercussions, the wife of Le Kam, a union official elected as a red municipal councilor in 1965, transferred her daughters from the state school to the religious school because one of them had to repeat a year.

The mother is the inspiration of scholastic advance in the family; here, too, women are leading Plodémet society toward progress.

FEMININE-MASCULINE

The use of make-up is spreading in various ways. Heavy make-up (lipstick, rouge, and eye shadow) is used mainly by the fashion-conscious women who have moved here from the cities. The old women say that make-up hastens the appearance of wrinkles, makes the face ugly, and wastes money, while the men believe that it is the mark of hidden eroticism. Make-up is used by bourgeois women over forty as a ceremonial mask for Sundays and feast days, younger women timidly apply a little lipstick, and teen-age girls use a little eye shadow—but only when they go dancing. Far more widespread and in daily use are the invisible cosmetics such as face cream, deodorants, and eau de cologne.

Women no longer restrict their visits to the hairdresser to the annual permanent at Easter but have a set once or even twice a week. The new habit has spread to the countryside, and in Menez-Ru where the men still cut each other's hair for a franc or a glass of red wine, the women now go to the hairdresser.

The two hairdressing salons in the town are expanding rapidly; according to one of the hairdressers, her clientele has increased by 50 percent each year since 1959. Both were modernized in

1966 and use the latest equipment. One of the salons even engaged the services of a beauty specialist in 1965, but the attempt was premature as only three women came in for advice. It is quite possible, however, that the specialist may have been visited by more women from Plodémet in the more discreet surroundings of Quimper. It is even said that one teen-age girl had her nose straightened!

The townswomen have varied wardrobes; some have dresses copied by a local dressmaker from fashion magazines. Young girls buy their sweaters, skirts, and slacks from stores in the larger towns. Fashion is triumphant even among country girls. Solange from Pors-en-Breval, who works in the fields, milks the cows, and consequently gets filthy at home, always arrives in the town impeccably dressed and never wears the same sweater or blouse two days running. "Here [Menez-Ru] you're supposed to wear everything out before you buy something new, but my sisters and I throw things away when they're out of fashion and buy something else" (Mimi, age 22).

The revolution in fashion and beauty care is following the urban norms. It is not confined to special occasions and holidays but is part of everyday life; women want to please not only others but themselves.

While developing their femininity, women do not hesitate to venture into masculine territory when they think it is to their advantage. Slacks, first worn by teen-age girls and later adopted by young married women, are the symbol of modernity, which casts off ancient proprieties for the sake of comfort. But slacks also express feminine rebelliousness; in appropriating the most masculine item of dress, women are attempting to abolish men's privileges by sharing them.

Young Mme. Le Bellec, twenty-one years old, from Lastronguy, works on the farm in slacks and a nylon blouse.

SHE. It's practical and warm.

HE. It's ugly.

HIS MOTHER. It's all right for everyday, but not for Sunday.

Smoking and drinking will soon be accepted publicly as feminine rights. For a long time and only at home, Bigouden women have been drinking "Catalunya," a sweet wine. More recently, smoking has been introduced, also in private, by women from the cities and young wives, but women are still not supposed to smoke or drink in public. Teen-age girls were the first to break the prohibition on their outings together. Cigarettes and drinks are now accepted accompaniments at teen-age get-togethers; in fact, smoking is a social activity before it becomes a private habit. Slacks, drinking, and cigarettes are stages toward the raising of the iron curtain that has long separated male and female society throughout the day, with the men reigning in the public forum —the *buvette*—and the women meeting for coffee in their homes. Women have now begun to broaden their world in the limitless areas outside the home.

THE DESIRE TO TRAVEL

The domestic revolution has increased women's mobility through the expansion of the range of acquisitions and by linking the home to the urban world—country to town, town to city. Both young women and old took to the motorbike as soon as it appeared. The car embodies the newly felt need for the outside world, a need as strong as that for the home. Women in their forties urge their husbands to buy a car, and younger women obtain their driver's license—the secret passport to freedom. Many women use the family car far more often than do their husbands, and almost all the wealthier women have cars of their own.

Women's slacks were symbolic of a desire for independence in the world; the car, another appropriation of male privilege, grants a spatial independence. It opens up the streets, the shop windows, the cinemas, and the amenities of the city; it bestows a measure of urban citizenship. Moreover, it stimulates a need for mobility as an end in itself—for a change of air, a change of surroundings. It offers a foretaste of travel, the desire for which recurred in our conversations with women of all ages, almost like an obsession. At a meeting of the agricultural information group, one speaker suggested a study tour to England. The general response (from men of twenty-five to thirty-five) was, "Oh, that kind of thing is for women!" We learned that a number of women had joined a previous study tour to Holland as a means of satisfying their desire for travel. The first organized tours to Spain and Italy were initiated by young unmarried and retired women.

The desire to see the world is also a yearning to see another more beautiful, more interesting, more romantic world which is also a theatrical world of landscapes and monuments, a cinematic world of moving images. The desire to travel in the real world takes flight on the wings of the imagination.

It is in the context of such dual perspectives, sometimes disjointed, sometimes intermingled, that women pursue expanding horizons. Bourgeois women are being led to read books and novels; they feel their minds a mixture of the real and the imaginary. The sales figures of the Café des Sports indicate that women's magazines are bought in overwhelmingly greater numbers than any other periodicals sold in Plodémet. These magazines satisfy both practical (fashion) and imaginary (romantic fiction) yearnings; they are a link with Paris and provide instructive models not only for fashionable dress but for conduct and daily problems. Models,and dreams are the stuff that great myths of the modern woman are made of.

THE DESIRE TO LIVE

The first wave of modernity had not yet completed its course when a second wave of young girls and bourgeois married women began to see the means for professional independence to add to their domestic sovereignty.

In the case of the married woman, a job fulfills a need which is not purely monetary. For teen-age girls and young unmarried women, a job has first priority, for it satisfies an immediate need for independence from one's parents.

A job is not only a course of self-determination but also one of contact with the world. The school has emancipated girls on a massive scale, turning them into teachers, nurses, secretaries. They have decided to put off marriage until they are twenty-four in order to lead a personal life that excludes having to prepare meals and tend babies.

The family unit no longer confines the new woman; it is now but the center of gravity of a system undergoing expansion and transformation. Will the job soon become a competing center of gravity? In any case, expansion is progressing simultaneously on all fronts in the search for freedom and happiness in ways both complementary and contradictory. And there are women who feel happy, in the euphoria of the upward movement, at having acquired over ten years electricity, a stove, running water, a washing machine, a car, television, a well-furnished home, freedom, and *embourgeoisement.*

Are these women a minority or a majority between those who are still prisoners of the old world and those whose aspirations are already too various and expansive to be contained within the little township of Plodémet? The girls both of Plodémet and the surrounding countryside are being catapulted into the big towns and cities by the schools they attend outside the township. And those who have not left, who could not leave, who followed their husbands to Plodémet, are already suffocating.

The countrywoman cannot find full satisfaction at home, and some townswomen already feel that the home is suffocating their lives. In both cases, feminine aspirations are well beyond current realities.

Lack of satisfaction in the home is incurable when it is not compensated for by love. And where is love to be found in Plodémet? The old married by parental decision most of the time. Nevertheless, many years of shared joys and troubles succeed in creating an emotional symbiosis between two people that is deeper than passion and can become love. Marie, of the Café des Droits de l'Homme, was transformed and utterly broken by the death of her husband, and found solace only in her granddaughter: "If it wasn't for my granddaughter, I'd have no interest in life." Of those under fifty—except for people who were forced to accept mates chosen by their families and those who felt predestined for the one they married—many marriages were contracted simply in order to escape from parents. They often chose, and still do, a profession rather than a man, a kind of disposition rather than desire. For some, marriage has brought communion, tenderness, friendship-love; for others it has created partial compatibility and partial incompatibility. A man of forty said to us in the presence of his wife, who was looking at him in silence: "Marriage is a lot of broken dishes and a lot of mended dishes." For still others, marriage is merely the juxtaposition of two solitudes.

Marriage is a life sentence, for there is no divorce in Plodémet. Even the return of the prisoners of war, when couples who had been separated for five years were reunited in dramatic circumstances, was not followed by separations. The five divorces registered between 1955 and 1965 involved a case of nonconsummation, a couple from outside the commune, and three marriages to merchant seamen. Divorce is sometimes contemplated by a few wives of alcoholics but always put off.

Adultery is limited by prudence and insoluble difficulties. Public opinion prohibits an open affair, and a secret one would be impossible to accomplish in the commune. Adultery could only be a precarious and foredoomed adventure, not a compensatory relationship. The stories one hears whispered concern rustic lewdness rather than lovers and mistresses.

There is a certain amount of "bovarysm" in Plodémet, which is a result not of the husband's absence but of his presence. In these cases, the woman's profound need for romantic love finds no expression, and marriage, home, and town form a triple but singular prison. Bovarysm plagues mostly women of the upper caste, but it can be found also among women in other strata. It ferments in women who are in their thirties and yearn without hope to lead their own lives, and desolates women who are between forty-five and fifty whose children have crossed the threshold of adolescence and are suddenly strangers to them, and who feel the approach of old age. It subsides gradually when old age really comes.

Bovarysm is not the only cause of loneliness among Plodémet women. There is the loneliness of the seaman's wife whose husband spends half his life away from home, and the inconsolable loneliness of young widows who do not remarry.

Besides these women whose loneliness is fundamental, one finds a different kind of loneliness in the prosperous bourgeois wife living here in "exile" who disdains the coffee meetings of the Plodémet women and whose friends and diversions are elsewhere, and the cultured, artistic woman who has no one to talk to about books and films.

Many Plodémet women say they are happy, and with the freedom and comforts they have acquired some are. This is not incompatible with deep and widespread dissatisfactions that emerged, sometimes unconsciously, in the interviews carried out by our women researchers, also confirmed by Dr. Lévi's findings. The results of the study conducted by Dr. Bourlière showed that "anxiety seems to be extremely strong among the women"; that women's dreams are more frequently unpleasant than men's; that 20 percent of the women take sleeping pills as opposed to 9 percent of the men. Thirty-five percent of these women are tradesmen's wives, 18 percent farmers' wives, and 7 percent seamen's wives. Among the men, there are twice as many farmers (10 percent) as tradesmen (5 percent) taking sleeping pills, and only 2 percent are seamen. If the sleeping pill is an index of anxiety[1] and anxiety an index of dissatisfaction, then more women than men are evidently subject to dissatisfaction, and frustration is more widespread among bourgeois than among peasant women, who still spend half their time helping their husbands on the farm.

The anxiety level of the farm population should perhaps be taken as higher than indicated by the figures, since the use of medicines in general is resorted to less often in the country than in the town. In any case, what emerges from these figures conforms with the findings of our inquiry: the two dissatisfied segments of the population are the peasants and the women.

Dissatisfaction is transformed into hope for the liberation of the children. The enormous emotional investment of the mothers in the schooling of their children is overdetermined by the transference to the child of their own unsatisfied aspirations. Dissatisfaction transforms reading and excursions into escape; reading becomes more an entry into a dream world than enrichment of experience; the car becomes a means of flight; the trip to Quimper is the oxygen mask for moments of asphyxiation. Generally, there is an ambiguity about escape as against an outing. A young woman of thirty is about to take her driving test: "I will go out, I love going out. I'm shut up here all week; on Sunday when my husband goes to the soccer game I'll go to the movies."

For these women, a job becomes an antidote without bringing salvation. The loneliest and most bourgeois are the most active ones, and they form the spearhead of modernization in Plodémet.

They evoke the heroines of the Italian novelist Cesare Pavese, who devote themselves to their professional lives in order to fill the void in their personal lives. In the first rank of these women are three widows, all faithful to the memory of their husbands. One became a widow in 1944 when the last German soldiers

---

[1] Another index: during our stay in Plodémet, only two categories of people entered the hospital for alcoholism: a few farmers and two married women from the town.

evacuating Plodémet fired on the premature Liberation procession. Subsequently, she turned her wholesale business into one of the three or four largest ones in Plodémet. She has now left business affairs to her son, lives alone in a large modern house, and goes off on organized vacation tours. She dresses elegantly and dyes her hair slightly. The second of these women came back from Nantes seven years ago after the death of her husband; she works with her father and has modernized his transportation business. She drives a Citroën DS station wagon, which is also used as a taxi. She likes to go to Paris. She is beautiful and elegant, and is regarded by the teen-age girls as "the most modern woman" in Plodémet. Her daughter goes to the university. The third widow, whose husband died more recently in a car accident, considered leaving Plodémet but decided to stay. She has transformed her café into a neorustic *crêperie*, which she is gradually modernizing; it was the first public building to have central heating installed in 1965.

Professional activity is the energetic transformation of an objectless love. Here, as elsewhere, work is an enormous expenditure of love. At its best, success in business becomes a substitute for success in love.

Dissatisfaction, which is one of the signs of the extraordinary increase in women's needs, exists in every sphere of expansion in Plodémet society. Dissatisfaction is as much a motivating force as aspiration, and it is part of the great dialectic of the transformation of women and of the evolution of Plodémet.

EMANCIPATION

However rapid and widespread the flowering of the feminine personality may be, it has not progressed in all directions. The psyche has become demanding, but Eros has remained discreet. The rustic-provincial environment, the old sense of shame, the fear of jealousy, and natural timidity limit the use of make-up, repress the instinct for personal adornment, and prevent all ostentation.

There would even appear to be a decline in the former wild sexuality of the countryside, if the decrease in the number of rapes does not mean an increase in consent. Tales of unmarried mothers and hot-blooded girls are not heard more frequently

today than in the past. The sexuality of the Plodémet girls seems
to be under strict control. One attractive, flirtatious young woman
had had no sexual relations before her marriage at the age of
twenty-four. Only the small *dolce vita* set, who are only loosely
tied to the commune, make their first sexual explorations during
vacations.

A veil of modesty covers everything concerning sex, including
birth control, a term still unknown in Plodémet in 1965. (A young
woman in the town thought it meant postnatal care.) Women
have an intense dislike of discussing these matters: "One doesn't
talk about such things, not even young wives among themselves"
(Jeannette, twenty-four, schoolteacher outside Plodémet). Some
who were questioned by a woman doctor who was on vacation
in 1965 eventually unburdened themselves: Couples still practice
the ancient method of *coitus interruptus* to control births. There
are exceptions, such as the man who has five children and does
not know how to avoid having more, but none of the women
mentioned family planning.

Sex could certainly not break up marriages. Divorce is utterly
condemned in this secular commune where everyone is married
in the church; the first civil marriage was performed for a couple
of schoolteachers three years ago.

Girls who defer their marriage do not question marriage itself;
the few instances where preference was expressed for the single
state may have been owing as much to a father-fixation or disappointment in love as to desire for total independence. They do
not envisage a rearrangement of roles between husband and wife.
Eliane from Menez-Ru, a philosophy student, reads Camus and
Sartre yet believes that "it is not a constraint but an obligation
to do housework; it's part of a woman's job, I think . . . Everybody accepts that . . . It's the man's job to make some decisions,
not absolutely of course . . ."

The old family has crumbled, but the old fortifications are still
intact around the new family nucleus. Will this in turn be
threatened by modern instability and anxiety? It probably will,
but in most cases it will act as a refuge against this very instability
and anxiety.

The woman who breaks with traditional womanhood does not
do so entirely. For example, whereas the emancipation of Plodémet society has separated man from religion, the emancipation

of woman has hardly affected her relations with the Church. Similarly, the expansion of the feminine personality is entirely apolitical. Women still do not participate in political and trade union activities. The women's information group was male inspired, and failed. Analysis of a particularly heavy voting turn-out on December 5, 1965, revealed that only two women had voted, one of them a teacher.

It is not only the dead weight of Plodémet society that still excludes women from civic activities and often includes them in religious activities. It is also that their aspirations are directed elsewhere.

It seems obvious that the personality of women is developing in essentially private and individual areas. Feminine aspiration conflicts totally with the old structures of Plodémet society, but not particularly with the Church. It expresses itself, not through political demands, but through a general opposition of the "modern" against the old.

There is no women's emancipation in Plodémet in the sense of aspiration for total and permanent professional and sexual independence and active intervention in civic and political matters. The desire for a job before, during, and perhaps even in competition with marriage may be the bait contrived to open up that avenue of development.

ONE STEP BACK, ONE STEP FORWARD

Most women in Plodémet are more deeply rooted in the old than are the men, but they are also more vigorously in favor of the new. A change in the personality of women has been effected even as they remain guardians of the Celtic household gods and of the Catholic home. This mutation was dormant during the 1950's but began to operate in the last fifteen years. The process is incomplete, but clear enough in outline: it begins with the matron-servant, passes through the housewife stage, and culminates in the woman with her own job. At the same time, the woman conquers new areas of femininity, abolishes male privilege, and even assumes a position of strength in the choice of a husband.

Feminine progress is a conquest. What women have acquired had never been offered freely; it had to be fought for. In the course of this conquest, ancient male rights have disintegrated little by little, even though, or because, they were linked to the traditions of a rustic-plebeian culture grounded in the Baillist era.

The conquest is inseparable from the modernist conquest that was begun by men in the technical field, and taken up and extended into other areas by the women. For example, the wife of Michel, a mason of Menez-Ru (age 40 to 50), decided to decorate and furnish the house; she wants a car, while her husband is quite satisfied with his motorbike; she wants to travel, while he is quite content to remain in the village. Although she resisted getting a television set, this was because her husband wanted to share it with all his neighbors, thus destroying the intimacy—and cleanliness—of their home. In their external and internal expansion, women are taking the whole of Plodémet society with them. They are confronting young men in general, and young farmers in particular, with the alternative of modernizing or leaving. By leading the revolution in domestic consumption they have revolutionized themselves; they are more dissatisfied than the men and therefore more modern.

The teen-age revolution in Plodémet is noisy, the women's revolution silent. (The public opinion polls would not even notice it.) But it is active in a different way, because it is ingrained in the local society. Through their aspirations, conquests, frustrations, activities, and dreams, the women are the secret agents of modernity.

9

The Red and the White

The Siamese Twins

With the Republic came civilization.
(Kerdan, age 70, Menez-Ru)

The flags of mutually hostile camps fly over Plodémet: the lily-white banner of the kings of France and the standard on which the red of the social revolution has been absorbing the blue of the Republic since the nineteenth century.

In Plodémet, political identity is defined by the colors red and white, before any other allegiance—left, right, Communist, Socialist, Radical, MRP, or Gaullist. The red and the white refer to a society divided into two parties and into two parts, and to an absolute conception of politics.

The white-red division originated in the antagonism between the landowners and the agricultural working class. The landowners held the economic and political power, enjoyed the support and endorsement of the Church, and formed a closed society. The small peasants waged a struggle for economic liberation, political emancipation, and social advance against the landowners. This peasant struggle was taken up and carried on in a hundred years of civil strife born of the Revolution in which the monarchy and the Republic were the figureheads of two past centuries contending over the nineteenth, of two worlds contending over France, of two Frances contending over the little commune at land's end.

On one side was a Catholic hierarchical, traditionalist France, her roots in medieval Christendom, propagating the idealized image of a community whose social, political, and moral life is infused with religious spirit, crowned by the monarchy of Divine Right. On the other side was a democratic egalitarian France that derived her humanistic and evolutionist principles from the great bourgeois revolution, crowned by the Republic of universal suffrage. The violence and intransigence of the duel were such that at the time of the separation of Church and State, White Plodémet and Red Plodémet made an attempt at separation and formed two societies within one—a "Siamese twin" society. The division opposed to each other two sources of authority, the town hall and the Church, with two militant organizations, two groups of families and villages, two networks for marriage, mutual help, suppliers, customers, tradesmen, craftsmen, and *buvettes;* there were even two doctors, two garages, and two hotels.

The separation was never total, however. White society, even at the extreme point of estrangement, could not place itself above the law of the Republic, while red society, even after it had expelled religion from political life, remained obedient to its sacraments. The separation could not be other than tenuous; it could only exist under the combined circumstances of a religious cold war and an undeveloped economy, and a social life that was still subject to the omnipotence of family and village clans.

Liberalization began when the war with Germany replaced local strife; it continued with the decline of the family-clan and with the development of the economy. Yet even today, vestiges of this fundamental division remain; even today, red and white represent two opposed political attitudes; even today, the break is most apparent over the question of secularization.

THE WITHDRAWAL

From 1914 to 1965 there was a withdrawal of the extreme red and white positions over secular and religious principles.

The quasi-proletarian meaning of the word "red" became first plebeian, then populist. It was still associated with the "little man," but in a general rather than a local sense; after all, by this time the little man was starting out on the road to becoming bourgeois. The decline of the revolutionary attitude was spasmodic. At first, the word "revolution" was weakened by the word "Republic"; the great intellectual impact of the Rights of Man dissolved in the windy discourses of radicals. Then, the communist movement among the tailors and seamen created a second upsurge of revolutionary fervor, yet even the great communist wave of 1945 did not so much subsume "Republic" in "revolution" as it did "revolution" in "Republic," where it was to remain, tamed once again.

The meaning of "republican" was not diluted to the point of being synonymous with "left" and "antifascist." Although its opposite, "monarchist," has long disappeared, red language retains the opposition between the Republic and its enemies. Republican feeling is a devotion to the original civilizing, emancipating Republic, whose features were unalterably fixed in 1905 with the separation of Church and State and the triumph of the secular school. Red Plodémet remained faithful to the Republic of 1905, but only indifferently attached to the later Third, Fourth, and Fifth Republics.

The word "white" has also been reduced in meaning, not so much through dehydration as through disintegration. The whites have abandoned successively the hope for a monarchy, the utopia of a return to the past, and the totalitarian myth of a Christian order. During the interwar years whites were identified with the national right wing but did not merge with it. After 1945, they did not even join MRP.[1] They drew inspiration directly from the Catholic Church, which has undergone a process of adaptation to the new bourgeois century.

Though considerably reduced in power, white and red allegiances still determine the political life of the commune. In 1965, the visitor found no Communist, Radical, Socialist, or MRP headquarters in Plodémet, for all political life is centered in the temples of the Virgin Mary and of the French Republic.

The Reds

The reception hall in the town hall is as bare as a Protestant church. The only decoration is a bust of Marianne above the mayor's chair. The sculpture is in 1900 style, one of thousands of reproductions of the same model. It was here that for the first time in my life I really looked at the face. I had no intention of

[1] Mouvement Républicain Populaire, a Christian Democratic party ranging from left of center to right of center.

pursuing an artistic or archaeological train of thought, but it occurred to me that the Marianne was like the Cybele or Isis of a dead civilization. At the same time, I suddenly discovered the beauty of this proud virgin's face and realized that it produced in me a state akin to faith, both encouraged and denied by my mythological reverie. I sensed the presence of a folk goddess, a rival sister of Mary.

Under the Occupation, Marianne was taken down by pious hands and hidden from profanation. She was put back in 1944.

Four framed portrait photographs dominate the bulletin boards at the entrance to the town hall. They are the solemn faces of the three Le Bail mayors, Lucien (1870-1874, 1876-1898), Georges (1898-1937), and Albert (1937-1952), along with that of Emile Loubet, President of the Republic from 1899 to 1906—the period of the secularization laws of the Combes government (1902-1905). The renaming of the streets, decided in 1965, retained only two proper names: the Avenue Georges Le Bail (founder of the CEG) and the Avenue Jules Ferry (1832-1893), the father of primary education at the beginning of the Third Republic. There are no streets named after Marx, Jaurès, Lenin or De Gaulle, and no Avenue de la Libération.

The town clerk, Le Nerf, retired in 1965. He is the son of a tailor, a puritanical activist and civil servant; he was entirely devoted to his office and his intransigent secularism suppressed everything that seemed to bear the clerical imprint. Mayor Maurice is sixty-four, and he was headmaster of the CEG Georges Le Bail before retirement. His deputy, Beuzec, is also a teacher.

Everything in the town hall evokes an active school as well as a long-gone but fossilized republic. At first sight, the clock seems to have stopped in 1905; the town hall is like a forgotten island of the Third Republic in the midst of the Fifth. This museum of a town hall is in fact a town hall-temple where the sacred is concealed behind a civic form, where the emancipating, educating Republic is sustained, commemorated, and celebrated in the forms of the bearded, stiff-collared gentlemen and a Marianne with a Belle Époque hairdo.

All the faces, living and dead—Jules Ferry's to President Loubet's, the three Le Bail mayors', the anticlerical town clerk's, and the schoolmaster-mayor's—celebrate the secular emancipating school, the secular Republic, and secularism. It is their unity that links the fossilized form and the living reality.

The unity in principle has been a unity in fact since 1959. Secularism is the political common denominator of the red party. The Secular Alliance (two hundred members) is the activist body that gives it intellectual leadership and forms the basis of the teachers' political power. The teacher has become both the administrator and the activist of the commune. Red politics produced the school; it is now the school that is producing red politics, for it is the major achievement of the red party. Even before it had electricity and running water, this small commune had a secondary school worthy of a large town. The two school buildings, which serve as both primary schools and CEG's, rule the town, one with 160 girls, the other with 330 boys.

The era that began in 1950 saw the triumph of a system of upward mobility through education, secondary and beyond. The whole of Plodémet society is eager to have its children pursue a secondary education.

The educational policy of the red party placed Plodémet in the vanguard of French secondary education, and the educational prestige of Plodémet is recognized even by the white party, which sent the girls of the Jeanne d'Arc School to the funeral of the tailor Le Moign. At the 1965 municipal elections, the red list won 1,600 votes, against 400 for the whites. The geopolitical network established at the beginning of the century still dominates the commune. Everything indicates performance, unity, vitality, and victory.

Yet from 1945 to 1959 the red party was split by dissension, and was in the minority in the general election of 1958. The CEG is threatened and no longer plays a key role in advancement. The hegemony conceals a crisis.

ELECTORAL INSTABILITY

During the interwar years, the Baillist municipal slate and the Radical candidate for deputy (for a long time, Georges Le Bail himself) won a constant 70 percent of the votes against 25 percent for the white slate. The Socialists, who came on the scene in 1919 with 58 votes (6.4 percent), remained atrophied at 3 percent of the vote until 1936. The Communists collected less than 1 percent of the votes until 1932, advancing to 82 votes (6 percent) in 1936.

Everything changed with the Liberation. The Radical vote in general elections toppled from 41 percent (1945) to 27 percent

(1946) to 19 percent (1956) to 12 percent (1958), and thereafter no Radical candidate was presented. The Communist won 30 percent of the votes in 1945; afterwards, it could count on 35 percent when it was in competition with a Radical and a Socialist candidate—in the first round of general elections[2]—but dropped to 28 percent in the first round in 1967. The Socialist Party, whose development was stopped by Baillism and then by the Communists, managed to reap some advantage from the collapse of the Radicals. It obtained 14 percent in the first round of the 1955 general election, but the absence of a Socialist candidate in the final round deprives one of an opportunity to measure actual Socialist influence that year. In 1967, a candidate of the alliance of the left which united Socialists and Radicals obtained 33 percent of the poll in the first round, but the unusually high figure may have been due to the fact that the candidate was the nephew of the local industrialist Azur.

Since the Liberation, the Communists on the one hand and the Radicals and Socialists on the other have been engaged in a sharp struggle for municipal control. In 1953, three separate slates were presented, the Radical Socialist (led by Azur), the Communist, and the white. The Azurists led the vote in the first round (926 votes), followed by the Communists (774) and the whites (630), and were elected in the second round with 1,272 votes against 910 Communist and 158 white votes.

The leftist alliance was formed in 1959 after a split in the Radical ranks, with one group joining an alliance with the whites in a common list, the other joining the new coalition. The red list was elected with 1,358 votes against 1,045. In 1965, the breakup of the Azurist-white alliance and disunity within the white party resulted in the debacle of only 400 white votes.

In 1958 and 1962, the leftist parties ceased to command a majority in Plodémet as Gaullism burst on the scene as a third force. Although it did not manage to take root in the political life of the municipality, it devoured both red and white votes in the general elections. In the first round of the 1958 election, the two red candidates—the Radical with 12 percent and the Communist with

2 The Communist Party obtained only 28 percent of the votes in the first round of the 1967 elections, against 33 percent for the Fédération de la Gauche (a left-center coalition, led by François Mitterand). It is difficult to know whether to attribute this inversion of the CP/SF10 + Radical ratio to the fact that the Fédération candidate was a local man, or to a slight decline in Communist support.

35 percent—gained only a total of 47 percent of the votes while the Gaullists obtained 35 percent and the MRP 15 percent. In the second round, the Communist was the only red candidate and obtained 46 percent against 51 percent for the Gaullist. In 1962, the only red candidate in both rounds was a Communist, and he failed to win a majority either in the first (43 percent) or the second (47 percent); the MRP candidate got 19 percent of the votes in the first round; the Gaullist candidate increased his first-round vote of 35 percent to 50 percent in the second. In the Fifth Republic referendums, the Gaullist propositions always won out—74 percent in 1958, 71 percent in 1961, 95 percent in 1962 on the Algerian policy, and even when the parties of the left formed an opposition block, 60 percent in 1962. Only in the presidential election of December 1965 did the candidate of the three red groups, Mitterand, garner 45 percent in the first round and then 52 percent in the second, when he won over more than half of the first-round voters for Lecanuet, the MRP candidate. In 1967, the reds gained a total of 61 percent in the first round and 51.5 percent in the second.

There is a clear contrast between the political situation during the twenty interwar years and that during the first twenty postwar years: a long period of dominance and unity was followed by disunity and instability. At first, the unity of the red party was broken, yet red dominance was maintained; then red unity was re-created in the form of a coalition, yet red dominance was jeopardized in the general elections. An inverse relationship came to operate between the communal political situation and the general one owing to the fact that the Gaullist factor was nonexistent in the former but of capital importance in the latter. Even in 1965, the union of the left gained only 963 votes (first round) and 1,175 votes (second round) in the presidential election, compared with 1,400 votes in the municipal elections of the same year. In the 1967 general election, the Fédération de la Gauche and the Communist Party won 1,118 votes in the first round, and 973 votes for the only left-wing candidate, a Communist, in the second.

In both interwar and postwar stages, a new phenomenon emerged as the result of war: communism after World War I and Gaullism with the Algerian war. The characteristic common to both was the disturbance of the traditional red-white division in both the municipal elections, when the two red lists fought each other and when red and white votes supported an Azurist list (1953–1959), and the general elections, in which, since 1955, an independent candidate has captured Radical and white votes and in which, at each referendum and each general election since 1958, Gaullism has emerged as a third, and major force.

The disturbances of the traditional division in Plodémet politics are linked to the appearance and increase of an unpredictable vote. The crises within the parties have freed voters from traditional allegiances; opportunist votes have mingled with votes of principle, and protest votes have joined with loyal votes. Gaullism has blown traditionally red allegiances (Communist, Socialist, Radical) wide open, and the breaches have not all healed. The floating vote has favored the reds in municipal elections since 1959, but Gaullism in general elections and referendums since 1958.

It is at the general political level that the red party no longer has a stable majority, though it is quite capable of recapturing it. December 1965 was both a victory compared with the referendums and votes of 1958-1962, and a failure in relation to the municipal majority, which itself was lower than the traditional 70 percent. Is this political crisis at the general level circumstantial or structural? Is Gaullism a temporary phenomenon or a new historical phenomenon?

On the other hand, at the communal level everything seems to have returned to normal since 1959. The red majority was never in danger, despite an internal crisis. The crisis was overcome by the formation of a coalition in which the Communists play a key role.

COMMUNISM IN PLODÉMET

During the war years the Communist Party was not regarded as the vanguard of a menacing proletariat, the fomenter of revolutionary disturbances, or the gravedigger of the old republican order, but as the vitalizer of the nation's energies against the occupier, the leader of the struggle for freedom, and the restorer of red tradition.

While the traditional parties were in eclipse, unsuited as they were to clandestine struggle, the Stalinist structure of the Communist Party transformed it into a war machine. The enormous energy concentrated in the disciplined, centralized apparatus could be used to optimum effect in identifying the national struggle with the pro-Soviet struggle. After the Liberation, the party capitalized on the fruits of struggle, sacrifice, and victory. It authenticated the years of distress by promising a future of rewards, not social revolution or socialist reform but a "free, strong, and happy France," with "bread, peace, and liberty for all." During the years of disenchantment that followed, the Communist Party became the party of frustrated, betrayed hope, and then the party of protest and demand. But it never departed from the Baillist tradition of which it claims to be the true heir.

Communism in Plodémet is in fact the sociological heir of Baillism, in that it spread first not among the agricultural proletariat or the semiproletarian factory workers but in activist republican circles, among the tailors and fishermen. It took root in all the social groups that had been united under the Baillist banner— tradesmen, craftsmen, smallholders, teachers; like the Baillists, it is an interclass party in a Plodémet moving toward a bourgeois society, not the party of an excluded or marginal class.

Communist agitation, far from being foreign to the republican tradition, evokes the ferments of the French Revolution; its attachment to the Russian Revolution revives Plodémet's own attachment to the emancipating plebeian revolution. The party does not offer Soviet-inspired collectivist policies. The U.S.S.R. is represented as the country where the little man has triumphed, not as the country of the Soviets. The Soviet state is not the Father-State that has replaced the republican state; it is rather a kind of Uncle-State. Stalin was the rough but goodhearted chief, strong and cunning, who embodied and magnified the image of the head of the rustic clan, the patriarchal educator and guide, the civilizing hero—and, like old Le Bail, a foreigner. The geographical distance made him as venerable as a patron saint or ancestor.

Destalinization was regarded as a family affair between father and sons, not as a problem that affected the existence of the party. Neither destalinization, nor Stalinism, nor collectivism disturbed the Communists of Plodémet; they regarded the embarrassing problems as the "internal affairs" of the great ally or as the "calumnies" of a lying enemy.

The war party of the Occupation era became the peace party of the cold-war era and has never ceased to organize peace campaigns. It is the only party to play on the trauma caused by two wars by constant denunciations of a militaristic Germany; it is the only party that has responded to fears of war by campaigns against nuclear weapons, German rearmament, the Korean war, the Vietnam war, the Algerian war. Its proclaimed pacifism is neither defeatist nor revolutionary; it is presented as being in the interest of the French people and the right of all nations to self-determination, and its proclamations never border on civil disobedience or subversion.

Above all, the "little people" of Plodémet have always needed a powerful ally, and the industrial worker is regarded not as a threat to this still semiplebeian society, but as an urban ally offering his organized strength. The alliance with the forceful and energetic party of the urban worker is itself sustained by the world-wide alliance of all working people and by the supreme alliance with the Soviet Union. The new alliance does not alter the old liberal-bourgeois alliance; it restores a total vision of the world that had been dislocated and fragmented by the radicalism of the interwar years. Progress, democracy, nation, and republic are the keywords that communism has reshaped into a coherent ideology: that of the French Revolution. Communism has revived the ideology that Baillism had allowed to die away.

The Communist message is that the achievements of the French Revolution are not only uncompleted but actually in danger. The party intends to defend what has already been won and to continue toward its completion. Progress is the key word by which it defines itself and by which it repossesses the key principle of the red party. It has taken over entirely the Baillist policy of upward mobility through education. Far from opposing the trend toward *embourgeoisement,* it encourages it.

What the party opposes is the decline of the smallholding. While white agricultural syndicalism has become the advocate of the cooperative and even of collective ownership of the land, the Communist Party is demanding that the State take steps to protect the small craftsman, tradesman, and farmer. One may well wonder about the meaning of a policy so foreign to the socialist spirit, when the need for modernization and cooperative methods offers a much more viable policy. It is difficult to decide whether refusal to reform in this matter is a mark of revolutionary intransigence, historical ruse, or inertia. Whatever the reason, the Communist Party is thereby stirring up recrimination and anger against the State in the small independent operator, from which it benefits electorally and which keeps the doomed small tradesman, craftsman, and farmer within the red tradition. By doing so, it sets up a crossfire to real Poujadism, which at the height of its influence won the votes of only 5 percent of the Plodémet electorate (1955). On the other hand, unlike real Poujadism, the party's policy also calls for the denunciation of a conspiracy between the State and big business—a matter having no relevance to local reform, but for that very reason enhancing local support by offering the image of a party struggling at the national level to free the state from the clutches of big business and guide it back to its parternal functions. Moreover, the protests of small businessmen help feed the party's overall policy of protest; transformed and channeled back to the grassroots by the central leadership, the basic components reappear as protests against the war in Indochina, Algeria, or Vietnam. This policy results in an opening up of political awareness whose scope is national, even global.

Therefore, communism in Plodémet maintains its universal principle by plunging into a particular local situation where it rediscovers, through Jacobin Baillism, the universality of the French Revolution. It has grown its roots by an extraordinary regression to 1905, not the 1905 of the St. Petersburg Soviet, Trotsky, and the battleship *Potemkin*, but the 1905 of Plodémet, when the victory of secularization confirmed that of the smallholders. Through the attachment of Plodémet society to *embourgeoisement*, communism returns to the plebeian ideological sources of that society. It is because Plodémet society is in the process of *embourgeoisement* that the Communist Party has remained so attached to its *petit-bourgeois* and plebeian aspect.

So the return to 1905 has linked communism to the French Revolution (from which, indirectly, it sprang and to which, through the detour of Stalinism, it returns) and identifies it economically with the declining small business. Nothing is less strange in Plodémet than a communism that assumes its past and at the same time looks forward to the future. And nothing would have been more foreign to it than the regime of Joseph Stalin.

Plodémet communism fully confirms at its own level the national claim of the Communist Party pronounced in 1945: "We are the sustainers of France." It is the heir to red Baillism in its social composition, its ideology, its policies. It brings, not a new gospel, but a new alliance. It restores, not transforms, red Plodémet. Once the problem of the division of power had been solved, communism could feel perfectly at home among the family portraits in the town hall, without wishing to add Lenin to the Le Bails, Loubet, and Ferry. Its entry into the municipal administration completed the integration of the Communist Party, which in turn became the reintegrator of the red party, by its being the best-organized, most stable, and most activist force thereof.

The influence of the party in the commune is based on a dual organization that has been expanded and consolidated through its entry into the municipal council. On the one hand, it utilizes the support of a body of influential notables, and has not hesitated to make use of the broker-contractor or the activist of the farmers' union for its purposes. At the same time, there is the party organization proper, directly linked to the regional section, which organizes strategy and political action. The center of power has shifted from Pors-Ensker to the CEG, and it is through the corps of Communist teachers that the great national campaigns saturate Plodémet.

However widespread Communist influence may be, about half of the red population refuses to recognize the image of its own tradition in it. They sense duality, not to say duplicity, behind essence and appearance, behind fidelity to the Republic and fidelity to the Soviet Union. It was to disarm or neutralize this distrust that the Communist Party renounced its claim on the office of mayor and accepted second rank in the municipal council, although it was the largest of the three parties.

THE BATTLE OF THE SCHOOLS

The mayoralty went to Maurice, a Socialist, whose nomination reaffirmed the primacy of the secular school which had been obscured during the Azurist hold on the town hall. The three parties of the left came together in a neo-Baillism centered on the secular school.

The alliance was not merely the cement of a rediscovered unity but also a self-defensive reaction, for the battle of the schools had flared up again.

In the 1950's Plodémet was unanimous in directing its children toward secondary education. The white party, after long opposition, joined in the movement and set up its own school, which posed a threat to the CEG. The triumph of the red ideology of education produced the ironic result of a challenge monopoly.

Until this event, religious education in Plodémet had consisted only of a small primary school for girls dating from 1928. Now, in 1957, not a hundred yards from the CEG Georges Le Bail, the Church opened the CEG Jeanne d'Arc, providing a primary and secondary school for girls in the heart of the red commune. Jeanne d'Arc grew from year to year, and in 1962 it had about a hundred pupils, which represented almost 40 percent of the total schoolgirl population, although the white electorate represents but 25 percent of the total. The state school for boys has no rival in the commune itself so far, but it is threatened from the outside. In 1965, the secular school in Lesnus was on the point of closing down because almost all its people had been drawn away by white Poulzic.

Moreover, the development of a longer course of secondary education has enabled the religious schools of the region, especially the famous Lykes *lycée* in Quimper, to lure the sons of white families away from the state school. In ten short years, a reconquest conducted both inside and outside the commune, in primary and especially in secondary education, has broken the almost total monopoly of the secular school.

The CEG is jeopardized not only by the Catholic reconquest but also by the increasing favor gained by the *lycée,* which has been turning the CEG into a regional rather than a communal school. While the buses are bringing boys from nearby rural communes to the CEG in Plodémet, three buses are taking Plodémet boys to the *lycées* in Quimper.

This depletion will be stopped in 1969, when the new law transforming the CEG into the CES (*collège d'enseignement supérieur,* the equivalent of a *lycée*) comes into force in Plodémet, making it obligatory that children attend the nearest local school. In any case, the CES will not play a central role in Plodémet's politics because it will be a national, not a communal, institution. The competition between state and private education will still continue, but the secondary-school teacher, who is an apostle of secularization, will be succeeded by the teacher from outside, for whom secularization is just one problem among many. The red municipality will be relieved of the burden of the CEG, but it will lose its power over the school and the power it derives from it. This power, at once cultural, political, and economic (awarding scholarships), has been diminishing ever since 1950. The influence exercised through scholarships has been circumscribed with the reduction of poverty areas and the expansion of student migration.

As the role of the CEG contracts, its liabilities increase. Competition and new requirements necessitate refurbishing and modernization, and in 1965 the school absorbed 20 percent of the municipal budget.

THE COMMUNAL STRATEGY

The problems of the commune have arisen simultaneously, suddenly, and on a large scale: backwardness, a crisis, and a need for development.

The backwardness of the infrastructure (water supply, roads) is felt most because it aggravates the agricultural crisis and hampers the advance of domestic comfort. The complex intermingling of causes and effects demands the creation of a communal development policy.

The municipality has taken steps to eliminate this backwardness. New roads and the installation of a public water supply will be completed by 1970. In both cases, the cooperation of the white party was essential, which indicates that all problems are no longer held up by the battle over secularization, and that the red party, despite its hegemony, cannot solve them all alone.

The revival of communal activity is complemented by a broad strategic move in agriculture, where the red party is emerging from thirty years of immobility by reorganizing its rural apparatus with the support of a number of middle-range farm owners in red areas, four contractors, two of whom are still farming, and an important official of the farmers' union, Le Kam.

This bridgehead strategy is based on agents of modernization who represent divergent tendencies. The introduction of Le Kam in 1965 was offset by the entry in the same year of two new contractors into the municipal council. The union militants are in a minority among the rural notables.

Land redistribution was one of the first actions undertaken by

the left-coalition council, and the first red initiative of an agricultural nature since the days of Georges Le Bail. But this initiative, in which, in any case, the town hall was as much concerned
with the building of new roads as with the modernization of the
land plots, was an isolated example. Whereas Georges Le Bail
envisaged postscholastic education for farmers in 1912, 1920, and
1927, the teachers of the CEG had no such notions. The red party
left the initiative in agricultural matters to the farmers' union and
the State. Communists and Socialists made no effort in favor of
cooperation; failing grants to white cooperatives, they could have
supported groups of producers and encouraged a red cooperative
movement. In fact, unionization has not led to cooperation, and
the alliance with the contractors is a move in the other direction.
The left-wing municipality bases its power on (and increases the
power of) four contractors, at a time when the parish magazine
is praising the first cooperative merger among farmers.

As for the communal problem generally, the same situation
exists as for agriculture: the red party has worked out no policy
beyond mobility through education, which in any case now takes
place of itself.

Yet the new direction taken by Plodémet already opens up the
prospects of a development policy that could benefit simultaneously cooperation in various economic sectors (as has been
proved in the intercraftsmen's group and the grocers' group),
technical progress, economic progress, and cultural activity.

Although under present conditions industrial development remains beyond the scope of the municipal council, everything
encourages a policy of tourist development. Yet nothing has so
far been done to signpost the coast road and historical monuments, or to draw attention to the commune's aesthetic resources,
its archaeological and folk heritage, or local products. The
eighteenth-century house which could have been restored or even
converted into a museum, the Maison Kérizit, was demolished as
a cumbersome eyesore.

The teachers, who made no attempt to set up in the CEG a
center of technical information for farmers, have not even thought
of establishing a cultural or educational center for adults, and
apart from a recreation center that was soon abandoned, they
have no youth policy.

Thus the hyper-Baillism of the left-wing coalition had not, in

1965, rediscovered the initiative and reforming zeal of the 1880-1910 period. Is it a sign of declining powers, or does the very movement of Plodément society oppose political solutions?

THE WITHDRAWAL OF THE ACTIVISTS

Red policy has not yet got its second wind; the activist apparatus is aging and thinning out in numbers.

In 1966, eight municipal councilors out of the total of twenty-three were over sixty; twelve were over fifty; and only one was under thirty. Several of the new councilors are local notables who succeeded the old activist guides of the great Baillist period. The last "tribal chief" is Michel Poullan, from Pors-Ensker, the sixty-six-year-old deputy mayor.

The backbone of the red party consists of a few activists between forty and sixty, most of them teachers. They are modest men, devoid of vanity and ambition, motivated by strong devotion to the public good—men of virtue in the sense in which Robespierre loved that Roman term. However, they are a vanishing breed. The teaching profession provides very few committed activists under forty. Activists feel isolated in a population where political affinity no longer inspires everyday loyalty, where television and trips in the car are far more attractive alternatives than meetings. This isolation is compensated for, in some cases by the multitude of tasks, and for the Communists by the comforting feeling of belonging to the giant beehive of the party. For others, whose activism has been stifled by the inertia of others, isolation has turned into discouragement. The photographer Menguy, for example, devoted himself unsparingly to the Secular Alliance, the Parents' Association, and the Holidays Committee, but gave up and now devotes himself to his job. The disappointed activist stops doing anything for those who will do nothing for themselves.

Our project was carried on at a time when a new generation of activists had barely surfaced. The takeover of the Holidays Committee by a new wave of young craftsmen and the combination of cultural and political action by a number of young teachers indicate that the breed of activists may not be dead but, like all else, changing.

Meanwhile, just as the political ideology has returned to the question of secularization, so the militant spirit has become concentrated among a nucleus of teachers who take on ever-increasing responsibilities. At the center of this nucleus, there is on the one hand a number of Socialist teachers, in the great tradition of the SNI[3], and on the other the Communist cell. This nucleus of teachers is the very center of red politics. It organizes national campaigns, such as the presidential election campaign of 1965. It keeps secular institutions alive. It runs the municipal council.

FROM THE SCHOOL AS TRAINING GROUND TO THE SCHOOL AS CITADEL

The teacher has attained hitherto unknown heights of responsibility and influence. Yet the vocation, the mission, the function of the teacher have been profoundly undermined. The teacher rules but no longer reigns over Plodémet. In the early years of the century, the teacher in Republican rural France brought with his teaching the tool of social emancipation, the humanist gospel of progress, and the enlightenment that would banish obscurantism and superstition. He was the magus, the priest, the missionary of secular authority. After 1930, he was promoted by and in the CEG, as the CEG itself became the instrument of advancement beyond the primary educational level.

But education has gradually ceased to be a total concept that encompasses knowledge, civilization, culture, and advancement. General education is no longer the pinnacle of culture, but a springboard to specialized careers. Advancement is coming to mean professional advancement. The supremacy of the teaching profession has suffered from the growing prestige of the technical professions. The sons of two successive principals of the CEG both want to become engineers.

The prestige of the teaching profession is now confined to secondary and higher schools. The increase in the number of teachers has already made them a common species in Plodémet. But it is above all the general acquisition of secondary education that is tending to reduce the Enlightener of former times to the status of lower-grade teacher. A fissure has occurred within the CEG itself, as the teachers are being supplanted by graduate secondary-school teachers who in turn feel at a disadvantage in relation to the graduate teachers in the *lycée*.

Thus, the teachers in Plodémet are losing their power and

[3] Syndicat National des Instituteurs, or national union of teachers.

prestige. In earlier times, the plebeian clientele received the
manna of scholarships according to their sons' merits and gave
thanks to the all-powerful schoolmaster. Today, the role of the
scholarship has diminished, the pupil himself or his family decide
on the career he is to take up, and the masters are less and less
honored and listened to by parents. The new common front of
parent and child in which the child is king is replacing the old
parent-teacher front in which the teacher was king.

MME. DURAZ. The parents just won't accept that their children
are being made to repeat a year.

LE GUILLAN. There's a different attitude. You find it everywhere.
People are more on the side of their children.

HIS WIFE. The kids are treated like film stars.

LE GUILLAN. If I got a spanking at school, I'd get another one
when I got home. Nowadays, if you lay a finger on one of them,
he'll go home and complain to his parents.

The authority of the teacher has been undermined by the advancement of the child within the family and by the desire of
the family for social advancement through the child. He is now
little more than an educating machine whose function is to advance the child as rapidly as possible, and any attempt on his part
to slow the pace of advancement is strongly resented by the parents. Deprived of his former prestige and authority, the teacher
is but a minor civil servant who enjoys excessively numerous vacations.

What is worse, the teacher's fund of culture is now being questioned both inside and outside the school. He was trained to
respect clear, rational ideas, the aesthetics of classical beauty,
and writers like Daudet, Maupassant, and Pergaud. He regards
contemporary tendencies in the arts as strange, mad, or dangerous. Only a few young teachers appreciate modern poetry, the
cinema, or photography. The rest regard art which dislocates
forms, the absurd questionings of Kafka or Camus, in short, modern culture, as barbarous.

Their senses are assaulted by jukeboxes, transistors, films, television, and the popular press. They perceive only hysteria in the
rhythm of teen-agers' dances, and stupidity or indolence in their
other recreations. "They spend their time watching television
when Zorro or some such nonsense is on" (Mme Duraz). "Young
people have changed so much. I can't get the kids interested in a

good author as I used to be able to, twenty years ago . . . I think
it will become more and more distressing to be a teacher. They're
not interested in Hugo and Maupassant any more" (Le Bellec,
age 54).

The teachers are being subjected to a triple cultural attack by
the specialized and technical professions, by the artistic and literary avant-garde, and by mass culture. They feel diminished and
unrecognized in a society that seems to them increasingly devoted
to material satisfaction, hedonistic activity, and selfish attitudes.
Moreover, they realize that secular education has been losing its
importance in French society, and the passage from the Fourth
to the Fifth Republic has merely confirmed their diagnosis of a
general regression. They also feel jeopardized within the teaching profession itself, threatened as they are by being pushed
out of the CEG, their own creation, by the graduate secondary-
school teachers.

Lastly, a break has occurred between the older and younger
generations of teachers. Those who have retained the activist
spirit complain bitterly that their younger colleagues no longer
regard their profession as a vocation but as a job. The young
teachers vanish as soon as they have corrected the students' homework. When I remarked to Maréchal, a teacher in his late thirties,
that the ecclesiastical teachers seemed more active than their lay
counterparts, he retorted, "I'd like to see them with a wife and
kids!" By nature an activist, he too feels discouraged and spends
his vacations working in a small family *crêperie* on the Pointe
du Raz.

The older teachers continue to fulfill their mission, but they too
are at least partially seduced by the bourgeois amenities of life.
They condemn television as "the scourge of the century," yet 50
percent of the teachers have it as against only 37 percent of the
tradesmen and 21 percent of the seamen.

The humanist apostolate is finished. The teacher is already too
committed to his role as civil servant and to *embourgeoisement,*
which he condemns but only partly resists. But it is the ideal of
progress that has been shaken by recent developments. To the
teacher, the idea of progress is contradicted by decline on a number of fronts, from the decline in the French language, which
children write less and less well, to the decline in politics. It is at
the heart of educational culture, the humanities, that an enormous

breach has opened under the combined assaults of technological culture, the avant-garde aesthetic, mass culture, the Catholic reconquest and bourgeois indifference.

Where are the new humanities in which the traditional humanities could be absorbed and transcended? There is no sign of them in the tiny besieged citadel of this western corner of France. At a time when the Church is undergoing a great modernization, secular humanism seems to be in final combat with the modern world. The mayor regards industrialization, contemporary urban living, subsidized housing, television, and mass tourism as signs of a fundamental turning away from progress, with material conquests being attained at the expense of spiritual values. While Plodémet society plunges totally into modernity, its secular guides are deeply disturbed by it and sometimes sink into apocalyptic or nihilistic visions of the future. They still believe in their values, but these values are in retreat. The teaching profession everywhere is on the defensive against the present and in fear of the future.

On the pedagogic level, the teachers cling to the principle of authority. Knowledge is held to be acquired first of all by discipline, and both old and young teachers reject new educational methods. In 1962, the Tricot study revealed that only one teacher in the state schools, as against three in the religious schools, based his teaching more or less on progressive methods. The great educational problems posed by the crisis in the humanities and by the transformation of society in general are not discussed by the teachers.

There is no initiative for cultural activity in Plodémet. The municipal library closed for lack of readers, and the closing took place without protest. There is as yet neither a cinema club nor a photography club (though the younger generation is going to change this). The Holidays Committee is left to the tradesmen. The municipality has not thought of turning the little school in Lesnus, which is about to close, into a vacation camp. "Once again, the priests will take over," its young teacher sighed. There are no extracurricular educational courses anywhere in the commune.

This cultural passivity reveals the depth of the crisis in the teaching profession. And the cultural retreat may well determine in part the political retreat, since in Plodémet the culture of the teaching profession has historically taken a political rather than an artistic form. Twenty years ago, the teaching body was a cauldron of political heterodoxy that was particularly susceptible to the minority currents of communism and socialism; at the 1946 elections the Trotskyite candidate won 24 votes in Plodémet, most of them probably cast by teachers. Neither Stalinism nor destalinization has affected the Communist teacher. Internal protest within the party has dried up, while Finistère, at least the north of the department, has become one of the first regions of dissident socialism in France, and in 1962 elected to Parliament the only PSU deputy.

The teacher has retreated to the old platform of 1905, to the detriment of any attempt to find a policy of communal-regional development in democratic-socialist terms. He has retreated behind the municipal scholastic citadel. The obsessive preoccupation with the principle of secularization—obsessive because it remains the only principle—reflects the difficulty of the teacher's situation. The teacher has become the scrupulous administrator of Plodémet; he is still something of a mentor, but he is no longer the Enlightener.

POTENTIALITY AND DELAY

At the beginning of the century, the red party benefitted from a conjunction of advantages in which the active agency of the tailors, the enlightenment dispensed by the teachers, the rise within Plodémet of the rural masses, the progress of the Republican State, and the dynamism of the Radical Party created the conditions for a communal policy. Today Red Plodémet lacks these conditions.

We have seen what has become of the teachers and activists. As regards the society of Plodémet itself, the small peasants, sailors, craftsmen, tradesmen, and wage earners are undergoing a process of *embourgeoisement*. The red party is already almost a middle-class party. The municipal council includes only one industrial worker (age 70), not a single wage earner from the private sector, not a single agricultural worker, and one smallholder in an assembly that includes three teachers, one post office worker, three tradesmen, one tailor, three sailors, four contractors, and five middle-range farmers.

Plodémet society is passing from plebeian homogeneity to bourgeois homogenization, without losing as yet its egalitarian characteristics. But *embourgeoisement* has destroyed the old plebeian homogeneity. We have considered the break that has occurred between bourgeois and rural people, and the professional retreat of the tradesmen and teachers. The new residential populations, whether they exercise their economic activity outside the commune (merchant seamen and some wage earners), or whether they are economically inactive or semiactive (the retired), have helped break up this closely knit society into a heterogeneous aggregate of social groups whose economic aims have become sectional. The breaks between the generations, within every social category, add to the sociological ruptures the conflicts of attitude between old and young. In the present puzzle of Plodémet society it is becoming extremely difficult to find a common (communal) policy beyond that of advancement through education. Neither the bourgeois nor the rural people can develop a coherent or bold policy that would be acceptable to the general consensus. The common aspiration toward a better standard of living may stimulate but cannot develop a policy. The widespread if not universal desire to safeguard the small business comes up against different and contradictory problems. The social struggle has died down, and there is no longer an internal class enemy that can arouse action. The new enemy is too far away, beyond the reach of communal action. Although everyone may accuse the State of helping the enemy, not everyone is agreed as to who or what the enemy is. The large outside firm that kills off the small firm can also save it by absorbing it. The new economy brings both ruin and better living standards. The outside world is becoming less and less decipherable to this society of small businesses, to which it brings both progress and death.

Technology still remains an enigma to this society, which is more modernized in its tastes and aspirations than in its material and mental equipment, and whose intelligentsia is nonscientific by training. Apart from the new generation of schoolchildren, who are turning increasingly to technical careers, only the advance guard of the farmers' union has made any attempt to understand the new world of technology. For the people of Plodémet as a whole, technology is not regarded as a means of political domination and action.

In fact, the economic-technological evolution has undermined the bases of any new communal policy. The commune is no longer a relatively autonomous cell. The municipality has been deprived, either gradually or suddenly, of much of its power. Decisions concerning agriculture are now taken outside Plodémet, in Plonéour, Quimper, or Landernau; it is already as important, perhaps more so, for the Plodémet trade unionists to have a bridgehead in Landernau as in the Plodémet town hall. The CEG will soon be outside the control of the commune, which will cease to be a center of school-oriented politics. The public water supply will be installed only with the cooperation of Poulzic. The commune can no longer envisage its development in an autonomous fashion, except in the field of summer tourism, where the possibilities have hardly begun to be exploited.

Plodémet is more and more integrated in a regional network, and must become integrated in a regional development policy. At present, it suffers from its position as an outlying region, subject to uneven development, not only at the national level but even within Brittany itself. The development of Sud-Finistère requires investment, redeployment, planning, programming— that is, the active intervention of the State. But so far the State has completely neglected Sud-Finistère, and consequently a commune like Plodémet, incapable of formulating its own development policy, is deprived of all help and guidance from outside.

Moreover, the great national parties to which the red party is attached have not yet come up with proposals for integrating regional development within national development. These left-wing parties, Jacobin and nationalist by tradition, have always mistrusted political provincialism. The Radical Party has left the field. The Communist Party, unlike its counterpart in Italy, which has regionalized its policy, hesitates to sacrifice concentrated activity to a geographical dispersion of energy.

Nothing is forthcoming, then, either from Plodémet itself, from the region, or from the national left-wing parties that might free the red party from its rigidity of approach. Moreover, although red power is threatened socially by the Catholic reconquest, the political disintegration of the white party removes the red-controlled town hall from all danger. It only takes a little strategy and a united front to retain the still secular power. The conservation of power encourages conservatism; political security sends politics to sleep. Finally, the conversion of the whites to evolutionism confirms the triumph of red ideas and transforms them into commonplaces. In these conditions, the bourgeois value system absorbs politics that are still plebeian at the level of principles and ideology, breaks up the old organic solidarity of the red

populace, induces people to withdraw into their private lives,
dries up the springs of activism, and reduces the political life
generally.

The bourgeois value system, the culmination of republican
emancipation, has become the gravedigger of the victor: the red
party is forced to navigate between an exhausted republican program and the absence of any new program. Moreover, the un-
realized part of the republican program is now left to the anonymous process of economic-social development; from this point of
view, the new direction is simply the integration of Plodémet
society into bourgeois society (the revolution in domestic consumption and almost universal secondary education). The new
direction dissociates the great processes of emancipation from
red political action, whereas until 1950 they were intimately
linked; the forthcoming takeover of the CEG by the national
government will complete the dissociation between social advance and communal politics.

However, this *de facto* dissociation is not a dissociation *de jure*:
the red party is not opposed to the current but in the current(not
in an active but in a passive capacity), since it has never ceased
to base its thinking on an evolutionism of social advance. In-
versely, but in a similar way, its small-business conservatism,
although against the current economically, is in the dominant
psychological current of present-day Plodémet society. The red
party is divorced from economic realities, but not from the consciousness of Plodémet society. This is why, although its political
field of action is considerably reduced objectively (new direction) and subjectively (fossilization of political consciousness),
it continues to express both the evolutionism and the conservatism of Plodémet, without exercising any real political action.

The new direction of Plodémet society carried within itself
either the renovation or the disintegration of the red party, which
had already been weakened between 1945 and 1958. The party
avoided both disintegration and renovation by a united stand on
the common Baillist past and an intelligent strategy that was
helped by the disintegration of the white party. The return to the
original principle of Baillist politics was a panicked regression,
in which a conservative withdrawal prevailed over the search for
new ways. But once again, premature innovation would have
meant rupture and disintegration. In fact, the regression was a

vital reflex, even in its fossilizing aspect, for fossilization is a phenomenon of resistance as well as of devitalization. In the event, the return to the vital principle and the fossil form of 1905 restored the unity of the red party, and enabled it to dominate the municipal scene against a politically disintegrating enemy.

The concentration on secularization is, similarly, an ambivalent sign of decadence and of the will to live. It is not an artificial or outdated question: the state school is in fact threatened, and nothing is more important to the two old party machines than their battle around the central point of Plodémet life—mobility through education. But at the same time this battle is no longer necessary to the future of Plodémet society, whose advancement no longer depends on the municipal school alone. It is no longer the Homeric struggle in which two civilizations concentrated all their social strength. It is not two types of humanity that emerge from the secular and religious schools, but two variants of the average bourgeoisie.

The red party has succeeded in re-creating its unity, but not in creating a policy. It has re-created its unity, not on a progressive basis, but on a regressive one. Could it have been otherwise, when one remembers that Plodémet society was deprived of the necessary external and internal agents of change? The undissociable half vitality and half fossilization of the red party make it possible to defer the definitive answer. This delay is itself ambivalent. The half vitality and half fossilization create a resistance, but form an obstacle to any profound change. They prevent the crisis from deepening and therefore from disintegrating, but they also prevent it from being regenerative. They both waste time and gain time.

Crisis, uncertainty, and prudence seem to merge in the policy of delay. "Everything will come in due course, first the water supply, then the roads, then things will come of themselves," said the mayor when we were trying to persuade him to adopt a policy for the development of tourism. He knows that sooner or later Plodémet will be integrated into the modern world. He also knows that the gains brought by the modern world will be offset by the losses. And for this man, who is experiencing more profoundly than anyone else in Plodémet the division, the contradiction between the crisis in progress and the faith in progress, delay is probably the only prudent policy.

Once again, we see Plodémet defending itself against the attacks of the new direction by a prudent policy of entrenchment behind the old structures. What will the future bring?

Diverse and divergent new forces are operating beneath the surface, not only in the Finistère region and Plodémet society itself but also in French political life (where the left-wing parties are also preserving themselves in a half vitality, half fossilization that postpones the arrival of their crisis—that is, their decline or their resurrection). Political immobilization is only a temporary immobilization. Political senescence corresponds to an extreme moment overdetermined by the aging of the cadres. There will be political change, if only through a change in the generations. But will this change destroy the red party or bring about its transformation?

The real problem of the red party is to rediscover itself in transforming itself. It could also be transformed in denying itself, or deny itself by simply rediscovering its fossilized form. It runs the risk of total disintegration or fossilization, as much by totally rejecting the new technological-economic-bourgeois direction as by totally integrating itself into it. In order to survive, a red party has as much need to resist the new direction to a certain extent as to adapt to it to a certain extent. It must therefore develop a technologized policy of communal-regional development, an advanced social policy (the cooperative movement), and a new cultural-civilizing mission.

While awaiting destruction or transformation, the red party is still in power because it is in the axis of Plodémet's rise and protest, because it benefits from the impetus acquired by Baillism and the influence acquired by the Communists during the Resistance, and finally, because the new direction has politically disintegrated its white enemy.

The crisis of unity has been overcome but not resolved by the union of the left-wing parties. The problem of the unattached vote has been partially and intermittently overcome, not resolved. The crisis of the political program has been fossilized on a regressive basis. The reduction of the red principle to secularization is not accompanied by a renaissance of the principle itself, that is, a renaissance of red enlightenment. Secularization remains dehydrated. The deepest crisis is to be found there. It is already felt by the teachers as a crisis of progress, but it is not yet recognized

as a crisis of ferments in culture and civilization, a crisis of the
revolutionary and universalist spirit, a crisis of socialist development—in short, a crisis of the principles of human development.
That is the true problem that may destroy the red party or the
red of the party. The answer is not to be found in Plodémet, or
even perhaps in France.

The White

THE PARTY OF CHRISTENDOM

The reds do not go to mass, but with a very few exceptions receive the sacraments of the Church. There is a religious picture
in almost every home. Most families, except for the CEG teachers,
a few seamen, and the Le Bails, contribute to the "vicar's basket."
The reds recognize the Church as depository of the great rites
of initiation and passage, as heir to a fundamental, primeval religion that preceded Christianity and was annexed by it, but they
challenge its specific myths and theology. Some are deists, others
are frankly atheists, for whom "God and the devil do not exist,
and when you're dead you're dead and that's the end of it"; but
deism and atheism are strata of clear consciousness superimposed
on strata of obscure consciousness in which the Celtic magico-
religious base blends with a Catholic base[4] and a naturalistic
cosmology.

---

[4] A dimension of major importance, that of the religious history of
Plodémet, is missing from our study. It would have enabled us to see how the
osmosis between Catholicism and the Celtic religions (similar to the pre-
Columbian magico-religious base of Mexican or Peruvian Catholicism) took
place. It would have enabled us to verify whether the Marian cult is a recent
implantation in a Catholicism that had long been archaic and in which the
cult of the local saint (Saint Démet) was predominant. There is no Notre
Dame de Plodémet, no Marian oratory, no Marian *pardon* (pilgrimage) in
Plodémet. The procession of August 15 is a meager affair, unlike the great
pardon in Penhors (September 8 in Poulzic), which is traditionally attended
by the people of Plodémet. It would seem that it was at the turn of the
century that the Virgin of Lourdes spread the cult of Mary and the attendant
iconography that still reigns in Catholic homes and in the Church itself.
According to this hypothesis, the cult of Mary flourished with the rise of
Bigouden rural civilization, from 1880 to 1910, of which it was the religious
aspect, and it was also an expression of the first Catholic counteroffensive in
which the Mary of the miracles was set up against the pagan Marianne.

· · ·

The whites are organically linked to the Church in both daily and political life. Whereas red means a duality of politics and religion, white means their unity. The whites constitute the party of Christendom.

The power of the white party extends over practicing Catholic families. According to the fiures published by J. Tranvouez and Monfortrain in *Au pays bigouden* (1964) Catholic practice in Plodémet is the lowest in the canton of Plogastel, but higher than in the southern Bigouden ports.

Twenty-five percent of Plodémet's population attends Sunday mass, which coincides exactly with the percentage of steady white votes in interwar elections, and with that of white votes in the first round of the 1953 municipal elections. The white party constitutes a solid minority bloc of one-quarter of the population, but religion extends to include women and children.

Geographically, the white world is heavily concentrated in the east of the commune, with totally Catholic villages; then disperses, with enclaves in the market-gardening area as at Kéringard and in the poorer land of the north. Most of the white population are farmers (according to Bourlière's sample, 46 percent of the men and 62 percent of the women go to mass), but there is a strong white minority in the town, especially among the tradespeople (29 percent of the men and 42 percent of the women go to mass). Like the red party, the white is an "interclass" party, but its spectrum is smaller and does not include the sailors or the state teachers.

THE MODERNIST TRANSFORMATION

The past seems to crystallize around the church in Plodémet. It is mainly to go to mass that the old men put on their velvet waistcoats and round hats, and the old women their tall Bigouden coiffes. Men and women are separated at church services, and not so long ago mass was still said in Breton.

Still, even the old church is modernizing. It is now heated in winter. Since the liturgical reform, mass has been said in French. The parish priest has promised that men and women would soon be allowed to sit together. The church council no longer consists exclusively of big landowners but is dominated by the activists of the farmers' union, including Kerzinou, the CUMA leader,

Demet, the president of the farmers' union, Gaelic, the model farmer from Pors-en-Breval, and Yvon Le Braz from Kéringard.

In addition to rejuvenating the old institutions, the modern network of social Catholicism has strengthened itself through Catholic Action, the Rural Family Movement with branches for tradespeople and workers, the Rural Movement of Catholic Youth, and the Catholic Parents' Association. There is a fund for loans to farmers and workers. The parish magazine has a monthly printing of one thousand, and copies reach practically every family in the commune.

Father Abel, the parish priest, and Father Azur, the curate, organize and control the white forces, assisted by the active nuns from the Jeanne d'Arc school. They are both social-minded modern priests. The curate has devoted himself enthusiastically to the cause of the modernizing farmers, urging them to form cooperatives. The priest, too, is willing to go along with the new, but is careful to preserve continuity with the past.

Defeated and disrupted politically, reduced to its religious basis, the Catholic party has found in that basis the principles and energies of a rebirth—not in politics, but in social action. Rebirth has been made possible by a crisis. In the course of the century, the Church has had to abandon its totalitarian theocratic claims, the monarchy as a principle, the hierarchies of the past, and the hope of maintaining the traditional agrarian society. Everything that it was still clinging to in the interwar years has been swept away. The time came when it was realized that democratic bourgeois evolution did not bring anarchy or chaos, did not destroy all hierarchy, did not bear within its breast the death of the Church, but gave it new opportunities—when, in other words, it became clear that conservatism could be saved only by compromising with change. First it became clear that the white party must modernize in order to survive; then, that is must modernize in order to revive.

The great reconciliation with the modern world began within the Church, not in political echelons. The new ideas of Catholic Action and Christian personalism spurred a revival that reached Bigouden Catholics during the Occupation and after World War II, and were put into practice in Plodémet between 1955 and 1960.

The breaking up of theocratism opened up a new pluralist field where the orders of faith, social action, and politics were associated and yet distinct. The Church wished to replace the believer with the believing activist. It wished to revive the faith that lay dormant beneath observance, and the action that lay dormant beneath obedience. The faith, the internal principle, was now addressed to modern bourgeois man, one who must live in a profane world and feel the Christian principle in his soul. It must take root in personal life, but not be enclosed by it. It must transform the Christian into a missionary in the modern world, an activist of a truth that must flow into every sector of social life.

The reactionary principle by which change is seen as deterioration was abandoned. There was not only a recognition of the *fait accompli* but support for it. A Copernican revolution took place in Catholic anthropocosmology: it was no longer the world that must revolve around the Church, but the Church that must revolve around the world. Christianity converted itself into progressive humanism—the first principle of red philosophy—but developed its own variant, evolutionist personalism. The Christian principle of improvement was now the rival of the secular principle of progress. The individual was no longer expected to integrate himself into the theo-socio-cosmological order, but became the keystone of the new Christian anthropology.

The Church concentrated its efforts on the family and home, which was still regarded as the primordial unit of all social order, but now, increasingly, as the central setting for human development.

The curate preaches participation in a world that God intended to be modern and which will go to its ruin only if the Church is absent from it. God wants science to progress, but this progress will be effective only if the quality of faith progresses. Science is useful, but its knowledge must be complemented by the teaching of the Church, which alone knows the true nature of man.

The parish magazine expresses this presence in the world along with support for technological and social progress by inserting information favorable to agricultural modernization and cooperatives, sports results, and funny stories among the pious exhortations. The "excesses" of the young arouse less disapproval from the Church than from the town hall. The Church has plunged into the modern world, and this enables it to rejoin the historical development of Plodémet and to intervene in it as a force of social transformation.

In 1950, the white party was still opposing land against school, traditional rural society against urban advancement, although the rural economy was declining and secondary education was becoming general. Of course, the Church still thinks that the education policy of the CEG was excessive and that it retarded the modernization of the commune. Yet the Church transformed its own agrarian conservatism into modernism, which is the only means of preserving a peasant class, and it now fully supports educational advancement.

The funeral of the old tailor Le Moign, the father of Brittany's leading academic figure, was attended by the whole population. Moreover, the school of Jeanne d'Arc sent its pupils as an act of homage. The state school was almost left out: it had not thought of organizing its own procession. Informed at the last minute of the white mobilization, it sent a young couple, both teachers, to round up the pupils, who were on holiday. The event sealed the integration of White Plodémet into the common educational destiny, but showed at the same time that its association with this destiny had become competitive.

THE CATHOLIC RECONQUEST

The opening of the CEG Jeanne d'Arc in 1957 prevented the state CEG from benefitting by the entry of girls into secondary education, increased the intake of the religious primary school, and triggered the Catholic reconquest.

Jeanne d'Arc has gained ground annually since its foundation, and even in absolute figures, there is a slight diminution in the number of girls in the state school. Jeanne d'Arc's 38 percent of all girls attending secondary school (1962) is already well beyond the traditional 25 percent of the white population.

The religious school presents itself as more modern, more humane, more devoted to the pupil than the secular school. The secularists denounce the "extraordinary pressure" exerted and the "disgraceful methods" used by the nuns to recruit students. The scholastic reconquest operates among families of red-white marriages, or families with no political allegiance where the parents generally solve the problem by sending boys to the CEG and girls to the Jeanne d'Arc. It makes its appeal to the women who are more religious than the men and can be made to see where the duty of a Catholic mother lies.

The scholastic reconquest is part of a general offensive of which

the woman is the prime objective, not only because she is more
religious than the man, not only because her role and her power
are increasing with bourgeois achievements, but also because she
feels more strongly than does the man the difficulties of the new
life: lack of communication, and solitude. The reconquest infil-
trates through the cracks and inadequacies in the bourgeois world
and establishes the Catholic protectorate.

While it advances in the bourgeois world, the Church does not
forget its rural bastions, for it has always wanted to prevent the
drift of the traditional Catholic peasantry to the towns. The paths
of conservatism are now leading the Church to modernism and
the cooperative. It all began in the JAC (Young Christian Farmers), through which the Church had been directing the white
rural youth of the commune, and which formed a phalanx that
was imbued with the new spirit. As we know, this activist group
succeeded in taking over the farmers' union in 1955 and completely changing its direction.

Since then, this corps has remained the permanent advance
guard of agricultural modernization. The parish church partici-
pates directly in the effort, both through action and through
publicity (the parish magazine), and supports not only the model
farm but also the cooperative. The curate, drawn into the dialectics of theological modernism and agricultural modernization,
is led to conceive of collective workers' control as the basic ethic
of work: "It would require a certain socialization, by which I
mean running a business in common. *What counts is work as a
common activity among individuals.*"

The Catholic revival has brought with it a noticeable increase
in religious practice in the radically de-Christianized area of
southern Bigoudennie, and to a lesser extent in the still solidly
white north. In Plodémet, according to the parish priest, the
situation seems to be stationary. I am inclined to think that the
stationary state conceals both the continuing de-Christianization
process among the women of the red villages and the beginnings
of a re-Christianization process among the women of the town. In
any case, the regression of Catholicism seems to have been halted.
While awaiting the upward trend, the parish priest believes that
the profundity of faith has deepened. In any case, a historic
transformation has been taking place in the Catholicism of the
commune, an extraordinary social revitalization accompanied, as
we shall see next, by political disintegration.

POLITICAL DISINTEGRATION

Catholicism is alive, but the right is in disarray. The white party no longer constitutes a homogeneous political reality.

The political crisis has a long history, and we reviewed it earlier in some detail. What is relevant here is that in the interwar years the white party maintained the national alliance with an urban right so remote as to be virtually foreign, while it retreated into a Breton-Bigouden regionalism in order to safeguard traditional values. Within the commune, the Church continued to depend upon the now wrecked great families, the big landowners now dispossessed of power and influence. The national right and Breton-Plodémet Catholicism combined to fossilize white politics until 1940.

The disintegration of the national right at the Liberation opened the way for a new policy, especially as the sudden rise of the MRP, a social Christian party, could at last have filled the white void. But the MRP failed to replace the network of traditional notables with its own activist apparatus, and possibly in consequence of that it failed even to rally all of the white vote in the general elections. By 1955, the traditional conservative right regained a good many white votes, and after 1958 the Gaullists split the white electorate. In the 1965 presidential election, the MRP's Lecanuet gained only 325 white votes against De Gaulle's 792; in the second round, the left-wing Mitterand captured a hundred of Lecanuet's votes.

The MRP never really seized a beachhead in White Plodémet. Unlike its counterparts, the German and Italian Christian Democrats, the MRP was a stillborn social Christian party; at the national level, it failed to take in the heterogeneous blocs of the Christian left, the various centrist groups, or the old right, and also failed to absorb the rapidly developing social Catholic associations which remained semi-autonomous between the Church and the party. Also, the white world of Plodémet was still too hesitant and already too divided between the old reactionary tendencies and the new social trends to be able to form a new political unity; the energies of the new Catholicism flowed directly from the Church into social action. Finally, the MRP aggravated rather than healed the division within the white party —one that was to be aggravated still more some years later by the traditional conservative right and the Gaullists. There is still no indication that the Gaullists will succeed in recovering the political heritage of a dismembered white party, on either the national or the communal level.

The first long political crisis of the white party was essentially a side effect of the Catholic Church's remoteness from the modern world; the second originated in the Church's reconciliation with it. The reactionary fixation in the first half of the century had isolated and fossilized the white party, whereas modernism saved it culturally and socially only to disintegrate it politically. It was inevitable that it should explode the old right-wing ideology to make room for a few reactionary enclaves, a conservative-evolutionist mainstream, and an agricultural advance guard.

Evolutionist conservatism is the dominant current. Even the old white chieftain of Poulzic, the boss of the cannery, feels at ease amid the change. When we spoke to him, he praised Pope John XXIII, expressed sympathy with the needs of the young, and reminisced with amused and unsentimental tenderness about the knife fights that used to take place between whites and reds. Evolutionist conservatism is a sort of centrist policy that seeks to reconcile stability and modernity, continuity and renewal.

The advance guard, which grew out of agricultural syndicalism, has passed beyond evolutionist conservatism. It was compelled to conduct the only instance of class struggle Plodémet has known since the decline of the big landowners, by confronting the industrialists of the cannery business, Hanff in particular. Whites against whites! Catholics against Catholics! The split manifested itself in a different form in the 1965 municipal elections, when the advance guard refused to back the right-wing list of traditional notables. Union action has led to strikes and proletarian solidarities; it has brought cooperation with the municipality over land redistribution and the attempt to infiltrate the red bastion (the election of Le Kam). The union advance guard already envisages a development plan beyond communal frontiers on a regional scale, and is already aware of national and European dimensions. By posing cooperation as the solution of the agricultural problem, it may well glimpse a socialist horizon. But this syndicalist advance guard is wandering in a political no man's land, beyond the MRP, and beyond the traditional left; it prefigures a new section of a new left, if such a thing were to appear; yet it always sees itself on the right.

"A Catholic must be on the right," said Yvon, the president of the AEP—a private school. "But I agree with the left's social policy and all that," he added. "The union was run by the right, wasn't it?"

"It still is as far as many of the leaders are concerned. Many of them used to belong to the JAC."

"You think the JAC is right-wing?"

"What do you mean by right-wing?"

The two ideas of Catholic and the right have not yet been separated because the great changes have been nonpolitical. But the signifier-signified relation has been reversed: Catholic once meant the right; today, the right means Catholic.

WHITE SECULARITY

A dialectic is developing the infra- and suprapolitical strength and influence of the white party while accentuating its political disintegration. It seems as if the energies that were immobilized by an obsolete political outlook had been freed by the great modernist transformation and transferred to new social activities.

The rejuvenation of the white activists contrasts with the senescence of the reds in the period 1950–1965. Whereas the apparatus of the red party contracted to a small nucleus of teachers, Catholic activists were emerging in both the town and the countryside, and the farmers' union was being run by young men in their thirties.

Yet even among the advance guard, the demographic gap in youth and the disappointments of 1962–1965 are producing a crisis of energy. The young men who came out of the JAC have lost much of their impetus; the pioneers are weary and have to struggle against discouragement. Kermelec feels old at thirty-eight.

Also, the crisis of the union advance guard goes beyond that of the activists. There is danger that native cooperativism will be swallowed up in the supercooperative of Landernau, and that the union movement will either become almost exclusively a technical-corporate activity or find expression in a political part that will concern itself with the regional development of Finistère. This would be another expression of the vitality of social Christianity, and at the same time testify to the insuperable difficulties facing any advance-guard action in Plodémet today.

The religious, cultural, and social vitality of the Catholic party is expressed in victories in every extrapolitical field—the school, the union, and the various lay associations. But the whites are still dominated by the larger following and political strategy of the red party. The breach between religion and Plodémet society has been closed, but the breach between religion and politics has widened. The separation of Church and politics came about through the reconciliation of Church and society. The religious, cultural, and social advance of Catholicism goes hand in hand with the political crisis of the white party. The whites have almost ceased to be a political party, but religion is seeping back into the infrastructure of both parties and trying to rise above them.

Bicolor-Tricolor

FROM SIAMESE-TWIN SOCIETY TO BICEPHALOUS SOCIETY

The two-party system continues to dominate the political life of Plodémet. For the intransigents in both camps, Plodémet is still two societies in one, every face and activity identified by color; the activist is often unaware of the changes in social reality.

A process of pacification between the two groups began in 1914, and the two wars united the civil enemies against the foreign enemy (with the exception perhaps of the perturbing influence of Vichy from 1940 to 1942). The interwar period brought political stabilization as well as increasing autonomy to the individual and to the married couple in relation to the patriarchal family and village. Political allegiance ceased to be an integral dimension of family identity and became subject to individual opinion.

The terrorism of collective opinion is being replaced by the tolerance of individual opinion. Still, individuality is suspended in the area between the person and his home; although everyone thinks he has his own opinion, there seems to be little difference of views within the family. A girl from a red family, for example, broke with her Catholic fiancé, despite her personal feelings, because he insisted that she become a practicing Catholic.

Nevertheless, intransigent parents or engaged couples are rare these days. We asked Mme. Traon, the wife of a white agricultural activist from Penquer, "Would you agree to your daughter's

marrying someone who has no religion or belongs to a religion
other than Catholic?"

"It's not up to us to decide for her," she answered. "It's our job
to bring her up properly. After that, she will have to decide for
herself."

Freedom of marriage has already created many mixed homes.
Intermarriage does not present special problems, as reds adhere
to church weddings and have not yet accepted divorce. The
principles of reciprocal tolerance and compromise are instilled
in the home; often, daughters are sent to the religious school and
sons to the state school.

Similarly, the old practice of economic segregation is breaking
down. The new psychology of money, profit, and necessities cuts
across the divisions of red and white. The younger generation of
tradespeople want to overcome the barriers that predetermine
their customers. The spirit of reconciliation—"being on good
terms with everybody"—is spreading among the tradespeople as
it is among their customers, some of whom patronize two or three
tradesmen in order to avoid "ill feeling." The reds' doctor is no
longer a red doctor, and no longer exclusively the red's doctor.

The decline of the patriarchal family and village and the advance of the monetary economy are factors in the rise of bourgeois
individualism. The focus of aspirations on private life brings a
diminution of public life. The great key idea of the personal life
competes with collective key ideas. The activists must take television programs into account when organizing meetings, which
in any case no longer attract the audiences they once did. Red or
white identity, in normal times repressed or forgotten, is aroused
only by the political passions of elections.

The younger the people, the less acute their political opposition. The youth club deliberately excluded white-red antagonism, even white-red distinctions.

At the same time, an uncommitted vote made its appearance
between the traditional allegiances, cast by those swayed by the
uncertain winds of national politics, by immigrants lacking local
affiliations or not wishing to alienate themselves from one side
or the other, by prudent tradesmen and craftsmen, and by mixed
couples putting their eggs in both baskets.

Reconciliation has even reached the Le Bail household. The
Le Bails have never had white farmers on their land, but recently

when Jenny Le Bail could not find a red replacement she accepted a white one.

"I don't give a damn if he's a Catholic," said Jenny Le Bail, and added, "This is the only house in the town where the priest has never set foot, but I don't feel as violently anticlerical as I used to."

But though reduced and weakened, the old party division has not been abolished. It is alive in the hearts of the militants and revives among the population generally at election time—especially at municipal elections. The old frontiers are set up and the old divisions reappear. In 1965, a red baker sent back some flour to a Catholic miller who was a candidate, complaining that it was "too white." But once the elections are over, peace returns.

What remains, then, of the long-standing radical opposition between two worlds, two doctrines, two political outlooks? The red or white identification is buried at an obscure level of consciousness, linked to family and civic identity. It is broader and deeper than purely political allegiance, less deep than family identity, and is part of both. The "Siamese twin" society has been replaced by a bicephalous society. The two have been reduced to mechanisms with sharply contracted fields of action and influence. One has virtually abandoned politics; the other is devitalized by loss of active support. Politics itself has become seasonal, sectorized, specialized.

The two great concepts have retracted into their inner cores: there is now the secular principle and the Christian principle. Erosion and evolution are doing their work.

THE GEL

In spite of erosion, the increase in the uncommitted vote, dislocation, and political fossilization, the two-party system still dominates the *politeia* of Plodémet.

France became tricolored when the development of the urban proletariat set the red worker in opposition to the blue bourgeois. In Plodémet, however, the plebeian red did not suppress the blue of the bourgeois revolution but integrated it into an emancipating republicanism. In fact, the fundamental orientation in Plodémet was never anything but emancipating in the context of the aspirations of the small landowner and bourgeois (blue), but the impetus was always plebeian (red). The red of Plodémet is distinguished from the red and blue of France in the sense that it is the common point of origin of both.

This lack of differentiation is understandable in that Plodémet society was able to achieve and maintain the French Revolution's principle of smallholder emancipation along with the Third Republic's principle of scholastic emancipation. Baillism had been responsible for this success, made possible only because Plodémet society remained as a sociological gel that maintained, protected, and fortified the egalitarian structures of smallholders until 1940. Outside Plodémet, republican bourgeois society allowed for educational development, and the industrial capitalism of the cities allowed for the emigration of the demographic surplus. By remaining outside, big capitalism did not bring in its ancillary urban inequalities, and undeveloped, seasonal local industry did not create a proletariat. The rural proletariat was absorbed by mobility and emigration while the emergence of the urban wage-earning class was a step toward becoming middle class rather than toward proletarianization. Moreover, the shared feeling of being abandoned and underdeveloped confirmed the emergent red *petite bourgeoisie* in its loyalty to the "little man" in general. In the final analysis, it was the conjunction of progress (emancipation and educational advancement) and lack of progress (absence of capitalist development, small-business economy) that safeguarded the unity of blue bourgeois and red plebeian in Plodémet.

After the Liberation, the Socialists and Communists revitalized the red party, which had lost much of its color during the last years of the Baillist era. They did not bring division, but reaffirmed the unity of plebeian red and republican blue. They did not reject *embourgeoisement*, but excluded from the alliance the upper bourgeoisie and big capitalism; this exclusion was confirmed by the threat to the Plodémet economy by the big firms of the richer regions. Socialism and communism entered and spread at a time when, far from wishing to overthrow the Republic, they claimed to have assumed its direction and to be pursuing its social mission. The fall of the red party between 1945 and 1959 was not the result of the Communists' refusal to join it but of the Radicals' refusal to allow the Communists to join it.

The red party was restored by the left-wing alliance of 1959, but left-right polarization did not supersede red-white opposition.

The notions of "left" and "right" are not deeply rooted in Plodé-met, although they serve as convenient code words to express local allegiances in national terms. Indeed, it needed the divisions of 1945–1959 within the red party for the notion of "left" to emerge as a new principle of reunification. But it became part of the notion of red, rather than replacing it. "Red" remains more precise and more institutional than "left," because it refers essentially to the Republic, to secularization, and to mobility through education. The alliance of the left-wing parties in Plodémet was formed to maintain this heritage, whereas the alliance of the national left-wing parties was formed some years later in an opposition to Gaullist power.

At the same time that the red party is drawing closer to the program of the national left without becoming absolutely indistinguishable from it, the white party is ceasing to be closely linked to the national right, what with the disintegration of this right and the Catholic renaissance. Politically last, it nevertheless remains more than ever "white" in the sense that the term identifies it with the Church.

In sum, the red and white in the Plodémet of 1965 were the old matrices that gave traditional forms to the new movements, and at the same time they were the crucibles in which the changes were taking place. Our analysis has attempted to embrace both aspects. The first of these is simple: the secular red and the Christian white are residues of an extensive political erosion that has reduced both parties to their nuclei. The second aspect is complex. The whites are undergoing a transformation in which religious-social rebirth and political disintegration are closely linked. The reds are at once neutralized, sustained, and modified by the dialectic between plebeian and bourgeois. They wish to maintain in a complementary, not antagonistic, way the dual consciousness, the dual reality of a Plodémet still half plebeian and already half bourgeois; and it is by maintaining the red in the blue and the blue in the red that communism has been able to take root and left-wing unity made possible, with the *petite bourgeoisie* continuing to lean toward the national left-wing parties, albeit with a new inconstancy.

THE METABOLIC DISTURBANCE

The opposition between the two parties is no longer an expression of an internal class struggle between the "little man" and the

big landlord; there are no longer any characteristic social inequalities between reds and whites. The opposition between the
two fundamental principles, the Christian and the secular, no
longer concerns the bases of society. Christianity and secularization are no longer the nuclei of two worlds, but two competing
principles within a single world.

Both white and red are now humanistic and evolutionist in
principle. They are both in favor of collective *embourgeoisement.*
Although they each have their own conservatism, the one a smallholder conservatism, the other a religious, they are both far removed from any extremism or adventurism. Although they both
claim allegiance to something more than higher living standards,
neither has a policy that goes beyond the attainment of such
standards. The red party has achieved its program of plebeian
emancipation and educational advancement, and has no socialist
program for the future. The white party has abandoned its policy
of a return to the past.

In these circumstances, the red party no longer automatically
attracts everything that is democratic, evolutionist, and progressive, nor the white party everything that is traditional, conservative, and hierarchical. The emergent agrarian capitalism of the
contractors is developing among red supporters, while the white
militants are the driving force behind the cooperative advance
guard and the struggle against the capitalistic factory owner.
There is even an inversion of progressive optimism and nostalgia
for the past among the older red teachers and the Catholic priests.

Moreover, the Plodémet party division no longer embraces the
whole of political activity. Until the war, the vote in communal
and national elections followed the same pattern: the reds voted
radical and the whites for the right-wing parties. Since 1945, and
especially since 1958, the reds no longer vote unanimously and
consistently for the left-wing parties (even in 1967 nearly four
hundred red votes went on the second ballot to the UNR); the
white votes are divided between the UNR and the MRP. Whether
it is a temporary or a lasting phenomenon, Gaullism has revealed
a double political consciousness; the national consciousness contradicts, to some extent, the communal consciousness, to the detriment of the traditional white and red parties.

Various erratic trends have been appearing on the ideological
level of late. In addition to the uncommitted vote which is largely
outside the influence of either party, there has been the emergence

of the neo-blues—that is, blues not in the sense of the Revolution
but in a sense that goes beyond both red and white. "We are
blues," said Alain, president of the youth club. "What we need
is a blue municipality," said Bonnard, whose family is red. The
neo-blues are generally men under forty; they condemn the sectarianism of whites and reds, and above all else, they want compe-
tence and efficiency. A young activist farmer said, "It doesn't
matter what political side they're on, so long as they serve people
well. That's what they're there for . . . There should be capable
people on both sides." Duloch, who is from a red family, said,
"You don't vote for the party nowadays, you vote for the man.
What matters is whether he's competent or not."

The blue tendency exists among both whites and reds, although its main source seems to lie in the social reconversion of
whites who have adopted certain red traits but want to eliminate
red sectarianism and immobility. The neo-blue gives priority to
practical achievements, modern technology, and development.
The oft-mentioned Le Kam is perhaps the first neo-blue politician
in Plodémet. He has been playing a leading role in the white
farmers' union; he was elected to the municipal council with
Communist backing. He supported the MRP candidate Lecanuet
in the 1965 presidential elections. The unifying elements in his
disparate political behavior are his attachment to the union cause
and the priority he gives to the problem of development. He told
us that he strongly approved the words of Le Braz, an old union
activist and the last of a long line of white farmers, who disavowed
both white and red: "The union has done more for this region in
a few years than politics has in decades."

The example of Le Kam shows that it is now possible to play
a political role without being confined exclusively to one of the
two parties. At the same time, it is impossible to play a role inde-
pendently of the parties. Le Kam has a foot in both camps.

THE POLITICAL NO MAN'S LAND

A total political crisis cannot be excluded from future possibility. A political no man's land between white and red, which
eats into the support of both, is occupied by unpredictable forces
(the uncommitted vote), by a virtual center, by opportunistic
notables, and by technologically oriented neo-blues. Will these

forces be absorbed into the system or will they tear it apart? In the latter case, notables and neo-blues, either together or separately, might play a polarizing role in the new combinations. Whether integration takes place or not, is there any chance of the emergence of an advance guard? In my opinion, it can come about only by a union of a cooperativist advance guard, a technological advance guard, and an advance guard of teachers.

The resolution of these questions will not come only or even principally from Plodémet. It will come partly from the nation, but it must also pass through the crucible of the region.

The region is the new economic and social context to which the commune is increasingly linked, and any policy of communal development—except for tourism—is now inseparable from regional poles of development and centers of decision. Moreover, a region like Sud-Finistère requires a development program involving both the full deployment of local forces and national intervention and investment.

Our project was carried out at a time when it was already possible to catch a glimpse of the sociological future of Plodémet, but not yet to decipher the new, contradictory political possibilities.

POLITICAL CIVILIZATION TO THE TEST

The old political division of Plodémet extended beyond politics. Politics itself constituted merely one horizontal level in a double system of vertical integration in which all the dimensions of social man were involved. It is precisely this that gave Plodémet politics its paleototalitarian character.

I have used the term "paleototalitarian" to signify that this totalitarianism was already archaic in relation to modern totalitarianism.

The white part of Plodémet was attached, not to the evolutive pre-Revolution monarchy, but to the medieval theocratic order that was still firmly rooted at the beginning of the twentieth century, and to the monarchist party of the nineteenth century, which was a rallying point for everything in religion, politics, philosophy, and society that opposed the French Revolution.

The old red totalitarianism was determined by the total struggle against white totalitarianism and by the quasi-religious affirmation of progressive-evolutionist humanism. This humanism was really religious, because it formed a unifying factor in a multiform struggle and gave an aura of sanctity and devotion to the New Ideas. It transferred to history—to progress—the victory over evil and poverty, that is, salvation. It made the people and the nation the source of all political truth. The People's State became the supreme sovereign power. On these bases, secular, democratic, republican, social, and revolutionary, humanism was able to provide not only a type of ideal society but also the advancement of man, as represented by the Individual, the People, and the State. Proclaimed first by the French Revolution; then by the Communist revolution, the religion of man—although opposed in spirit to the religion of God—has been the second religion of the West. Just as the first religion extended its scale from the Anabaptists to the Catholics, the religion of man extended its scale from libertarianism to totalitarianism. It was in its organicist form that it spread to a large part of rural-plebeian-republican France, where the great archaic family-clan itself constituted a totalitarian microsociety. This is why, despite its Bolshevik–post-Tsarist–Stalinist foreignness, the virtual totalitarianism of French communism was able to harmonize so well with the old red base in Plodémet.

Red politics has amply fulfilled its civilizing mission, and Catholic civilization has been amply political. This little outlying commune is still a center of political civilization, where people are still more politically educated than in many towns. Political participation and an interest in general ideas, in principles, institutions, and social development, have been very strong here. Hence the atrophy of artistic and literary culture, which have been sacrificed to political culture. It is even possible that the existence of these two political civilizations has spared Plodémet, since 1950, from the outbreaks of political barbarism (of the Poujadist type) that might have been provoked by the tragedy of the small business.

The red civilization flourished in the CEG. The CEG was an instrument of social transformation through the emancipation-advancement-transformation of the rural populace, a temple of learning, a center of humanist philosophy and of political influence and action; it became the Kremlin of the red community. The Church, too, is still a center of civilization and culture, and, with the advent of social Christianity, more so than ever.

And in Plodémet, neither the humanist religion nor religion turned humanist is condemned to death in the new age. Already the old Catholic religion has accomplished the Copernican revolution that integrates it into the future; it is now within bourgeois society, manipulating its tools, slipping into its cracks, lying in wait for its weak points. The younger humanist religion is still fighting a rear-guard action; it is entering its own crisis and may need its own Copernican revolution, in which the world will cease to turn around man so that man, the seeker in time and space, may turn around the world. Will humanism be able to accomplish its cultural revolution?

The two centers of culture-civilization-ideology are not, then, on the point of dying out. The new direction of Plodémet society —and of French society—is moving toward a breaking up into specialized, autonomous sectors of what was once organically linked in each of the two systems: the political, social, economic, cultural, educational, religious, and philosophical. Will the empirical-technological politics that is bound to develop sooner or later break up the two old parties, or will the red and (or) the white party succeed in integrating the future policy of development? But the question of the future can no longer be asked in symmetrical terms for red and white. Will the white party cease to be a political party? Will the red party cease to be a center of civilization?

10

The Modern Age

Time

THE PRESENT

"What is modern?"—this was the only question that we constantly
asked the people of Plodémet; the word "modern" aroused almost
universal approval among them before any attempt was made
at definition.

Modern denotes the ideas of evolution, progress, and well-
being. For the old plebeians, the evolution has come from progress, that is, from the actions of the red party, from new ideas,
and from education. The modern is generally identified with the
twentieth century and contrasted with "the old days," which are
seen as dark, barbarous, and poverty-stricken. The popular consciousness retains the feeling of having emerged from the Middle
Ages at the beginning of the twentieth century. For the younger
generations, progress is not so much a fighting ideology as a
result; it tends to be identified with evolution, which is the natural
or "normal" course of modern society. The change of attitude in
the Church has brought evolution and the modern world into
universal favor. For everybody, evolution and progress are seen
as a state of general well-being.

Technical progress, economic development, education, and
social security converge in well-being, which takes the form of
material comfort and greater autonomy in work and private life.

This conception of modernity, fundamentally recognized and
desired by all, is the basis of two belief systems, each with its own

connotations. The old world-view, what we might call the "paleo-modern belief system," regards the modern as a vast civilizing-cultural-economic-social entity in which the Republic, for example, cannot be dissociated from technical progress. It is ruled by a constellation consisting of enlightenment (education, Baillism), collective advancement, technical achievements, and social security (from scholarship to retirement pension).

The contemporary world-view, or "mesomodern belief system," which developed largely after 1950, is centered on the individual attainment of well-being and private autonomy. Education remains a value of prime importance, but it is dissociated from the notion of enlightenment and becomes centered on advancement through professional qualifications. Technology is regarded as the new nature of evolution and progress. The young accentuate the tendencies toward technical advancement, personal autonomy, and leisure activity, together with a strong taste for the new, the fashionable, the ephemeral present, the diverting. The older generations identify the modern with the twentieth century, while the young reduce it to mean novelty, the avant-garde, youth itself. "The youth center and modern mean the same thing," one of them said to us.

The acceleration of modernization can become perturbing in the sense that it requires a continuous adaptation to innovation and change. "You always have to move faster . . ." "You have to modernize all the time . . ." say those under thirty-five, such as Cloédic, the manager of the furniture factory, and Donatien, a craftsman. But for men over thirty-five, "Everything's changing too quickly" (Bozer, wine merchant).

There is a fear of speed, of excess itself. "People want to go too far, be too modern . . . they want to have everything" (Mme. Michel, from Menez-Ru). "The young want everything, and at once" (the mayor). The teacher Le Bellec fears that excessive comfort will result in a crisis of morality.

For others, such as merchant seamen whose jobs are jeopardized by automation, progress is beginning to seem ambivalent. Technology makes work easier, but adaption to it is difficult. "In one way it's easier, in another it's more difficult; you have to work with your head," one of the three brothers-in-law of the GAEC cooperative told us. Moreover, some farmers and teachers feel that in the last ten years a dissociation has been taking place between the two components of modernity that were indissolubly linked in the Baillist era: progress and evolution. "We follow evolution, but not progress; only the big fellows can follow progress," said Duloch. For the old teachers, the dissociation even becomes a partial divergence, and they discern a new opposition between material and moral progress. Some of them even form a conclusion that contradicts the overwhelming evidence of most of the population of Plodémet. "People are not happier today," said the mayor, a belief also expressed by Narour, a young farmer, and in a different way by Jean Kéravrec, a young merchant seaman, who has visited the United States and decided that Americans are "not happier than the French," although they are more advanced technologically and have higher living standards. At the extreme, crisis becomes the most striking aspect of progress, even for those who have carried its banner for half a century. They share Le Bellec's terrible definition: "What is the modern? The bomb!" But he added at once, as if to correct a flippancy: "Labor-saving devices."

Doubts, even when extreme, are not cast on the fundamental nature of the modern, only on its ambivalences and perils which are projected into the future. It is remarkable indeed that despite the disruptions that technological progress has brought to the commune during the past fifteen years, there is no apparent fear of or revolt against the machine. Essentially it is politics, not technology, backwardness, not evolution, that stand accused. It is the insufficiency and not the excess of modernism which is the cause of discontent. There is no nostalgia for a pretechnological world; the people of Plodémet feel and know that they are caught up in an ascending spiral of well-being. Evolution, progress, and well-being are no longer absolutely unitary as they once were for the red populace in paleomodern days. The different forms of progress (collective, individual, technological, moral, material) can, as the teachers realize, either collaborate or oppose each other. On the other hand, progress is no longer regarded by the mesomoderns as the monopoly of a single political party, but is becoming embedded in the nature of society itself.

THE PAST

The nineteenth century has no defenders in Plodémet. Duloch is considered a fool when he declares that "People were happier then; they were free . . . What's the use of education? . . . There's too much of it." Among peasants, craftsmen, tradesmen, and seamen, there is no wish to rehabilitate the past. Young people do not dream of a bucolic world where man lived in harmony with nature; the experience of the old is still present to remind them that the past meant poverty, ignorance, and subjection.

Only a few formerly large landowners are wistful about the past. Even the whites agree that life is pleasanter today, and the crisis of small business has not undermined this belief.

The ethical rejection of the past has come to include an aesthetic condemnation of everything that seems to belong to it. This does not apply to traditional Bigouden arts and dress which, as we have seen, flourished with the modern awakening (1880–1910) and are regarded as links to the genuine, historical past. It does, however, apply to old houses, old furniture, old objects and utensils, all made old-fashioned by the new suburban styles. It is not so much the old as the old-fashioned that has come to be regarded as ugly.

Houses from past centuries, some of them decorated with Gothic ornaments, which are still to be found in the countryside, are regarded by both townspeople and country people as old, dark, and dirty. They are converted into stables or sheds, and those that are still lived in will not be renovated but abandoned when the new, impatiently awaited modern house is built. The Renaissance manor of Kerzibou is used as a farmhouse; "It's too big and too cold, and the ceilings are too high," its owners say disdainfully.

The affair of the Maison Kérizit was revealing in this respect. An early eighteenth-century three-story house, standing by itself opposite the crossing of the Ensker road, it was the oldest secular building in the town. The municipality had bought it in a dilapidated state with the intention of demolishing it to make way for a parking lot. Jean-Claude Le Bail, who is an architect as well as municipal councilor, failed to persuade his colleagues to preserve the building. He appealed to the Ministry of Culture, and the day before the demolition was to begin a telegram to the mayor placed the house under the protection of the State, pending further decision.

From then on, passions were inflamed against the house that had been preserved by a "plot"; only a small minority led by

Jenny Le Bail and Mme. Luc, a retired schoolmistress, wanted to save it. Mme. Luc launched an "appeal to the authorities to restore the Maison Kérizit to its former splendor," and proposed that it be converted into either a Bigouden museum, a youth center, or even a town hall. Eventually, the obstinate municipal council succeeded in having the old house demolished in March 1966.

The few supporters of preservation were not to be found among the teachers, despite the campaign led by Mme. Luc. They were isolated individuals, like the educated farmer Cloédic ("It's got something about it"), a union activist ("The façade is beautiful"), the proprietress of the Ty-Koz *crêperie* ("It's very beautiful, we ought to save it"). Among the old peasants, we noted respect for the size of the building, rather than aesthetic admiration. Among the tradespeople, there was marked dislike. "It's a horror. It ought to be pulled down," said Marie of the Café des Droits de l'Homme.

"Certainly, the Maison Kérizit has to be pulled down, mainly because it's ugly. I can't understand how people can like such things," declared Hervé, the pork butcher.

The working-class teen-agers of the town all found it "old, ugly, and ready to be pulled down." The teacher Le Bellec said, "In my opinion, it's not a beautiful building." In the course of the debate in the municipal council a majority judged it to be ugly. "I've no artistic education," one councilor said, "but ordinary people know what's beautiful—Quimper Cathedral, for example."

The anti-Kérizit group published an article in the newspaper *Ouest-France* (December 1, 1965), complete with photograph, claiming that "this decrepit building stands in the way of traffic development" and "detracts from the beauty of the church and the war memorial." The final outcome was, above all, an aesthetic condemnation of the old-fashioned.

Outside pressure alone compels people in Plodémet to respect old architectural forms; local taste favors the modern suburban style, and only the state-imposed regulations concerning traditional forms and colors slow down and limit the suburbanization of the landscape. Construction norms established by the State control the vicinity of the church, much to the chagrin of the electrician and the pork butcher, who were forced to alter the original plans for their store fronts. The admiration of tourists has also helped to cast new light on old buildings in local eyes.

The convergence of opposite currents has resulted in the appearance of new-old houses in the town, which combine bourgeois comfort and neon lighting with ancient elements such as jutting eaves, tiled mansard roofs, and bonded stonework.

The aesthetic reaction against the old-fashioned is evident inside the house also. Beams and hearths are held to be not only useless but also symbols of poverty and therefore ugly. The fireplace is blocked up and concealed behind a curtain or door. In the first stage of modernization, old furniture was thrown away, used as rabbit hutches, sold for very little, or exchanged for new department-store furniture. In the last ten years, however, the abuse of old furniture has stopped, as Parisians—whether originally from Plodémet, summer visitors, or retired—have displayed admiration for old furniture and objects and actually sought them out. Eventually, country people began to realize the value of their old clocks, dressers, and copper pans, and refused to sell them.

In this manner, the break with the past has been halted by urban economic demand and aesthetic intimidation. Objects once judged to be obsolete have acquired dignity by acquiring market value. The native estimates aesthetic dignity on the basis of the amount and quality of manual work put into the object: "It's all handmade!" Or he discovers the special nobility of the old, and the idea of a thing being old and therefore ugly is converted into its being old and therefore beautiful! And even in this, in the return to the past, Plodémet follows the direction taken by modern urban mythology.

Certain pieces of furniture that have been rehabilitated, especially those associated with the great flowering of traditional crafts at the turn of the century, are viewed as manifestations of ancient Bigouden sentiment. Most houses are furnished in a mixed style: the kitchen is ultramodern, a laboratory for household appliances; the dining room is department-store modern; and here and there one sees an old dresser, an old clock, and sometimes an old cupboard.

While Plodémet wants to do away with outward signs of its former poverty and sometimes of its rusticity, it has not lost its nostalgia for the old communal events: harvest festivals, "high days," village wakes, and Sunday games in the village square. All these festivities had begun to die out even before 1939, but the old people who reject the past and its deprivations without reservation still regret the passing of the great collective festivities.

This nostalgia is no doubt enhanced by the nostalgia for childhood and youth common to all adults and enhanced by the aging of a commune where the villages are in decline and the young are absent, and which has lost the collective gaiety of the summer holidays when the young amused themselves, by themselves and in their own way, and in which the new culture (television) encloses the individual in his own home. This nostalgia is centered particularly (as is the aesthetic recovery of the craftsmanship of the past) on the great period of rustic and popular culture which flourished with and in the post-1880 improvement in living standards and with paleomodernism, and which declined between 1930 and 1950.

This nostalgia is not turned against the acquisitions of the modern age, or even against the new domestic privacy, which is deplored but practiced. The fact is that domestic privacy is chosen no less than merely submitted to. Still, one is aware of the lack of festivities and communication.

It is the migrants who are beginning to develop an obsession with a past which they identify with family roots and Bigouden origins. Besides the usual urban nostalgia for a rustic, simple, healthy, "natural" life, the migrants yearn to recover their abandoned roots.

The rejection of the past in Plodémet had struck at black bread, *bouillie,* and crêpes, but the migrants who come home are reclaiming these banished foods. During the summer vacation of 1965, the Kéravrez baker baked black bread three or four times a week for the first time in ten years. Since 1964, he has been baking *kouigne* once a week at the request of summer visitors who remember the Shrove Tuesdays of their youth. The crêpe has returned also; the Ty-Koz *crêperie* makes crêpes every day in the summer and twice a week during the rest of the year.

The migrants are also avidly interested in folklore and in brushing up their dialect, and their interest may increase with the distance and degree of uprooting. For example, the son of a migrant, who goes back regularly to Menez-Ru for his vacations, has begun to learn Breton, wants to improve it by taking a course in Paris, and would like to take part in a *bagad,* or folk-music group.

The recovery of the past—which is an attempt to safeguard one's identity from the threatening anonymity of city life—can only be aesthetic in nature, that is, experienced in a split of consciousness wherein the uprooted urban component remains present if not dominant. The neofolklore of black bread, crêpes, *kouigne*, *bagad*, and the Breton language is an appeal from the outside, not a tradition maintained from within. Aesthetic recovery betrays the distance that separates one from the past that one wants to bring closer by imitation. It is because the past is dead that it can return in an aesthetic form.

The inhabitants of the commune, half belonging to the past and half committed to modern civilization, are divided between the parallel ethical condemnation and aesthetic cultivation of the old. Under the influence of the migrants, they have been led to reconsider and révaluate their heritage and to make a new distinction between things associated with primordial identity (to be preserved and honored), and things that result from backwardness (to be condemned). Thus on the one hand Plodémet is exorcising its "medieval" period, and on the other, claiming its heritage.

The growing pains of integration in a world where Bigouden features are beginning to blur within the larger regional framework, the widespread scholastic emigration of teen-agers, the early stages of an adaptation to urban models, the dissolution of rustic-plebeian culture—all these factors are creating initial conditions for the emergence of a concern with identity. Plodémet is now beginning to desire an identification with Bigoudennie, which has been taken for granted until now. There are teen-agers nowadays who insist on using Breton as the language of friends and family and on going to watch the bonfires on Midsummer Night, while at the same time being devoted to the absorption of urban culture.

The custom of bonfires has been successfully revived. Besides the sad spectacle of fires built of old tires and assorted rubbish, surrounded by a circle of silent figures, there are many lively bonfires, as the one attended by Jenny Le Bail and her Parisian friends. Sweet Breton melodies sung by old women alternate with patriotic songs of old men and pop songs of the young.

In Menez-Ru bands of teen-agers go from bonfire to bonfire on their motorbikes, acolytes in quest of the divine fire. Nevertheless, Saint John's fires—as they are called—are no longer the fires of

Saint John. The old secret has been lost. When asked, "Why do you have bonfires on Saint John's Day?" people have no real answer, only a generality such as "to show the young what it was like in the old days." The bonfires are a sort of rekindling of the flame of the unknown Celt, of primordial identity. Plodémet is entering a stage of modernity in which people turn to the past because it is dead, to their roots because they are threatened, to their identity because it is perturbed.

THE FUTURE

The vision of the future has always been an optimistic one in the red consciousness of Plodémet. Baillism was based on the idea of progress; socialism and communism prophesied a revolution that would transform mankind; during the first half of the century, there seemed to be a harmonious conjunction of personal-familial, professional, communal, and general visions of the future. Today, on the contrary, one can distinguish four separate futures.

The future of the individual and the family is one in which the most emotional capital is invested. It encompasses a span of ten to twenty years, which is looked forward to with confidence. Well-being will improve further; the different stages of life will be protected, with education providing a good job, and the job providing a secure retirement; family advancement will take another leap forward with the secondary or higher education of the young and with the attainment of the bourgeois condition.

Personal-familial optimism parallels professional pessimism in the case of farmers who foresee the end of peasantry, a great many tradesmen and craftsmen who are witnesses to the decline of their business, and merchant seamen whose livelihood is threatened by the automation of shipping. Yet despite widespread professional pessimism, personal-familial optimism remains dominant.

The communal future of Plodémet provides another contrast to personal future. The hope of industrial development has now been abandoned, and the transformation of the commune into a vacation and retirement resort, viewed as a symptom of economic decadence and demographic aging, presents a picture of irremediable decline. Most of the people we talked to manifested a certain fatalism, and foresaw a stabilized future combining good and bad elements stretching over ten or twenty years, beyond which they saw nothing. "Come back to Plodémet in twenty years and you'll see houses for rats," predicted Gaelic.

These prophecies are limited to one decade or two, demonstrating the magic of round figures (in 1962 Kourganoff was told, "In ten years there'll be no one left here at all"), but they point to a belief in a discontinuous future. Ten to twenty years are seen in a semicrystallized, "reified" way, but beyond that comes the abyss of the unknown and the unknowable.

Individual prospects are rising, but the future of the commune is in doubt. Few people would regard the present decline as the first stage of a rebirth. The crisis of the old economy still conceals new possibilities. Long-term thinking is left to the regional experts, who emphasize the processes of decline. The town hall is too busy overcoming the backward state of the commune—roads, public water supply, schools—which is still hampering immediate development. Only the advance guard of the farmers' union, assisted by study groups throughout Finistère, has made a proper study of long-term development, but it knows that hope is subject to factors beyond the communal and even the regional level.

The preponderance of optimism over pessimism indicates that the personal-familial world can now distinguish and detach itself from the collective world, and even contradict it, expressing its supremacy thereby.

The general future lies outside the field of consideration in Plodémet. The future of France is hardly thought about; it does not seem threatened in any particular way, or destined for any particular mission or grandeur. In the course of our inquiry, the future of mankind did not arise spontaneously in conversation. The subject of the world in the year 2000 was met with surprise and silence. "Whoever's alive then will see" (Le Braz). "It's too much to ask" (Mme. Le Kouign). "I can't see as far ahead as that" (Mme. Bourdain). "I've never thought about it" (Annette Robic). "That's a philosophical question" (the notary).

During our first meeting with the teen-agers, I asked them how they saw the year 2000. Three answers emerged spontaneously and lightheartedly: "The atom bomb"—"Retirement"—"I'll be a grandfather." On another occasion Alain Le Calvez answered, "Retirement ... death not far away."

In the preceding answers the subject was the individual, not mankind. To four young people, the year 2000 suggested personal destruction, either through individual decline (old age) or general disintegration (the atom bomb).

Besides egocentric reactions, prophecies follow two lines of thought, that of continuous progress and that of fear and anxiety. In the first case, the belief remains widespread that progress will continue. It could be threatened only from the outside, by nuclear catastrophe, or for some, by the "yellow peril." Progress is seen as being beyond politics, though political action can accelerate it, improve it, correct social or geographical injustices, and avoid wars. It has its own dynamism, which is already at work in the present, and present development is projected into the future as continuous progress. "Things get better all the time . . . the future will be even better" (Kéramadan). "Things will always get better, I think. Every year there's change, it gets better and better" (Henri Michel). "Things will continue to progress, there'll be even more leisure and facilities, more holidays" (Hervé). Education will expand: "People will stay in school longer and longer, and civilization will get better" (Thérèse). Domestic comfort will become more widespread: "No one will be without anything —everyone will have a car" (Madeleine Clopin). Work will be automated: "You'll run the machinery by remote control, like they do with the rockets" (Duloch). "A combine harvester will work by itself, without anyone attending to it, just like a robot" (Leclerc). "Perhaps people won't have to work any more, everyone will be like the birds. Robots will do the work" (Le Neur).

To all this progress in everyday life is added the cosmic expansion of mankind. "It makes you think of the moon" (Jean Kéravrec). "Interplanetary travel" (Jeannette Robic). "People will go to the moon or to Mars for their holidays" (old Le Neur). "People will be living in the cosmos, or in the sea" (Mme. Mascoler).

In the cosmic and domestic future technology is the common denominator and motivating force of progress. The two kinds of progress are seen as parallel, not convergent; between improved living standards and cosmic expansion there is a great void; no social change, moral progress, or revolution is envisaged. Human nature, like biological nature, is regarded as immutable. No one doubts that man can create the most perfect robots, but most people doubt whether he can create life by artificial means. A

Rand Corporation study foresees the eradication of natural death between 1995 and 2025. To Plodémet death is inevitable. Old Charles Autrez exclaimed, "Nothing will stand in man's way," but added, "There's nothing you can do against death." Only Menguy, having said that "you can't bring back the dead," postulated the possibility of human amortality: "They manage to do such incredible things nowadays that I don't see that it's impossible." But his daughter protested: "You can't do anything against nature! The body wears out, the frame won't hold up." Death is nature. Man can tame nature, but not change it.

Among the old, it is generally the immutability of the laws of nature that tempers optimism about progress. Among the others, anxiety is focused on man rather than on nature, or remains obscure and unexplained. It is usually the women who express this type of anxiety, perhaps because the present is a lesser cause of anxiety for them than it is for the men, who are concerned about specific economic and technical problems. "It's frightening to think of a time as far off as that" (Marcelle). To her husband's statement, "Every year things get better," Mme. Michel retorted, "Or the opposite, perhaps." Mme. Soizick: "We lose in one way and gain in another." The daughter of the butcher Le Kouign: "Moving forward as they are, they'll get hurt and then have to go back again." Antoinette Berger: "There may not be a year 2000."

The most acute anxiety is felt by the teachers, who are all too aware that progress is no longer guided by reason, but is being corrupted and derailed by egotism, irresponsibility, and loss of moral sense. Among other people, as indeed among the teachers, anxiety centers on the all too concrete threat of nuclear weapons.

It is understandable why the consideration of the long-range future of mankind should be repressed in favor of short-term prospects. Commitment to the world of today not only compensates for the failure of messianic hopes but also represses apocalyptic fears.

In the final analysis, an optimistic view predominates, based on a conjunction of the near certainty of personal-familial progress and the self-propelled movement of technological progress. What has been dissipated is the great hope for a golden age, for a new humanity, once held out by the secular teacher. Having fallen from its ideological heights progress has become consolidated in material civilization. The egocentric view of a personal-familial future which does not look beyond the next generation is realistically based, despite the threats that hang over the professions, the commune, and the region, and it is propped up by a view of the general future which seems to be caught up in self-propelled progress, despite the ambivalences and fears expressed.

The "medieval" past is still condemned, which means that it is not forgotten, romanticized, or mythologized. The *archē*-identity is still sustained, but is already threatened by the new regional concept. But the preservation of identity and the aesthetic recovery of the past, together with the nostalgia for old communal festivities and communication, betray the rupture only now breaking apart the present and the past, and also foreshadow the new union that the present wants to contract with the past.

The Inheritors of the Cosmos

FROM THE OLD WORLD TO THE NEW

The spirit of the new times carries humanism within itself. Humanism—the conception that makes man the privileged subject in the world—continues to erode and disintegrate the underlying archaic cults that were retrieved, curtailed, but not dissolved by Christianity.

The ancient view of the world attached the human being to a cosmos where sun, moon, earth, and sea, personified or not, were powers with which communication was continually possible through occult forces and spirits, especially the spirits of the dead.

Christianity adapted itself to this cosmoanthropology by making itself the necessary and supreme mediator between man and the cosmos. Even today, prayers and *pardons* appeal to the Virgin Mary or the saints to intercede with the sea, the earth, the sky, and the sun, to bring farmers a rich harvest, fishermen a good catch, even good weather for the vacationers. The saints who drove out the god-spirits appropriated some of their magical attributes, particularly those of a therapeutic nature, and hundreds of little miracles are evidence of the complicity established between religion and nature: thus it never rains at the *pardon* of Penhors on September 8. The Church brought an abundance of divine attention and a new promise to the dead, but the dead remain ghosts that continue to appear on the moors or in dreams, bringing the secrets of time (premonition) or space (teleinformation).

Moreover, Christendom consolidated the integration of man into the cosmos by crowning the individual, the community, and the world with a universal monarchical principle hierarchized by the Church and governed by almighty God. Until the twentieth century, Christianity confined its own historical principle (the creation of the world, the Fall, Christ's intervention, the Last Judgment) in this doomed cosmoanthropology.

It was only in the middle of the present century, under the terrible blows dealt it by modern evolution, that the theocratic order fell apart: the world, the community, and the individual began to go their own ways, and God withdrew from the external world in order to permeate man's inner life more deeply. Christendom, in the sense of an integrated universe, subject to the rule of Christ the King, disappeared, but Christianity survived, in the sense of a Church that left technology to transform the world, accepted the evolution of society, and recognized the sovereignty of a State which did not itself recognize the sovereignty of God.

But the Church was slow to divest itself of its prodigious ethnographical and medieval load: it maintained and will continue to maintain the old cosmoanthropological relations until they are finally exhausted. It provides the great initiation passage rites that separate man from the cosmos (baptism) and rejoin him to it (burial), or unite the biological act and the social act (marriage). However, Christianity is re-emerging on the surface of the century by rediscovering and modifying the anthropocentric and historical principles that had become petrified in medieval Christendom. All it had to do was to transmute anthropocentrism (the privileged attention paid to the destiny of man, man made in the image of his creator) into personalism and to conceive of history, not as a fall, but as a quest for a progressive humanism that could be both specifically Christian and a variant of modern humanism.

THE RED WORLD

In the nineteenth century, it was not humanism that flourished in the hearts and minds of the reds of Plodémet but a conception of the world whose originality (and in my opinion, its richness

and beauty) lay in the ability to graft onto an archaic cosmology
a modern and revolutionary anthropology.

The erosion of Catholic faith and of ancient Celtic beliefs
among the red seamen and peasants at that time brought about
a flowering of pre-Christian cosmological tenets, but divested of
gods, genii, and spirits (except for the presence in the household
of the spirits of the dead). According to this naturalistic cosmology, the cosmos was both order and energy. Order controlled
and directed energy, but it could be, and on certain occasions
had to be, subjugated by it. Times of chaos with a superabun-
dance of energy succeeded times of order according to a law of
alternation. Alternation was probably the supreme law of this
universe, but it always led to a restoration of balance, not to
evolution, according to a quasi-Empedoclean cosmology. Earth,
sea, sky, sun, and moon were natural realities of infinite power,
on which seamen and peasants depended entirely until modern
technology began to emancipate them and social security to
protect them.

A man depending on the cosmos is also part of it. He is a natural
animal who is born, lives, copulates, procreates, and dies without
any particular attention being paid him by the cosmos—without
any privilege other than the natural ones of his head and hands.
Man the animal feels related to the other animals. Even today, old
peasants talk to their horse and their wives talk to their cow in a
symbiotic manner that is quite different from the urban tenderness shown toward pets. Even today, the old people in the countryside regard the education of children as being no different
from the rearing of animals. "You have to train them. Look at a
horse; if you don't beat it, if you don't train it, it'll wander all over
the place, it won't do anything and won't want to work" (Duloch).
As with animals, "You have to get children used to it while they're
young or they won't want to work later" (Kerveil).

All living beings are subject to a fundamental polemical law
of nature: Everyone is a potential enemy to everyone else. The
solidarity of those of the same blood or common interest makes
survival possible. It is also possible to be on good terms with
one's neighbor, on condition that there is mutual recognition of
the differences and rights of others.

But, among men as among animals, a permanent struggle between big and small goes on without mercy.

"It's like in the sea, the big ones eat the little ones. It's the same with people" (Yves Michel). "On the land and in the sea the little ones are eaten by the big ones" (Le Brez). "It's always been the same and it always will be" (his son Alain).

Past experience has verified the truth of this law for the little men and present experience sustains it, even if they are young or white. The small farmers see that the larger ones are ready to devour their land, and the larger ones see the industrial producers and Landernau ready to absorb theirs. The small businessman sees big business from outside ready to squeeze him out.

The war brought these cosmobiological laws to their culmination: man fights his neighbor; the big ones start wars in order to divide the small ones among themselves, to destroy as many of them as possible and then subjugate them; war is the expression on the human plane of the great law of cosmological alternation of order and chaos. War is not an accident or a mistake. It is part of, and expresses, the very essence of the world.

The red cosmoanthropology is naturalistic and materialistic. It is a fundamental challenge to religion, which it accuses of masking the world as it really is by adding to it a providential deity. It is not so much the idea of a god who "is in control up there" that is absolutely rejected, but that of a good, humane god. "The god here is money. If you haven't got any, you get kicked around. If you have, you can do what you like," said one man from Menez-Ru. Religion is "claptrap, myth," because it neither expresses nor explains the pragmatical, cynical reality of the world and of man. The cosmological critique is linked here with the political; religion claims to base the domination of the powerful on law and justice, whereas it is based simply on the relation of forces. The new anthropology based on historical analysis contradicts, but is in essence linked to, the old naturalistic anthropocosmology.

The idea of progress was instilled by the Revolution, in the course of the struggle between the big and the small. It was consolidated and extended with the first victories of the Republic and eventually became the humanist key idea. This original progress, which is still embedded in the paleomodern ideology, is not based on nature; it is a deliberate, violent progress that is brought about by the implacable struggle between the small and the big. It is because the small have finally learned to unite under red leadership that the Republican State broke the power of the big for the first time, imposed progress on the human jungle, and initiated the reign of civilizaton. Progress then gradually developed, diversified, and extended through enlightenment, education, technical development, and better living standards. It was at the mesomodern stage that progress finally became natural to society, confirming the break between the human world and the cosmos.

The cosmological law of balanced alternation is gradually being superseded by the new human law of evolution-progress; the pragmatical-biological law is being superseded by the law of pacification through the growing solidarity of the small and the imposing of limitations on the power of the big.

But the law of pacification does not enjoy the same untroubled progress as the law of advancement. France experienced three wars between 1870 and 1945, and since then there have been other wars in various parts of the world. War is still the stronghold of the old cosmology and of the pragmatical law of the human world.

War is almost regarded as a regular cyclical phenomenon. Many old people believe that since 1870 a cycle has been operating which predetermines a war every twenty years, with the built-in possibility of "missing" a war, as between 1870 and 1914 and in 1965.

"There'll always be wars," said Jean Bars, a retired seaman and a Communist.

"The war could start in India. Russia and the United States could poke their noses in, everyone else would be dragged in after them, and bang! That would be it! I think the war will start in that part of the world, not next week, but it will come," said Michel Poullan at the time of the Kashmir crisis.

The red patriarchs who await the next war with Empedoclean serenity remain faithful both to the old law of alternation and to the new law of progress when they state that the wars of 1914 and 1939 were followed by general improvement. Kéramadan declared that "the improvement came from education and the war." Menguy carried this still further and declared that an age of enlightenment must now succeed the pragmatical law: "War makes the advance of civilization possible . . . After every war there's progress in the countryside . . . Now it's by education that we'll move forward."

The attitude toward war swings—sometimes in the same person—between cosmological fate that makes it inevitable and progress that makes it possible to overcome it.

"As long as there are two men on earth there'll be war . . . [later] It's the big fellows, the arms manufacturers and industrialists who start wars when things are not going well for them. After the war the small fellows pay for the damage through taxes . . . [later] I don't know why they have to fight—Americans, Russians, Germans—they're all buddies really! But they don't all speak the same language. They don't understand each other, so they fight. If they all spoke the same language there'd be no wars" (Yves Michel).

The multiplicity of languages is not regarded here as a natural law but as an artificial obstacle to understanding between peoples. As Duloch put it, "If I took a rooster from Menez-Ru to Germany, he'd understand the other roosters. I don't know why it is, but men aren't as clever as animals. They don't speak alike, so they don't understand each other and start knocking each other about."

A common language, that is, an understanding among the little people of all countries, would end war. Above all, peace would result from transforming wars between countries into a worldwide struggle of the little against the big.

The threat of future war is envisioned as the overrunning of Europe by the hungry of Asia, in other words as part of the eternal conflict of hungry and rich. For Brezec, war is "to destroy people when there are too many of them, that's all it's for," but he added, "The little men do the fighting, the big fellows are behind the lines."

Red Plodémet, which has always been resolutely on the side of the little man, is perplexed when confronted by the "threat" of the hungry. They too are little people and they should not be condemned. "If they haven't enough to eat, they're bound to revolt." Yet at the same time they are foreigners and too foreign, and they are a threat to the world as a whole, of which Plodémet is a part. A few old ex-colonials are obsessed with the "yellow peril," and it relieves them that "the Yellow River and tigers kill a large number every year" of the seven hundred million Chinese. But most of the people in Plodémet believe that the hungry should be helped and a solution found that would avert war.

Thus evolution in the world, far from reducing the risk of war, increases it. Fortunately, given the atom bomb, war no longer works to the advantage of the big, "Because it would destroy everybody, big and little . . . the big will never want to destroy each other" (Yves Michel).

Curiously, the atom bomb is a demarcation line of sorts between the paleomodern and mesomodern world-views. For the red patriarchs, it is not so much nuclear warfare that is the chief danger as the nuclear experiments of today and the moon rockets that run the risk of disturbing the cosmos and, consequently, the man-nature balance. For the mesomoderns, the atom bomb is the sword of Damocles that hangs permanently over progress, arousing vague fears of annihilation.

The mesomoderns wish to exclude war from their field of vision and thought in order not to have to question the future of progress. For the patriarchs, war and progress are the two fundamental experiences of this century, each as inevitable as the other. For the mesomoderns, war can only be regarded as an anomaly and can be caused only by backwardness or the madness of the superpowers.

The plebeian anthropocosmology of Plodémet might be described from a certain point of view as a "primitive Marxism."

Marx's point of departure is a "critique of religion," which leads him to base his anthropology on a materialist naturalism. For Marx, the dialectic of conflict reigns over nature as it does over society. The history of man is the extension of the history of nature; its motivating force and its keystone are the class struggle between exploiters and exploited. The development of man takes place in and through this conflict. The great difference here is that for Plodémet development (evolution) is a late product, following the Revolution, and not the axis of anthropocosmology, as it is in Marx. But there is also a similarity in the idea that the modern world has made possible a decisive change whereby the conflict of the big and the little will culminate in a new society. At this point, there is another divergence: for Marx, the decisive step is marked by the formation of an industrial proletariat in capitalist society, which leads to a specifically socialist premise (socialization of the means of production, withering away of the state, etc.); for Plodémet, it is a question of fulfilling the promise of the Revolution and of creating an egalitarian society under the guidance of the republican, socialist State. But there is agreement on the theory of war, which is seen as an inevitable result of conflict in history, and which can be abolished only by a historical change in which the community of the little men would impose unity on mankind. The red ambivalence of Plodémet, divided as it is between the inevitability and the evitability of war, is reflected in present-day communism itself. On the one hand one can affirm, as Stalin did and as Mao does now, that (imperialist) wars are inevitable, while on the other hand one can advance theoretically, as the Communist parties of the Soviet Union and France do, that the progress already achieved (by the "forces of peace" of the "socialist camp") makes it possible to avoid war.

Finally, there is one more point of agreement between the two anthropocosmologies, namely, the formulation of a progressive anthropology on top of a materialist cosmology controlled by a fundamental law that opposes big and little in an emancipating struggle for mankind.

This makes it even more easy to understand why part of the red populace in Plodémet passed quite naturally from Baillism to communism. Communism took root in Plodémet, not only through a propaganda campaign adapted to a given historical situation, not only through the similar emotional appeals of Stalinist communism and red paleototalitarianism, but through its similar anthropocosmological foundation.[1] It is in and through

[1] It may seem incongruous to bring together a developed political theory and the conception of the world produced by the collective experience of the rural populace. But the secret and multiple relations between collective world-views and the great philosophies have not as yet received sufficient attention. Moreover, we have seen in the twentieth century, and on the non-European continents, that Marxism has been capable of adaptation to pre-industrial social groups. Also, the ideology of Plodémet was not produced in isolation but nourished by the thought of the French Revolution, which provided a popular version of the philosophy of the Enlightenment. Marx, too, was a partial heir of the philosophy of the Enlightenment and of the French Revolution, but he based his thinking on something radically original, the dialectical theory. Similarly, Plodémet based its world-view on something radically original, the secularized archaic anthropocosmology. It is not surprising that the lessons derived from the French Revolution by Marx and the people of Plodémet should be parallel. The most surprising and remarkable thing is the parallel between two cosmologies of such totally different origins. Yet here too there is a relationship between the quasi-Empedoclean cosmology of Plodémet and the materialist cosmology established by Marx, through a return to the pre-Socratic cosmologies, that is, to an emergent

its ambivalence as the party of the social-struggle-of-the-little-man, and as the party of the conquest-of-progress-and-peace, that communism has espoused the red philosophical duality.

The duality between immutable cosmology and constantly changing history tends to dissociate the two aspects. With the passage from equilibrium to contradiction between man and the cosmos, the crisis of paleomodern cosmoanthropology begins.

The contradiction may have created a fatalism in the little people, who despite their faith in progress no longer expect to end war or abolish the power of the big. The decline of small business marks the conquering return of the big, and many people doubt whether it is really possible in the end to eliminate the big, who although they have lost their omnipotence are still the stronger, while the little remain divided.

"What do you expect? That's how it is. It's always been the same. That's history!" (Mme. Gaelic).

Was there ever a time in Red Plodémet when the messianic hope in the triumph of the little man surmounted cosmologic fatalism? In any case, the red patriarchs hardly expect such a triumph, but their loyalty to the party is unshaken. The party and the little man have won the victories, even if they have not won the ultimate victory. It is the party of the Soviet Union, whatever may be happening there, which has given the big the greatest shock they have suffered.

The same patriarchs who are fatalistic about war and the impossibility of really eliminating the big also sing with the greatest enthusiasm the praises of a progress that has transfigured life in Plodémet. This is because for them contradiction is being subsumed once again into a great equilibrium.

This contradiction between progress and war, between cosmological anthropology and progressive anthropology, which is felt so acutely by the patriarchs is also present in an attenuated form in the minds of many natives of Plodémet, for they have all to a greater or lesser degree been imbued with the paleomodern cosmological anthropology. It arouses deep questionings. If philosophy is more than a discipline reserved for a university group of

---

philosophy that secularizes an archaic cosmology. Both contain the fundamental polemical law. The great difference is that Marx is Heraclitean and overcomes law and alternation through the dialectic of development, whereas Plodémet opposes alteration and progress in a struggle in which each remains partly victorious and partly vanquished.

specialized, paid intellectuals called philosophers, there is a real philosophical search being carried out in Plodémet, where the patriarchs, superior in this respect to most contemporary thinkers, are concerned with the question of what unites and opposes progress and war. They conceive of the twentieth century not only as the century of industrial societies of consumption and high living standards but also as a century of permanent conflicts and wars; they try to discover whether the immutable has succeeded in becoming the changing or whether the changing is a mask for the immutable; and they see neither absolute continuity nor an absolute break between the cosmos, life, and man.

HUMAN, ALL TOO HUMAN

By the tenets of the new anthropology, society is no longer governed primarily by the pragmatic law, which survives nevertheless as a secondary law. Progress brings the peaceful evolution of society. The big-little conflict ceases to be radical; the big have certainly not disappeared, but a *modus vivendi* can be established in the general interest, and they can be allowed to run the large business concerns on condition that they respect the vital interests of the little people and assure the common development of the economy. The little people have not disappeared either, but their penury has; they have become "medium-sized." They are little people who have been promoted and now benefit from certain advantages of the big. They no longer hope or wish for a society governed by the little, but they do hope and wish that in the future all the little people will be integrated into a society of the medium-sized.

Society is now democratic, and economic and social development is an inextricable part of its future. Progress is now rooted within it as an internal, fundamental law, and could be challenged only by an incomprehensible external accident.

Mankind has succeeded in establishing its own order, its own laws, and its own harmonious development. It deserves to extend its sovereignty over the world. Man is not a superior animal. He is superior to the animals. He is no longer a fragment of the cosmos, but the subject of the world; secular humanism and the new Christian humanism, despite their divergences, are now variants of one humanism that proclaims the truth and the law of man.

The cosmos becomes the theater of man's adventures and is

no longer seen as an organic whole. The earth is becoming material that is being worked by technology, and is no longer the Ancient Power. The behavior of the sea is increasingly being predicted by meteorology, increasingly overcome by radio and radar. The socialized human universe becomes the living universe, while the cosmos that rose up in the physical power of material laws falls back into the material inertia of physical laws. Television pictures, rending the celestial vault, open up the infinity of the stellar void.

One of the final breaks took place during our research in Plodémet when the first cosmic pedestrian left his space capsule and the first journeys to the moon were announced. Regarded as the body that regulates climate and the rhythms of the sea, as the star of fecundity that determines the time of planting, the moon was the keystone of the old system of natural order and forces, and in addition was invested with the magic aura of pre-Christian beliefs. In Menez-Ru, most of those who did not have television doubted that man would ever reach the moon. "In my opinion they'll never get to the moon" (Leclerc). "I don't believe it. The papers are just saying that. They can say what they like, since they know very well that no one will see!" (Duloch). Bozer, a worker in the cannery, said, "I don't believe it. They'll never get there," and added, already conceding the success of the astronauts, "And getting there isn't everything. They'll still have to get back." Even Mimi, a young teacher, betrayed skepticism: "They say they'll go to the moon. I don't mind, but I don't think they will."

The patriarch Michel Poullan admitted the possibility of a landing on the moon in the near future, but suspected it would lead to catastrophe: "In a way, the moon is something for nations to quarrel over, and we'll all be destroyed afterwards."

For old people, but also for those of the young who still retain an ultimate fidelity to the old cosmology, there is an equivalence between space rockets and nuclear tests in that they both lead to a disturbance of the seasons, that is, of the fundamental law of alternation. "There's no weather any more. Don't you think it's all the things they send up there that's making everything go wrong?" (an old woman in the laundry in Pors-Ensker). "A man to the moon? That's why the weather has changed" (old Le Bars). "It's not warm enough any more in Brittany. It makes you wonder. Perhaps it's the atomic explosions" (Mme. Pouldrenzic). "The atom bomb! This year we haven't seen the sun. There was a time when it was fine for two months on end" (Mme. Goémon). "Terrible weather! Whoever's in charge up there perhaps wants a vacation, too, or perhaps he's not pleased with the rockets and things we've been sending him" (old Gaelic).

Rumors attribute agricultural accidents (scorched harvests) or maritime ones (dead fish) to nuclear fallout. During the harsh winter of 1962, large numbers of dead fish were cast up on the beach at Menhir. Le Brez said they were killed by nuclear debris, or that perhaps somewhere they were doing experiments on fish before doing them on men. His wife was more realistic: "I think they froze to death."

Space ships and nuclear tests provoke reactions that accelerate the decline of the old cosmology. "They're trying to bring down the moon," said Le Bars, the old seaman. Indeed, man is bringing the moon down, off its stellar throne. The dethronement of the moon is at the same time the enthronement of man who is taking possession of the cosmos. "In the end, they'll manage to catch the moon!" (old Gournet). "Nothing can stop man. He's bound to get there" (Charles Autrez).

Patriarchs are to be found among the enthusiasts of technological conquest. This is because belief in progress has been no less total than in the old cosmology, and as cosmology begins to disintegrate, faith in progress remains.

The reaction of most of the others toward a fallen, emptied cosmos is one of indifference. "What's the use of the moon now that you can live on it?" (La Braz). "There are better things to do on earth" (Guillou).

One should be concerned with the human world above all. Of course, the great exploits of the astronauts confirm man's unprecedented license in the universe, yet the dominant tendency is not toward a Promethean conquest of the planets. Moreover, the two humanisms that rule Plodémet both warn man to beware of excess. He must not wish to equal God, says one; he must not go beyond reason, says the other.

PLANET AND NATURE

The collapsed cosmos is being replaced by physical matter and space, and time is becoming autonomous.

Television and the automobile have made Plodémet aware of

outer space as well as of the world. Now the young want to travel —to Russia, to China, to the United States. The earth is beginning to be perceived as the common ground, the living space of mankind, no longer as the cosmogonic Mother Earth or the Human Fatherland. It is not so much planet as nature.

As the cosmos disintegrates, it is being transformed not only into a planet but also into nature. This transformation has not been a rapid process in Plodémet. The rediscovery of nature began in the cities. The new nature, although assuming certain regulatory properties formerly attributed to the cosmos, is more womblike, maternal. It is becoming a source of inner peace and aesthetic sentiment, and turns into landscape. The neo-Rousseauism that has been spreading in the cities has now reached Plodémet. Already, there are many people in Plodemet who no longer regard the city as a fabulous metropolis but as an artificial and unhealthy environment where one cannot live "naturally." The town is drawn rather to the delights of suburban life where urban civilization blends with the green spaces of the countryside.

Country people prefer to walk in the woods, *their* countryside, to sense and observe the animal and vegetable life around their land, and pay less attention to the landscape. The bourgeois are discovering the landscape and go on excursions to the tourist areas of the region, such as the Eckmühl lighthouse, the Pointe du Raz, and the Ile de Sein.

The aesthetic discovery of the landscape of the commune is just beginning. People who are very much aware of the human charm of their commune were extremely surprised when I told them that the landscape of the lanes leading to the sea is among the most beautiful I have seen.

The town already feels a need to participate more closely in nature; the bourgeois—three times as many of them as farmers —go hunting, and many townspeople go fishing. The purpose of modern hunting and fishing is the expression of aggressive and acquisitive drives and the sustenance of an animal relation with nature, not to disregard its aesthetic values. Also, vacationers want to fill their lungs with *natural* air and eat the *natural* foods of the farm. Plodémet itself is beginning to like, admire, and breathe its own pure air, regarding it as a source of health, vitality, and even youthfulness. "It makes you live longer," old Poullan declared proudly.

SOCIAL NATURE

The ordering, regulating principle of the old cosmos has now been assigned to society. Its law and order seem almost as firm and even more reasonable to the mesomoderns than those of the cosmos were to the paleomoderns. The infinite forces of earth and sky, on which farmers and seamen once depended totally, have been transferred to technology and the State.

The new lobster boats are equipped with radio, radar, and deep freezers, the new oil tankers are floating laboratory-factories, the new stables are cattle factories. The Provident State dispenses functions that go beyond those of the cosmos and partly take over those of God. The Provident State must not only guarantee the order of the social universe but rectify disturbances, protect, cure, compensate, pay, improve, and guide. It must respond to the requests that were once intoned at altars for harvests, catches, security, and prosperity. In a secularized and socialized form, the State even embraces in its sovereign power the occult forces, genii, and spirits that directed the Breton world. These are the "they" so often evoked by the people of Plodémet. "They say that man will reach the moon"—"They are preparing for war." "They" run the world. Who are "they"? The big people? The powerful? Nothing as precise as that. These "they" are as innumerable as the primordial spirits that the Old Testament refers to by the unique plural of *Elohim*.

DEATH

While medical science has stayed the power of natural death to some degree, unnatural death has come closer to home.

In the interest of the community, the regional pages of the newspapers give predominant attention to auto accidents. Indeed, accidents occur in the region every day, and in 1966 Plodémet was stunned by the accidental deaths of young Le Kam and Michel Poullan's grandson, a few short years after a fatal accident nearby that also cost two young lives.

For the old people the car is simply an instrument of death, and in Menez-Ru this amounts to an obsession. "That's all you read about, car accidents, that's all there is in the papers" (Brezec). "They won't need wars any more. Cars will do the job for them" (Le Grevez). "There's no point in buying a car. There are already too many of them. They're all right if you want to break your neck" (Duloch). "We don't want him [their son] to buy a motorbike. It's dangerous. Road accidents are all you hear about" (Mme. Michel).

For the old people, the car is a terrifying death machine. In the words of Le Braz, "The car is replacing war." From a different point of view, one might almost say that for the young, too, the car replaces war in the sense that adventurous driving offers a risk of death that normal life excludes. The car has reintroduced the implacability of fate, and in a way the daily reporting of car deaths by the papers plays the role of human sacrifice to the invisible.

As death has become a social phenomenon through the car, so it has become internalized with the maladies that obsess the modern consciousness. In the times of frequent epidemics, death seemed to strike from outside and the adult who had escaped childhood death felt armed against attack. Today, as general anxiety increases, producing death fantasies, the fear of heart attacks and cancer places death inside the individual. Both doctors in Plodémet mentioned the recent dramatic increase of this syndrome; they attributed it to the medical programs on television, and found its most frequent forms in fears of cardiac infarction, excess cholesterol, and cancer. In our opinion, the success of these broadcasts shows only that the psychological terrain has become fertile and that people have become conscious of their internal panic. "When people have a little sore, they start talking about cancer right away" (Mme. Tykoz).

Two types of modern death reign in Plodémet. One, by heart attack or car accident, evokes the cosmologic fate that struck blindly; the other, by cancer, is new in that it is internal, proliferating, unnamable, and unclean, and it indicates that the fear of disturbance, which used to be projected onto the cosmos, has now entered deep inside modern man.

Death, internalized and socialized, remains irreducible; like war, it is coming to be regarded as abnormal and absurd by the modern consciousness. But, like all unbearable absurdities, death also is retrieved by cosmology and religion, which enable progressive, humanist optimism to flourish. Death remains the citadel of cosmology and religion within the humanistic universe. It is through death that the Church so dominates a red commune that only two graves in its cemetery bear no cross. It is death that holds on to the umbilical cord to the cosmos. The conquering human order has replaced the cosmic order but can do nothing against death. Human progress always circumvents the island of death in its advance. Cosmos, nature, and religion share the invulnerable citadel of death.

The Upheaval of Modern Man

THE PALEOMODERN INDIVIDUAL

Humanist advancement, in the paleomodern sense, is the united advance of State, society, and individual. Society is not so much a collection of individuals as a collective body, itself made up of aggregations whose primary cells are families. The authority of the father in the family seems natural, almost biological. The paternal principle rules the clan-village and the commune, extending to the Republican State, which is both father and guide.

The process of family liberalization began at the end of the nineteenth century, free choice in marriage being the first fundamental step of emancipation for the individual. Soon after, a conflict developed between two family needs: the need to succeed the father and the need to enter the educational process. The obligation to succeed the father, although substantially weakened, still survives, and we met men, not all of them over fifty, who had had to renounce their personal aspirations in order to preserve the hereditary right.

"I wanted to be a policeman. I had enough schooling. But at home they said, 'And what's going to happen to the land?' If I'd become a policeman, I'd have retired long ago" (Kéramadan). Goémon wanted to be a teacher; Kerfuric came back to the farm against his will.

In the town the law of succession still applies, even among the progressive tailors. Michel Loïc wanted to continue his education and become a teacher: "I cried every night." Caradec had to take over his father's hotel. Clopin, a grocer and baker, had his draftsman's diploma at the age of twenty and still regrets that he came back; now he thinks he should have left in spite of his father. Erwan remained, also against his will, in the family bakery.

Nowadays, it is not so much the decree itself but the death of the father that forces the young man to come home. Or else timidity, fear of the unknown, or failure in examinations brings him back to the family business. Solange would have liked to study literature and live in a city but had to work in her mother's hairdressing salon. Annick Le Gal was attending the *lycée* in Quimper when her mother died, and she came back to manage the Hôtel des Voyageurs. Pouldraizic wanted to be a taxi driver in Paris, then thought of emigrating to Canada. "If there'd been an immediate opening and a place to live, I'd have gone." He is resigned to working with his father, a mason, and he and his wife live with him.

The constraint of the family business on the individual has remained strong only because paleomodern individualism was also dependent on the independence of this business. The great red effort was directed first of all at achieving independence for the small proprietor, and it resulted in the formation of a society of small individual businesses in which personal autonomy (that of the head of the family) was equivalent to family autonomy. The pleasure of owning one's business was at its peak during the interwar period of stability. Everyone was pleased at being his own boss, using his own methods, and organizing his own operation. It was more than proprietary autonomy, it was also self-expression through the full use of the personality in work.

The mesomodern period, characterized as it is by the extension of individualism, begins paradoxically by reducing, sometimes even destroying the individualist foundation. Small businesses that want to avoid ruin must resign themselves to affiliation or cooperation, subject themselves to proper accounting, efficiency, and in many cases mechanization that destroys craftlike qualities in work.

Plodémet feels the decline of the small individual business very strongly, yet it is more and more willing to see the younger generation abandon private business in order to gain a higher standard of living, greater security, and other forms of freedom.

At the same time, the new direction shifts the base of individual autonomy to the ownership of one's house and its domestic equipment (furniture, labor-saving devices, a car), and the personal life coincides more and more with the private life. Even those who have jobs that are both interesting and profitable try to reduce their hours of work and increase their leisure, that is, the autonomy of the private life. Thus the old freedom gained through work is added to, and partly replaced by, the freedom gained from work.

MESOMODERN INDIVIDUALISM

With mesomodern developments, the threefold balance between State, society, and individual is not destroyed but modified to the detriment of local society (the falling off of political activity) and national society in favor of the individual. The idea of individual happiness is linked with that of collective happiness. "People are happy here," I heard repeated several times in the town. This theme of happiness expresses the good humor of the people of Plodémet, conceals their deep dissatisfactions, and reflects the satisfaction derived from the first acquisitions of domestic comfort and the beginnings of an individual feeling of happiness.

The feelings of satisfaction produced by greater security and comfort have brought the first signs of a relaxed individualism in which the sensible enjoyment of life becomes the cardinal principle. "You only live once," "Make hay while the sun shines," are maxims of a tempered Epicureanism that is beginning to sample the pleasures of comfort, while the young indulge in more obvious forms of hedonism.

This sensibility is broadened by well-being and also includes an increased awareness of not feeling well, of cold, fatigue, and pain. The rustic who would go to the doctor only when he could bear his pain no longer has been succeeded by one so susceptible to discomfort or anxiety that he runs to the doctor at the first disturbing sign. The dentist now uses anaesthetics routinely. However, in 1965 painless childbirth methods have not yet been introduced.

Aesthetic-recreational pleasures are already an important part of Sundays and holidays, and of café culture. The aesthetic field has extended to caring for one's garden, to the house (furniture, flowers, pictures, ornaments, use of color), to enjoyment of the countryside as landscape, to tourist excursions, to the revival, for pleasure, of old practical activities (hunting, fishing, boating), to the recovery, in general, of nature and the past, and to the semi-aesthetic consumption of the world in the form of television. Already among the young, vacations are regarded as times of specifically aesthetic-recreational activity.

An artistic current is noticeable in the taste for pictures in the house, photographs, and reading, especially among women, who consume variously the short stories in women's magazines, novels depicted in comic-strip fashion, and novels proper. The beginnings of a literary culture are to be found among girls and young women in the town, and the municipal library that closed down is being substituted for by book buying. Among the younger teachers, one can discern an attraction toward modern poetry and writing, the newer arts (photography, films), and the arts of the past (archaeology).

Thus the mesomodern current brings or accelerates a great thaw of sensibility which evokes, even in its still semiplebeian form, the awakening sensibility in the privileged circles of the aristocratic-bourgeois world in the eighteenth century.

The development of this sensibility, whether it is sensual, emotional, or aesthetic, flows from a state of subjective individualism where the individual is the focus of innumerable sensations, feelings, and pleasures, and is also an egocentric subject in relation to others and to the external world. The need for greater personal privacy arises in this state.

The mesomodern individual also demands increased autonomy from society and wider protection from the State. He is less disposed to devote himself to public affairs; he feels less loyal to his class, his profession, and his native community; his need for protection nevertheless keeps him in his class, his profession, and his community.

The decline of the big family continues, but the family unit is not dissolving. It is being transformed into a network of trust, security, and mutual help in a world far too big, where strangers and neighbors are still potential sources of threat.

The new home, a result of the domestic revolution, is producing a vertical split in the big family by ending the practice of the young couple living with the parents. The new symbiosis between individual life and family life is taking place in the basic family unit. By delaying marriage to age twenty-five, the younger generation is expressing the wish to reserve a slice of their lives as strictly autonomous, but they are unanimous in their desire for the personal-family life. None of them questions as yet the unity and permanence of a life whose need for autonomy, participation, and protection is focused essentially on the house, the car, and the television set.

THE HOUSE

The house represents more than ever a need for personal ownership, and for the overwhelming majority in Plodémet it is inconceivable to rent out or even share the ownership of a dwelling.

For the mesomoderns, the model house is the suburban villa with enough rooms to assure the autonomy of the wife (kitchen), the husband (workshop), the couple (bedroom), and the children (additional bedrooms). It must also be possible to receive guests (dining room, and already here and there in the town, a *salon*, or sitting room), and the house must have sufficient grounds for a garden.

The break with the big family is consummated not only by the fact of separation but, when possible, by the choice of a new home according to the pleasantness and convenience of its location—that is, by the fact of free choice, as opposed to the former predestination.

The domestic revolution has concentrated an enormous emotional investment in the home, shown not only by the capital expended on it but also by the constant attention it receives. The wife focuses her activity on cleaning and furnishing, and the husband on improvement, repairs, and decoration. The house is a place of love that arouses, even ensnares, the passion, tenderness, attentions, and fetishisms of a love that, if it does not attach itself to the partner, will certainly attach itself to the child and the house itself.

The door of the old farmhouse was kept open during the day. The door of the villa is kept closed; one has to ring, and is sometimes peered at through a peephole. Some couples put off buying a television set for fear of being invaded in the evenings by neighbors. The house has become a refuge, and fewer and fewer people come to the meetings arranged by the few surviving militants. The cellular house is becoming the insular house.[2]

[2] As yet there are practically no telephones for private, nonbusiness use among the seventy-two subscribers to the service in Plodémet. Are we to see in this a combination of the old mistrust of a technology whose practical use one does not understand and an old way of protecting modern domestic insularity?

The house on which so much loving care is expended and which satisfies so many convergent needs is closed against neighbors but open to the landscape. The door is closed, but the windows are large, and inside is that window on the world, television. Domestic rootedness is parallel with modern uprootedness, with the new mobility, precisely in order to allow for them and to give shelter from them.

THE CAR

The car and the house are growing up together, and there is as much demand for car equipment as for domestic equipment.

Mesomodern man has the same kind of obsessional attachment to his car as he has to his house, but perhaps to a lesser degree. This attachment is expressed in conversation about it and in some cases by washing, polishing, and other attentions, and also in inordinate use. Like the house, the car is a source of various gratifications: a strong sense of individual existence, expressed in the pleasure of mastering the steering wheel and accelerator; a strong element of play, expressed among the young in fast driving, whereby risk becomes the antidote to domestic security. The car corresponds perfectly to the structure of mesomodern individuality.

The house is the base of rooted autonomy, the car is the instrument and symbol of mobile autonomy; the house provides the internal freedom, the car the external one.

The old life was confined not so much to the home as to one's land and village. Many older people even today cannot understand the attractions of the Ile de Sein or the Pointe du Raz. For them the only purpose of travel is either to look for work or go on a pilgrimage (Lourdes, a battlefield, the German farm where one was a prisoner of war).

On the other hand, the new desire to travel is touristic and vacational. The desire to travel and the desire for vacations are linked in Plodémet. They cannot be regarded as a desire to flee the noisy, stifling city for nature and the sea, since Plodémet has both, which draw vacationers and tourists from the cities. They correspond, rather, to a new need which in the past was felt only by the tailors: to see and know the world—the provinces, neighboring countries, Europe, and recently, for the young, America,

Russia, and Asia. This nomadic need is combined with that of the aèsthetic-recreational life of vacations: landscapes, museums, buildings, entertainments, games.

The fact that in Plodémet the busiest season coincides with the nation-wide summer vacation is the greatest obstacle to travel. Thus, the mesomodern individual tends to express himself through the antithetic and complementary means of home and car, of sedentary and automotive activities, of routine daily life and vacation trips.

TELEVISION

Despite a slow beginning, almost a quarter of Plodémet homes now have television, penetration having followed the same lines as the domestic revolution. Television performs a function of acculturation by introducing all the elements of modernity from the space rocket to the obsession with cancer. It improves the French of old women who spoke only Breton and keeps Plodémet up to date with events in the world. Country people often remark that television "teaches you things." "I go to school every day, thanks to my television set," says eighty-year-old Thérèse.

Television enforces the isolation of the home from the community by opening it much more to the world at large. It arouses a desire to travel, and those who travel most and farthest are the avid viewers. Television tends to stifle local politics, but it stimulated heavy participation in the elections of 1965. Whereas old people without television remain fixed on the regional page of the newspaper, others read about the underdeveloped countries, the Vietnam war, and the race riots in the United States.

The exploits of the astronauts and the discovery of the hungry Third World are the twin poles of a new planetary consciousness. "When I see on my set little children dying of hunger and think that here we've got more than we need, it's too sad. Tears come to my eyes" (Thérèse). "They showed us the Congo where people are dying of hunger, and here there are too many cauliflowers which would be very welcome to those dying of hunger" (Mme. Kéravrec).

It is especially among those who still nurture the old red feelings of solidarity with the little people that television arouses planetary consciousness and a sense of community.

Television strengthens all the formative forces of the meso-modern personality, bringing information, participation, and aesthetic pleasure. It confirms the new *modus vivendi* between man and the world, and in that sense, it has replaced the *buvette*.

The *buvette* was a forum of culture at the district and village level, where ideas and information were exchanged, where red wine encouraged practical and political communication. The *buvette* is not dead, of course, and television, though it deprives conversation of much of its charm, does provide subjects of conversation. Television is a source of culture to the individual in his relations with newly discovered space and time. As wine can bring poetry or lethargy, so can television bring new perspectives or new bromides.

THE MODERN STATE

In Plodémet, then, there is emerging a type of man still imbued with rusticity, for whom the human universe has emancipated itself from the cosmos, who is progressing in ways both encouraging and dangerous. He is fully devoted to the present but wants to sustain his identity from the past and is beginning to invest this past with aesthetic nostalgia. He has confidence in the personal-familial future, but adheres more to progress than to the future as such. It is in progress that he finds and conquers his new autonomy, his emancipation, his advancement. The State, society, the family, and the individual constitute the new humanity in which the individual, while entrenching himself in an ever cosier placenta-family, asks society and the State to guide and protect him in space and time. The house is always his refuge. But house, television, and car are the new instruments of a superindividualization and are becoming integral parts of the new, developing being.

Marcelle and Antoinette, both eighteen years old, explain what it means to be modern: to have a modern house, to be properly dressed, and to buy the finest television set.

"It's the bourgeois mentality," said Antoinette.

"It's part of everybody's mentality," said Marcelle.

11
Permanent Modernity

Three Islands

Electronics and automation have not yet reached Plodémet. Large economic concentrations have enveloped and infiltrated the commune, but so far have respected individual ownerships. New inequalities are just now emerging out of the newly conquered egalitarianism.

What concerns me here is the emergence of three islands: the patrician home of the Le Bails; the modern villa of the dentist; and the pseudo-Breton house of Dr. Lévi. Three islands showing signs, if not of new times, at least of new problems.

The fine upper-bourgeois residence of the dynasty that once reigned over Plodémet has become an artistic island. Jenny Le Bail is a painter in her thirties; she is married to Marc, who works for a literary publication; her father-in-law is Jewish. She lives in Paris and works part time in the dressmaking business owned by her mother, who has remarried. With her husband and their friends, Jenny often comes to Plodémet, for which she has a deep affection. The triple corruption—Parisian, artistic, Jewish—that broke up the provincial bourgeois dynasty spared Jenny's rustic simplicity and saved her from a sheltered bourgeois existence in Passy or Cornouville.

The big Le Bail house is almost a museum of Bigouden furniture collected by Jenny's parents. It is looked after by Gaîte, Jenny's "second mother," a handsome Bigouden woman. Jenny spends her time in Plodémet, not in the house, but in a barn she has converted into living quarters. While fireplaces are being demolished throughout the countryside, she has built a rustic fireplace in the barn. They have barbecues over wood fires, although firewood is no longer used in the commune. The beams, customarily hidden throughout Plodémet, are well in evidence here. Jenny lives, paints, eats, drinks, and rests in this barn–studio–living-room with her friends, who are devoid of artistic ambitions and without any rule other than the will to live outside bourgeois constraints. The phonograph plays Johnny Halliday or Bach, the Pernod is at the disposal of all, a parrot observes, comments, shrieks with laughter, or sings the first few notes of the "Marseillaise," while a group of women friends from Plodémet and Paris paint or sit around talking. Friends drop in, spend a few days, and pass on. In social background and position they are varied; they are not from the Saint-Germain-des-Prés set where people are more taken with the pen and the camera, but predominantly from the Montparnasse where professional intellectuals are rare. They have much of the bohemian and hippie about them; they are more concerned with living according to a certain concept than with brandishing ideas, more anarchistic and Trotskyite than Stalinist. Marc likes literature and hides—and reveals—his philosophy beneath the placid appearance of a libertarian. It was in this fashion that Montparnasse came to Plodémet.

The dentist's house represents the vanguard of comfort and modernity, though in other respects it is a conventional villa. In his profession, he uses the latest equipment, and for his own pleasure he has assembled a panoply of equipment including tape recorder, 8-millimeter camera, and underwater fishing gear. He is thirty-five years old. His wife looks after the house, reads a lot, and sometimes helps him with his work. They have two children. They are from Normandy and they feel isolated, not only because they are strangers to the region but also because they are modernists. He is absorbed in his work, and is overworked.

Dr. Lévi is from Paris. His Jewish name and Christian religion disturb some of the natives, who refer to him as "the Jew." Like the traditional *penty*, his house has no upper floor, but it is much bigger. He collects paintings (he has a Daumier), antique furniture, rare stones, and old pistols. He lives with his wife, two teen-age daughters, and an old dog. His parents were deported during the war and died somewhere. He himself was a prisoner of war. He is haunted by the war. During adolescence he was drawn to occultism, but was converted to Catholicism by a reading of the gospels. His approach to religion is a syncretist one, in which he tries to combine the teachings of the Hebrew prophets, Christian evangelism, and scientific rationalism into a universal religion. He believes in the unlimited possibilities of science, in extraterrestrial beings, and thinks that one day "it will be possible to direct life and create new beings. There will be beings that are different from men—it's inevitable." But only religion can save man from the annihilating war that threatens him.

In each of these three islands, the mesomodern satisfactions of the *petit-bourgeois* world have been transcended. The dentist feels a fatigue that is not physical, a sort of unsatisfied tiredness produced by overwork, to which is added a feeling of futility both in work and outside it; he deplores the fact that he does not do anything really thoroughly in his spare time. The couple feel strongly the absence of any true communication with others, and in the course of a long talk they said a great deal about the absence of happiness in the midst of symbols of modern bourgeois happiness.

The dentist finds satisfaction for his curiosity and aesthetic needs (photography, films) in the latest technical equipment. The doctor's and Jenny's cult of art, on the other hand, is their response to mass-produced culture; for both, art is not a complement to modern bourgeois life but an antidote to it. It becomes a vital secret. They both feel that modern bourgeois life bears within itself an artificiality, a dissociation, a separation of man from his own nature, whereas art expresses an archaic principle by which the human being and nature—the human being and his own nature—are, or can be, in fundamental harmony.

For Jenny the barn, the wood fire, the unkempt garden are a transcending of the weekend vacation life of the urban bourgeois, for these signs of rusticity and neo-archaism are part of the artistic life, between the bohemian and the beatnik, already described: living with one's friends, in spontaneity, play, art. Of course, this life is made possible by the previously acquired wealth of a great bourgeois family, but it has detached itself from bourgeois life.

It is, therefore, through both a continuity and a break with bourgeois life that a desire to live in accordance with a sort of primordial neo-Rousseauist human nature has emerged, a principle of vitality, authenticity, and truth, which, as in the case of Rousseau himself, appears as a primitive, ideal model. Jenny Le Bail's view of life is existential and confined to a small group of friends, whereas that of the doctor wishes to embrace the entire anthropocosmological relation. The doctor feels a cardiac discomfort that he attributes to strictly physiological causes. Personally, I see the cause of this discomfort in an original anxiety that led him, before the war, to theosophy and which was increased to its extreme point by the shattering experiences of war, captivity, and the death of his parents. This anxiety finds appeasement in the Plodémet countryside and expression in the doctor's indefatigable activity and extensive collections. But it is also nourished by the ambivalent and solitary identity of the uprooted Jew, who in this case is all the more uprooted because of his conversion to Christianity.

The doctor's anxiety animates his spiritual quest. For him, the modern world is indissociable from the madness of war, the threat of which continues to hang over mankind and which shows that man is suffering from the absence of a fundamental truth. The doctor continues to seek the answers to his questionings in religion, mysticism, and science. For him, the problem of regulation (which is already emerging in Plodémet) is being transformed into a search for the rule and ground of all being, for the being of nature and of the nature of being. The doctor's metaphysical quest is inseparable from the search for the collective salvation of mankind, which he sees only in the creation of a universal religion: for him, this religion is Christianity. Only Christianity can save the world from the cataclysm that threatens it. In a sense, it is because he is a Jew that the doctor is a Christian—that is, not out of self-interest, as the naïve anti-Semites suspect, but out of messianism.

Thus two principles emerge: one in Jenny and the doctor, the other in the doctor alone.

The first, formed by a more or less unconscious convergence of the existential, aesthetic, and philosophical drives, might be called neo-archaic, in the powerful sense of the Greek *archē*, meaning a principle that is at once fundamental, primitive, and ideal. With the doctor, the search for the *archē* is combined with, is almost indistinguishable from, the search for the historical ark, the heir of the Hebrew Noah's Ark and the Ark of the Covenant.

Do these three islands, so foreign to Plodémet, constitute a neomodern advance guard?

Will people encounter difficulties with a high standard of living—people who are still at the early stages of the conquest of well-being, who are still grappling with deprivations and still remember the past servitude only too clearly?

Will we see the appearance of the dissatisfactions of private life and the problems of married couples, which are now stifled and hidden when they emerge?

Will we see an expansion of the void already present among the young?

Will we see an increase of anxiety, which is now barely apparent and is projected onto an indeterminate future or the atom bomb?

Will we see more spontaneity and joy—once confined to festivities and now emerging timidly in leisure pursuits and vacations?

Will we see crisis, transformation, or a transcending of bourgeois civilization?

In any case, there will be an increase in all kinds of technological development, and in this respect the neomodern will be ultramodern. There will be an emphasis on the search for the *archē*, already indicated by the return to nature and to the past, and for the Ark, already apparent in the yearning for a viaticum that would stimulate or complement the idea of progress.

Must modern man return to his own origins in order to transcend himself?

Plodémet will enter that new adventure later.

Reintroduction

Plodémet is changing and will continue to change. This change is producing the greatest transformation, the greatest disturbance, and the greatest progress in its history, involving not only the transformation of a local society but the final and decisive stage in a process of integration.

Plodémet is entering a period of urban civilization. It is entering bourgeois society, and *embourgeoisement* is transforming not only daily life but the relations of man with himself, with others, and with the world. Plodémet is entering the circuit of the generalized economy and generalized capitalism, which is penetrating through every crack, destroying, annexing, vassalizing, developing. It is entering the revolutionizing adventure of technology.

The new direction, initiated by a national, even an international process, is becoming one of the many different aspects of this process.

This integration is not an integration into an anonymous world —that world too has its problems and its history. Plodémet is moving not toward a static equilibrium but a problematic future. What lies before it is not simply the society of consumption or the benevolent rationalization of industrial society, but, in and through the industrial society of consumption, change. Technology means not only equipment and modernization but permanent transformation. *Embourgeoisement* means not only a higher standard of living but new problems in living. Capitalism brings not only economic adaptation but new antagonisms and new inequalities. As Plodémet enters a period of total change, it will feel directly its modifications, progress, setbacks, breaks, and crises.

Problems that are peripheral today will become central. The positive and negative of today will become ambivalent, perhaps even inverted. As always, the progressive will give rise to the regressive.

Moreover, the great process of integration and the extremely active forces of homogenization now in operation are certainly not destroying all the inheritances of the past, the local and regional differences, the fundamental metabolisms of the personality of Plodémet, or even all the artisanal and individual modes of production. As we have said, the great currents produce, by action and reaction, countercurrents that oppose them as well as merging with them. Indeed, the countercurrent is also the current itself, a fact that escapes the unilateral theories of modern times and societies. In Plodémet, the change is fantastic, but the resistance to certain aspects of this change is no less fantastic, and the true change is what results from both the change and the resistance to change.

The disintegration of archaic Bigoudennie and the breaking down of the isolation of Plodémet are not being succeeded by a homogeneous space stretching from the Pointe du Raz to the Odet, or even to the Oder, *although and because* an ever more homogeneous infrastructure is forming from the Pointe du Raz to the Oder.

A new regional reality is emerging from the economic, administrative, and tourist areas to the detriment of the communal and Bigouden areas. It shows awareness of its common origin in its spectacular displays of folk art (the annual Cornouaille festivals held at Quimper), and of its common future in the specific and urgent problem of its economic development. It is on the basis of this new economic awareness, and of its enlarged ethnic awareness, that the identity of Sud-Finistère is being formed. In turn and by the same process, the department too is becoming increasingly aware of itself as a part of the province of Brittany. The equally new feeling that Brittany has its own economic problem leads to the idea of a provincial policy based on an economic program and militant action. The equally new idea that the Breton cultural heritage, even the Breton identity itself, must be saved has led the young to place the Breton word *Breiz,* which once adorned the old standards, on the hoods of their cars.

Plodémet is becoming conscious of itself as a part of Sud-Finistère and of Brittany. This process tends, of course, to reduce the importance given to the originality of Bigoudennie and of Plodémet, but at the same time the wider departmental and provincial identities serve as a protection for the narrower Bigouden and Plodémet identities. In addition, the urban-bourgeois homogenization, the diaspora, and intermarriage are initiating a revival of the cult of the Bigouden *archē* and maintaining the Plodémet identity. For although the new transformation of the Plodémet personality is taking place within a process of urbanization and *embourgeoisement,* the residential and touristic development, which contributes to this transformation, also brings the urban desire for a return to nature and the past, which revitalizes native values.

It would seem that the transformation of Plodémet must bring with it the general liquidation of an economic system. But cheap mass production (the canning of vegetables, peas, pâté, and fish), which became totally irrational on the basis of the small business and such extremely diversified land, is condemned far more radically than artisanal or semiartisanal production. Plodémet is unsuited to large-scale production: if there is an economic possibility other than commerce, the crafts, and the services required by a residential and vacational population, it lies in the field of small-scale quality production.

The new urban demand for "natural" and quality products is bound to increase. Once again, the backward movement produced as a reaction to mass-production is complementary to and therefore a part of the modern movement itself. It is in this field that there is a possibility for the revival of artisanal and semi-artisanal production in agriculture, cattle rearing, canning, and furniture making, but only provided it is integrated into the modern distributive system.

Thus the fate of Plodémet is not limited to a decline through the emigration of its young, absorption by large-scale business at every level, and transformation into a bedroom suburb. On the contrary, it will play its part in the dialectic of modernity.

This dialectic is all the more open in that Plodémet remains extremely diversified and has at its disposal a wide range of possibilities. It is for this reason that I believe municipal political action, despite the reduction in communal autonomy, could play a decisive role in the future. It could either activate or slow down the dominant currents and, above all, could control the counter-currents produced by the current.

The political problem is not only that of economic development. The economic-social dialectic, which on the basis of the egalitarianism of Baillist times is producing new inequalities and new antagonisms, has already appeared in Plodémet. Finally, there is the problem of civilization: is the political civilization of Plodémet going into decline? No one knows whether important new measures will be taken, as at the height of the Baillist period, whether the red party will lose its political dominance to the blue party or be diluted into pink. Personally, I would regret the disappearance of the spirit that could inscribe on the historical escutcheon of Plodémet "The Rights of Man" and "The Love of Humanity."

APPENDIX

The Multidimensional Method

The principle of the method employed in Plodémet is to encourage the flow of concrete data, to capture human realities on various levels, to bring out and reveal the features of the terrain, to begin with the sociological individual, which is a commune, to recognize the original features of the double nature, unique and microcosmic, of the phenomenon studied.

Interpretation and research cannot be separated in time. The corpus of hypotheses cannot be established once and for all, but must be capable of development and modification as the inquiry develops, and in turn modify the course of the inquiry and even the techniques of investigation. In short, it is a question of finding rigor, not in rigidity but in a strategy of permanent adaptation.

This means that the standard method used in inquiries is not only inadequate but distorting. It seeks verification by means of a questionnaire addressed to a sample of the population.

The instrument of verification, the questionnaire, is as insensitive to the various concrete features of a local society as it is to sociological multidimensionality. Above all, the standard inquiry reduces the true research to the preinquiry phase when hypotheses are formulated, methods worked out, and a sample of the population picked. From then on, the inquiry refuses any retraction, correction, or innovation. The phase of collecting the questionnaires is an intellectually passive one. Thought comes back into its own only later.

We therefore abandoned initial programming and the use of a questionnaire, though we did not preclude the possibility of using one as a final check.

We retained the use of the sampling method, as a population

of 3,700 is too large for a direct house-to-house study. We built up the sample in the course of the inquiry in such a way as to respect the special problems of the terrain.

THE MEANS OF INVESTIGATION

An investigation must encourage the flow of concrete data, and therefore it must be flexible enough to include on-the-spot documentation (descriptions of actual events, tape-recorded discussions, conversation with a minimum of direction).

It must capture the various dimensions of the phenomenon studied and make use of different approaches.

It must be capable of correction and vertification in the development of an interpretation. The variety of approaches allows a confrontation and concentration of means on points of verification.

We made particular use of the following:

1. Phenomenographic observation (which is related to methods in use in ethnography but neglected by standard sociology).

2. The interview.

3. Participation in group activities (social praxis).

PHENOMENOGRAPHIC OBSERVATION

The investigation should be applied as much to the various centers of social life as to the individual household. It should be complemented by other methods of investigation, but remain autonomous. Ideally, it should cover the totality of the objective, including the observer in the act of observing.

It should try to be both panoramic (capturing the whole of the visual field) and analytic (distinguishing each element in the visual field).

The visual sense is so atrophied among sociologists who depend on the questionnaire and the tape recorder, or conversely on unsupported speculation, that they must learn to observe facts, gestures, dress, objects, landscapes, houses, lanes. We believe in the need for a Balzac-like and Stendhal-like approach in sociology.

The Balzac-like approach is encyclopedic description; the Stendhal-like, that of the "significant detail." To these should be added a sense of the sociological snapshot.

As the terrain becomes intelligible, the mass of accumulated documentation becomes a breeding ground in which data are transformed into signs, and in which the detail becomes less and less incidental and more and more rewarding.

The qualities needed in observation are those needed in the inquiry as a whole: an interest equally sustained in general ideas, concrete realities, and men and women in their uniqueness. The purely professional attitude, on the other hand, atrophies perception; a monomaniacal interest in a single idea distorts that idea; indifference to human beings is blindness; indifference to ideas blinds one to the proliferation of signs of which the phenomenal world is composed; an inadequate capacity to interpret leads to an inadequate capacity to perceive, and vice versa.

Each worker recorded his observations in a personal diary, which was not an accumulation of notes but a narrative that led of itself to the recall of a series of unconsciously recorded facts. The diary, complemented by subjective accounts of impressions and feelings, provides the external eye—which may be the second sight of the observer himself—with material that can assist in the elucidation of the observer-phenomenon relationship. This subject-object relationship is the key to any effort at objectification in research.

THE INTERVIEW

The interview was used throughout the inquiry, and it was for this purpose that we built up a population sample based on the usual categories.

The choice of interviewees was made (1) by chance (and throughout the inquiry we left room for chance); (2) by scanning diverse areas (Menez-Ru, Kéravrez, Bravez, Kerminou); and (3) by systematic selection.

In the case of villages, groups, and individuals, the criterion of choice was not average representativeness, as in the method of quotas or random selection, but maximum significance. We looked for extreme cases that would allow the formation of typological poles of opposition (young-old, modernist-traditionalist, bourgeois-rustic). We looked for subjects that were experiencing the crucial conflicts most closely (in Plodémet, these conflicts are linked to the development of modernity which constitutes the main theme of our study); for social leaders (union and party

activists, initiators, and not only Lazarsfeld's "leaders of opinion"); for deviants, passive or rebellious; and, of course, for key
persons occupying socially strategic positions, and those at the
center of multiple communications.

According to opportunity and circumstances, we made use of
the pseudoconversation, the limited interview (asking a limited
number of open questions that could be used in all fields), and
the interview in depth.

The function of the interview in depth is to reveal the personality, basic needs, and view of life of the interviewee. Our
great problem was to direct the interview toward areas of non-
directivity. We tried to confine our own role to that of initiating
rather than directing the conversation, letting ourselves be guided
by intuition rather than by preconceived rules. In fact, patience
and sympathy, not technique and skill, were the determining
factors of success.

The interview succeeded from the moment the speech of the
interviewee was freed of inhibition and embarrassment and
became communication.

It was usually after one to two hours that the struggle between
inhibition and exhibition was resolved to the advantage of the
extravert forces.[1]

It appeared to us that the interviewee was fully satisfied with
having talked to us only when he could himself ask questions,
either to get to know his observer or to learn something from a
"scientist." On our side, we felt embarrassed at making the interview a captive operation. The fact of having an interviewee who
disliked letting himself be manipulated and an interviewer who
disliked manipulating drove us to introduce dialogue as the final
stage of the interview.

[1] We had the good fortune to be studying an open, good-natured,
curious population, which helped us to gain access to the need for communication that exists in most human beings. Communication was helped
by having the interview take place in the home of the interviewee, in the
presence of two or three research workers; the participants were able in this
way to help each other get over their nervousness. The tape recorder is both
the "spy" that sets up inhibition and the microphone that arouses the desire
to communicate and gives the interviewee a stronger sense of personal
existence. The art of the interview is to overcome inhibitions and to appeal
to the interviewee's need to communicate. We have examined some of these
problems in "L'Interview dans les sciences sociales et la radio-télévision,"
Communications, 7, 1966, pp. 59–73.

The interview, regarded as drudgery by sociologists and market researchers, was for us one of the essential means of communication. These "dives," with tape recorder as oxygen tank and microphone as harpoon, led us to the secret dimension of lives that seemed two-dimensional at first sight.

GROUPS AND PRAXIS

What we have retained from Marxism (which we assimilated and integrated in an anthroposociology) makes us attentive to the social praxis, to the reality and action of social groups. Action not only reveals realities that rarely reach the level of verbal expression and consciousness, but it is also the dynamic reality of social life.

Through the methods of investigation outlined above, we were able to get hold of groups in an indirect way only, but when possible we did so directly through professional, political, ideological, religious, and other bodies. We tried to discover the conflicts and tensions they aroused in action: in the case of the youth club, internal class conflicts, tensions with adults, difficulties in relations with teachers, the municipality, the clergy.

Within the social praxis, on-the-spot events or on-the-spot reactions to external events provided us with spontaneous social tests. Land redistribution (1961–1966), for example, was regarded as a great multipurpose test of peasant life and consciousness in Plodémet.

In addition to observation, we also provoked test situations, like the showing of the film *The Wild Ones* to the teen-agers, or the plan for a holidays committee, which we proposed to different social groups. As observers of group behavior, we were sometimes led to intervene as purveyors of information and even as advisers. Our experience with the provoked tests and the youth committee brought us to the conclusion that intervention should be a necessary method of research. We used the basic idea of interventionist psychosociology, that of action-research, but without confining ourselves to the precepts of any particular school. Our principles of intervention were the following:

1. The maieutic principle. We were led to intervene when we thought we detected a situation pregnant with change or innovation.

2. The nondirective principle. Our intervention had to be cata-
lytic. It could initiate movement, but not fix its norms and program. It could help, but not orient.

3. The principle of primitive experimentation (test situations
or paraexperimental situations).

4. The principle of psychosociological "Socratism." The intervention must lead those involved to reflect on their principal
problems.

5. The principle of utility, common to both research workers
and their subjects.

We caught only a glimpse of the possibilities and difficulties
of intervention-research. *The difficulties:* The experience of the
youth club, however moderate its disturbing effect on the commune may appear to have been, presented us with a problem in
responsibility and prudence.

The possibilities: One envisaged the formation of "general sociological states" in which the various groups of Plodémet society
would be led to formulate and compare their aspirations and
needs.

Intervention needs a policy that goes beyond the framework of
immediate utility for the group under study. A norm should be
conceived that should not necessarily be the reduction of tensions
and conformity to the general norm.

SUBJECTIVITY AND OBJECTIVITY

Our method seeks to envelop the phenomenon (observation),
to recognize the forces within it (praxis), to provoke it at strategic points (intervention), to penetrate it by individual contact
(interview), to question action, speech, and things.

Each of these methods poses the fundamental methodological
problem: the relationship between the research worker and the
subject.

It is not merely a subject-object relationship. The "object" of
the inquiry is both object and subject, and one cannot escape the
intersubjective character of all relations between men.

We believe that the optimal relationship requires, on the one
hand, detachment and objectivity in relation to the object as
object, and on the other, participation and sympathy in relation
to the object as subject. As this object and subject are one, our
approach must be a dual one.

In most of our methods a lack of sympathy would be a grave obstacle to communication. We wanted to stimulate reciprocal sympathy by using the technique of drinking together and eating together. Drinking together is necessary everywhere, and especially so in Plodémet. The *buvette* is a forum, a center of comradeship. In Bigoudennie, a man who drinks well is accepted as a naturalized Breton. Eating together is an occasion of warmth. Unfortunately, I was not able to carry my efforts in this direction far enough. On the one hand, my digestion still suffers the effects of such previous research into human communication, and on the other, financial disbursers appear not to realize that expenses for entertainment are a sociological investment.

Apart from these friendly encounters, our immersion in the life of Plodémet by virtue of our extended residence there (adoption of customs and sometimes participation in work) was also a subjective immersion. Our sympathy with the future development of Plodémet not only made us wish to assist the development, it also made us in a sense naturalized citizens of Plodémet.

The scientifically indispensable dissociation between observation and participation is an intellectual divorce which does not exclude effective participation. Yet participation requires a sustained and permanent effort of distancing and objectification. The researcher must constantly elucidate what he feels and reflect on his experience. He cannot escape his internal duality. Moreover, this duality must be apparent to the subject-object of the inquiry. The fact that he carries a tape recorder with him wherever he goes designates him in his objective capacity as a "scientist," while daily contact shows him to be a human being like everyone else. In fact, he must be both practitioner and friend. He must be like everyone else and also the possessor of special knowledge like the priest and the doctor. The art of the sociological inquiry is to experience this dual personality internally and express it externally, to dialectically enrich participation and objectification. We do not claim to have succeeded; we do claim that it is necessary to attempt to do so.

In one sense, the subject remains an inaccessible object: this is reflected on the part of the research worker in a cynical desire to know. This is why we must counterbalance this cynicism with a device to obtain the flow of everything that is in the nature of a confidence, or exchange. Exchange is our key value, although it does not settle our problem of dual responsibility to knowledge and to those whom we are studying.

THE RESEARCH WORKERS

Standard inquiries take elaborate technical precautions about obtaining their data, forgetting that this also depends on who is obtaining them. We paid more attention to the personal qualities of the workers we recruited than to their technical qualifications. The multidimensional method requires a curiosity open to all dimensions of the human phenomenon, and the full use of varied aptitudes. Each worker is versatile in that he must practice observation, interview, and group action, and be a specialist in whatever sector suits him best.

We had to struggle against too great a need for mental security on the part of the younger workers who expected schemata and programs drawn up in advance, work that might be boring but easy to separate from the rest of one's life, or an assurance at the outset of the validity of the method of analysis and of the theoretical value of our final conclusions. They were disturbed by the freedom of initiative they were given. The open attention to facts struck them as "impressionistic"; the open attention to ideas, as "experimental." They failed to see that these impressions and experiments, as well as errors of intelligence, must be used, criticized, and integrated, not rejected. They understood the method only when they began to feel personally involved in the work.

Curiously enough, the resistance to the full expression of sociological aptitudes among young research workers is a result of their sociological vocation, serving as a religious conversion rather than an elucidation of consciousness. In such cases, devotion to objectivity is too closely linked to the repression of a guilty subjectivity. Mathematical order and ambitious intellectual structures exorcise the disorder of the world and internal disorders. Their mistrust of their subjectivity leads them to mistrust their professional gifts.

DEVELOPMENT OF THE INQUIRY

The research developed in successive stages, which we called "campaigns." In 1965, there were six campaigns, separated by periods of methodological elaboration or correction, examination of collected data, criticism of the methods used, re-examination of hypotheses, and the drawing up of strategy for the next campaign—the sectors and populations to be studied and the problem to elucidate.

Within each campaign, the day-to-day orientation and regulation of our work was assured by our presence and participation in the field, by meetings of the research team, and by the intercommunication of the inquiry diaries, including my own.

By means of innumerable day-to-day confrontations, an overall control was established whereby norms could be laid down, dissipation of effort avoided, and errors corrected. Control and progressive focalization gradually reduced the element of error in the inquiry (but the principle of the open door to the unexpected was maintained to the end).

Thus the constant effort to elucidate a social personality is one designed to isolate the subject's uniqueness and understand its metabolism, and to see it as well as a microcosm of the social macrocosm.

Is it paradoxical to affirm that the more particular a study should be, the more general it should be?

Without a general constitutive model that is both complex and articulated, one does little more than carry out a census that would be inadequately catalogued in any case by schemata based ultimately on private ideological commonplaces and the journalistic ideas of the specialists themselves.

The constitutive model is that of French society, but it is not a strictly national model; it is the French variant of a Western model, and more widely still, of a technological, industrial, capitalist, urban, bourgeois, wage-earning, statist, consumptionist civilization whose fundamental dimensions must be articulated, rather than largely excluded in the manner of single-dimensional minds.

In order to articulate our constitutive model, we had to historicize our study of Plodémet. We had to study the past (and here previous historical research was most valuable), and above all, at the level of our own research we postulated space in relation to time. We wished to situate the data we collected in relation to evolution.

This led us to elaborate a multidimensional battery of indicators of modernity in relation to a tradition; to use as much as possible the oppositions of generations as indices of transformation; and finally, to use the heterogeneities of the terrain as temporal landmarks. Thus Menez-Ru, a backward village, and Kerminou, a highly advanced hamlet, helped us to chart a whole process. Inequality of development is the spatiotemporal notion that enabled us to transmute space into time and to integrate change into space.

In concentrating our work on the elucidation of the personality of Plodémet, we remained at the crossroads of space and time; we tried to encapsulate this tiny society within its own future and its relation to the general future.

Finally, the question "What is Plodémet?" implied the question "What is the modern world?" It was this dual and inevitable question that we tried to press as far as possible.